Praise for *Your Child's Strengths*

"This is a brilliant, innovative, enormously practical, and hugely important work. Where positive psychology and strength-based philosophies usually stumble, this book soars, namely, in practical application. If teachers and parents would all read this and implement its suggestions, our broken educational system would be fixed in no time. Truly, this book could change the world."

—Edward Hallowell, MD, author of *Driven to Distraction: Recognizing and Coping with Attention Deficit Disorder from Childhood to Adulthood*

"With this important book, Jenifer Fox expands the strengths revolution to our children. *Your Child's Strengths* is a smart and useful guide for any parent—full of great exercises that will change the way your kids think about themselves and their future." —Daniel H. Pink, author of *A Whole New Mind*

"*Your Child's Strengths* contains clear, interesting, step-by-step techniques for identifying and utilizing children's cognitive and emotional strengths—an excellent starting point for any parent, teacher, or student who wants to take the more effective step of focusing on assets rather than liabilities. The wisdom contained in this remarkable volume will be a godsend, not only for those who are just beginning to try to understand a child's learning style but also for those already battered by a misguided educational system."

—Dan Kindlon, Ph.D., coauthor of *Raising Cain: Protecting the Emotional Life of Boys*

"*Your Child's Strengths* puts in plain view what has been in front of us all along—that education and character development always do best to first identify and deepen strengths, rather than to first (and too often exclusively) focus on deficit and weaknesses. Fox's approach is more interesting, more effective, and ultimately more humane."

—Michael Riera, author of *Staying Connected to Your Teenager: How to Keep Them Talking to You, and How to Hear What They're Really Saying*

"When I was labeled 'learning disabled,' the educational system tried everything to fix me, from giving me purple-colored reading glasses to putting me through hundreds of hours of remediation. Through all these efforts to fix what was supposedly wrong with me, my strengths, gifts, and talents were not

D0041360

simply neglected or ignored, but negated. Jenifer Fox has taken a groundbreaking and important stand against the standardized deficit and remediation education that dominates the lives of millions of students. Philosophical yet extremely practical, innovative yet grounded in solid research on effective pedagogy, *Your Child's Strengths* is a must read for any student, parent, and educator."
—Jonathan Mooney, author of *The Short Bus: A Journey Beyond Normal and Learning Outside the Lines*

Praise from Parents and Teachers for *Your Child's Strengths*

"*Your Child's Strengths* is a book that will be on my bookshelf as my children grow older. It is one that I hope will help me alter my parenting style to one that is rooted in positivity and loving my children for [their] strengths."
—Stephanie, mother of Ryan, age eight, and Natalie, age four

"Filled with practical advice and thoughtful exercises to help parents change the way they and their children approach life, learning and relationships. This book primarily . . . is about a vision . . . of seeing things in a positive light."
—Maryanne, mother of Alexander, age six

"We live in a world that is focused on the negative. Schools are designed to identify what is 'wrong' with a child; parents tend to try to 'fix' their children. As Jenifer Fox argues, what is needed is a fundamental shift in attitude. Parents and teachers should focus on a child's strengths, not their weaknesses. . . . Not simply skills that the child has developed an acuity for, but rather those skills which . . . provide them with a sense of accomplishment and excitement."
—Jeff, father of Jessica, age four

"I am reading your book and I LOVE IT! It speaks to my heart and my beliefs about children and education! This is perfect for teacher training since it has theory *and* practice in it."
—Lynn Varner, Thad Cochran Center for Rural School Leadership and Research

"As a career middle school teacher, I know how challenging it can be to manage a classroom full of diverse learners. It is easy to focus on 'fixing' what is wrong with kids. What Fox does in this book is offer a practical program to build on students' strengths. She shows us how to discover them with great activities and exercises and also makes a strong case that building on student strengths lays the groundwork for students to improve their performance overall. I, for one, am looking forward to sharing this book with the parents of kids I teach and using the exercises and ideas in it to partner with them to see our students in a new light. Great book, groundbreaking."

—Paul Nicholson, middle school teacher

"As an educator, I always believed that every child and student should have the opportunity to achieve great things. Unfortunately, our educational system just isn't set up that way. *Your Child's Strengths* is part of an amazing educational movement that is calling parents and teachers to see what their children do well and utilizing that to help them learn. My daughter will be entering some type of preschool program this fall. And you can be certain I'll be observing how they capitalize on her strengths."

—Kristen, music educator and mother of Quinlan, age four

"The message and resources in this book are clearly what the California State Public System needs to embrace as a way to address our struggling system."

—Yale Wishnick, Ed.D., California Teachers Association Institute for Teaching

"It is difficult to deny the potential for success that Fox writes about in her new book."

—California Teachers Association Foundation for Teaching and Learning

ABOUT THE AUTHOR

Jenifer Fox is an educator and public speaker who has worked in public and independent schools as a teacher and administrator for twenty-five years. She is currently the international leader of the Strengths Movement in K–12 schools. She holds a B.S. in communications from the University of Wisconsin–Madison, an M.A. in English from Middlebury College's Bread Loaf School of English, and an M.Ed. in school administration from Harvard University.

For more information, please visit
www.strengthsmovement.com

YOUR CHILD'S STRENGTHS

A GUIDE FOR **PARENTS** AND **TEACHERS**

Jenifer Fox, M.Ed.

PENGUIN BOOKS

PENGUIN BOOKS
Published by the Penguin Group
Penguin Group (USA) Inc., 375 Hudson Street, New York, New York 10014, U.S.A. • Penguin Group (Canada), 90 Eglinton Avenue East, Suite 700, Toronto, Ontario, Canada M4P 2Y3 (a division of Pearson Penguin Canada Inc.) • Penguin Books Ltd, 80 Strand, London WC2R 0RL, England • Penguin Ireland, 25 St Stephen's Green, Dublin 2, Ireland (a division of Penguin Books Ltd) • Penguin Group (Australia), 250 Camberwell Road, Camberwell, Victoria 3124, Australia (a division of Pearson Australia Group Pty Ltd) • Penguin Books India Pvt Ltd, 11 Community Centre, Panchsheel Park, New Delhi – 110 017, India • Penguin Group (NZ), 67 Apollo Drive, Rosedale, North Shore 0632, New Zealand (a division of Pearson New Zealand Ltd) • Penguin Books (South Africa) (Pty) Ltd, 24 Sturdee Avenue, Rosebank, Johannesburg 2196, South Africa

Penguin Books Ltd, Registered Offices:
80 Strand, London WC2R 0RL, England

First published in the United States of America by Viking Penguin,
a member of Penguin Group (USA) Inc. 2008
Published in Penguin Books 2009

10 9 8 7 6 5 4 3 2 1

Copyright © Jenifer Fox, 2008
Foreword copyright © Marcus Buckingham, 2008
All rights reserved

Photographs from BigStockPhoto

The experiences recounted in this book are true. However, in some instances, names
and descriptive details have been changed to protect the identities of the individuals involved.

THE LIBRARY OF CONGRESS HAS CATALOGED THE HARDCOVER EDITION AS FOLLOWS:
Fox, Jenifer.
Your child's strengths : discover them, develop them, use them / Jenifer Fox.
p. cm.
Includes index.
ISBN 978-0-670-01876-5 (hc.)
ISBN 978-0-14-311517-5 (pbk.)
1. Child development. 2. Ability in children. 3. Child rearing.
4. Teaching. 5. Education—Parent participation. I. Title.
LB1117. F69 2007
372.21—dc22 2007032337

Printed in the United States of America
Set in Dante MT with AG Schoolbook
Designed by Daniel Lagin

Except in the United States of America, this book is sold subject to the condition that it shall not, by way of trade or otherwise, be lent, resold, hired out, or otherwise circulated without the publisher's prior consent in any form of binding or cover other than that in which it is published and without a similar condition including this condition being imposed on the subsequent purchaser.

The scanning, uploading, and distribution of this book via the Internet or via any other means without the permission of the publisher is illegal and punishable by law. Please purchase only authorized electronic editions, and do not participate in or encourage electronic piracy of copyrighted materials. Your support of the author's rights is appreciated.

For J. B.

Foreword

After twenty years of researching, studying, and delivering the message about strengths, I look around and see that we still live in a world that is obsessed with remedying weaknesses. There is no place where this is more disconcerting than in our schools. Most people reach adulthood with no idea of what their strengths might be; yet, they are painfully aware of their failings. In 2006, with the creation of my series of six short films called *Trombone Player Wanted*, I set out to reignite the Strengths Movement by organizing people around the positive power of identifying and developing their strengths. These films stress the power of playing to one's strengths at work, using as a backdrop the story of a young boy miscast in his school orchestra. He starts out playing trombone but discovers his strength really lies in playing the drums.

Shortly after the release of this film, I received a stack of over forty letters from a group of students in Pottersville, New Jersey, who, after viewing *Trombone Player Wanted*, asked me to come and visit their school. The students wished to show me how they practiced the message professed in the film. What I found at the Purnell School inspired in me a new hope for the future of the Strengths Movement. The entire organization is set up to build on the strengths of both students and teachers. This school is quite unlike any school I have ever encountered, and the Head of School, Jenifer Fox, is determined to ensure that the success her students have experienced transcends their New Jersey campus and spreads out in revolutionary fashion across the United States and around the world.

As an author and speaker whose focus is on strengths, I naturally feel energized by this much-needed book. However, it is as a father that I am most enthusiastic. Jenifer's understanding of strengths development in children is refreshingly original. She has extraordinary insight into the minds of young people and an unshakable belief in their potential. She provides a compellingly convincing argument for changing the way we approach children. Jenifer's call to action couldn't be more sincere. When I initially spoke with Jenifer in October 2006, she explained in detail her desire to change the conversation in this country about how we raise and educate children. As you read this book, you will no doubt become part of the new conversation—one that will echo into the future, making the world a better place for all of us.

The Affinities Program outlined in the appendix is as creative as it is necessary. This is the one program that schools must have. It has the ability to change the landscape of American education from one that focuses on deficiency to one based on developing student strengths. Even though my own children are still young, I eagerly anticipate the implementation of such a program in their schools, one that is wholly engaging and designed with a watchful eye on the future.

Clearly, the next twenty to thirty years will bring fascinating opportunities to those who are ready. Schools and families that have the wisdom to place deliberate emphasis on organic identification of personal strengths will be the ones best preparing our children to take full advantage of those opportunities.

As you read this book, you will recognize yourself and your own experiences as well as those of your children. You will alternately feel frustration at the current situation in many of our schools and hope for what is possible when strengths are spotlighted. The unique quality of this book is that it reveals a new model for interacting with and teaching children. In this model, students who excel in traditional school settings work alongside students who learn differently, and everyone is successful. While it clearly demonstrates how teaching strengths is pertinent to all students, this breakthrough model has a special ability to alter the course of how schools teach students who learn differently, moving from an international deficit model to a strengths-based one. I hope you enjoy and benefit from reading this book as much as I did.

Marcus Buckingham
Los Angeles
June 2007

Preface

DO YOU RECOGNIZE THIS STORY?

THE NEED TO DEVELOP CHILDREN'S STRENGTHS IS A STORY THAT cuts across economic lines and knows no racial, gender, or cultural boundaries. It is every child's story, and the time to tell it is now. Ultimately, it is a story of joy and fulfillment, but rarely does it begin that way. Most children today feel weakened and depleted by their experiences in schools. My hope is that this book will convey the serious need for parents and teachers to join in an effort to change the way we understand children. The world is changing, and the only way to guarantee children success in the future is for parents and schools to change as well. What children need most are families and schools that demonstrate unconditional belief in their strengths.

My story is included here because it is reflected in the literally hundreds of similar stories people have related to me in my twenty years as an educator. All these stories have one thing in common: a child who was misunderstood. Here is a glimpse into why strengths development is so important.

I can remember the very first moment I knew I had talents inside me. I was in first grade. One day my teacher, Sister Jonah, tapped me on the shoulder and asked me to come to her desk to speak with her about a story I had written. In the story, I described a place populated by numbers instead of people. In this land, only eight varieties of beings existed, the numbers 1 through 8. I described each number's personality in relationship to its shape. In my story, the 8s were supreme and had achieved perfection. They represented what all the other numbers strived to become: perfect in their roundness and complete in their shape, an infinite flow. This made the 8s the leaders in the Land of Numbers. Meanwhile, the 1s, 7s and 4s—having achieved no roundness—were the members of the lower class, furthest from the ideal. Of that group, the 4s were the least outcast because they had managed to close the top part of their figures. I wrote a rather lengthy story for a first grader, yet I recall feeling it was incomplete because I had not explained why the 7s, who should have evolved from what looked like an obvious progression from the 4s, 5s and 6s, nevertheless took a step backward. They had lost all the momentum toward becoming an 8. Perfect form was a result of effort, and lack of effort resulted in exile. At the time, I had little idea that this was the meaning of my story. I do recall having some anxiety that the teacher would chastise me for treating the 7s so brutally.

Sister Jonah asked me if I would please read my story to the eighth-grade class. To a first grader, the eighth-grade classroom, situated down a long hallway on the second floor of the school, seemed to me as far-off a place as the Land of Numbers. I was simultaneously surprised, nervous, and thrilled to accept her assignment. Sister Jonah walked with me up the stairs to their classroom. I will never forget the feeling of facing those twenty-five eighth-grade students. Standing before Bobby Hackett, a big red-headed kid who once ran past me so carelessly on the playground that he knocked me down and didn't even notice, and Nell Jennings, a girl with shiny blond hair that reached down past her hips, I couldn't help but tremble. I read my story, stopping every now and then to hold up a page and show the little illustrations I had drawn in the margin. They laughed when I read the part about the 3s and the 6s ganging up to confront the unruly 7s. At the end of my story, they burst into applause, and at that very moment, a puff of strength blew through me. I discovered the power of my imagination. It was then that I began to believe I had something worthwhile, even creative, to say to others.

I began my education convinced that there was something extraordinary about me. Despite my having received a D in penmanship in the second grade and a C– in spelling in the fourth grade, I nonetheless believed that I had a talent for communicating ideas in writing and proceeded to live my life as though that were so. By the time I left grammar school, I had developed a strong set of skills in most academic subjects. I enrolled in the prep school where generations of my family had been educated. I was fourteen years old.

The self-confidence I developed over eight years of grammar school took just five months to crumble into self-doubt, anxiety, and depression. As vividly as I can recall the moment when I first experienced the swell of my own strengths, I can recall the moment when I no longer cared about developing them.

As social beings, the worst thing humans can experience is the act of betrayal. In most communities, the consequence for an act of betrayal is exile. This principle is at work in such simple situations as a group of girls no longer speaking to the one who broke their confidence, or a wife divorcing her husband for cheating on her. In profound instances, societies isolate prisoners who fail to comply, and for the grandest act of betrayal, humans reserve the right to employ the ultimate form of exile: the death penalty. Regardless of the circumstance, betrayal always constitutes a deep breach of the social contract.

In 1975, I spent day after day in my algebra class with my hand thrust in the air hoping the teacher would call on me. Mr. Hayes was a longtime, well-loved veteran of the school. My father was proud of the fact that I went to the same school he did and took math with the same teacher who taught him. My father is a well-respected, very successful man, so I assumed that Mr. Hayes was the absolute best as a math teacher. Naturally, I wanted to be successful at math. I remember hoping Mr. Hayes would call on me and value my contribution to class.

When Mr. Hayes wrote $6x + 5x = 33$ on the board and asked us to solve for x, my hand shot into the air. "I don't understand what x means," I said.

He answered my question by demonstrating how to work the problem. When he finished solving the problem on the board for all to see, he asked me, "Now do you see?"

I told him I didn't. I explained that I understood what he'd done, but I still did not understand what x meant. He turned to the rest of the class and asked them as a group, "Do you understand?" They all nodded their heads in agreement, and he said, "Well, let's move on then." This was the way the math class went for most of the first half of the year. Initially, my difficulty was not with solving the problems, although this is what it became; instead, I struggled at first to understand the way one might think mathematically. Up to that point, I had thought in words and visual images. I grappled with understanding how people thought in symbols. I had the same experience learning music. I couldn't understand how a musician envisioned notes and music. To me, learning a math problem without understanding the overarching framework was like learning to read music without ever having listened to a song. Until I had some grasp on that understanding, solving the problems didn't make sense to me. At fourteen I wasn't able to articulate this struggle, and I asked many questions. Mr. Hayes thought I asked questions to intentionally distract the class from learning. His mounting frustration eventually led him to ignore me when my hand went up. He moved my seat to the back of the room, and I began to fail my quizzes as he moved on to the next problem and the next section, leaving me behind.

This was the first time I felt betrayed by a teacher—a betrayal that plumbed so deep that I feel prickles of anger in dredging up its memory even today. In response to my teacher's betrayal, I unconsciously exiled him in that I no longer cared about math. My grades began to reinforce this exile. After that, my self-confidence was the first to go; next was my respect for school as a place where good things happen. I then lost my motivation, and eventually I turned my strengths elsewhere. Adolescents with low self-esteem and undirected strengths in leadership will become leaders in negative places. When they begin down this road, we label them "at risk."

When it was clear I was not going to succeed in any arena, I left the independent school by my own choice.

A switch to the public school the following year did little to improve my feelings. I hated the sound of the banging lockers and that the teachers didn't know if I was in class or not. I hated that kids smoked pot in the bathrooms and that teachers never even came by to kick them out. I took only the classes I needed to graduate from high school. In my senior year, I was enrolled in geometry, which I recall liking, but I attended only the minimum number of times needed to pass. My journey through high school had more low points than high ones. Month after month, year by year, the overall experience threatened to suck all the life and enthusiasm right out of me. I actually think my father ended up bribing the geometry teacher in the end to pass me with a D so I could finish high school.

This is how my story began. The details are unique, but the general themes are becoming more commonplace each day. I write this book with the hope that it can offer a clear and well-lit path to a new way of teaching and raising children. This book is written with the conviction that if we can retell the story of schools and homes as places that revel in the strengths of the individual, and recast the characters as people who have intuitive knowledge of the activities that cultivate their potential, then we will truly create a society where no child is left behind. The anecdote you just read began in frustration, but my discovery of personal strengths, as you will see, takes my story somewhere quite different.

In 1979, the University of Wisconsin at Madison, a state-funded school, guaranteed admission to almost every high school graduate who could afford to enroll. With my life's belongings stuffed into large brown trash bags, I boarded the Badger Bus for the ninety-minute ride to Madison in search of the strong person I had left so far behind in the first grade.

At the time, course registration at the University of Wisconsin was like an initiation ceremony. This involved following an unclear map across several miles of campus that had over one hundred buildings. It led to various rooms where one waited in long lines and, at the end, received a stamp on a schedule, granting permission to enroll in your chosen course. Students had to prepare several schedules based on the possibility that when they finally found the registration room and suffered through the line, the course might already be full—or, worse, the class meeting time changed to the same time as the class for which you registered two miles, forty buildings, and a thirty-five-minute waiting line earlier. Due to my dismal performance in high school math, I had to enroll in a course called Math 99-100. In order to earn an undergraduate degree in English, I needed to pass this, and only this, math class. It was the last math class I would ever take, and it would take two attempts to pass.

By the time I found my way to the Helen C. White Library to register for an English class, the one subject I looked forward to taking, all the courses I had circled in the registration booklet had filled up. The only class that was still available was an advanced-level course in Nineteenth-Century British Literature taught by a professor who at first glance seemed crustier than burned toast. His name was Standish Henning. I couldn't believe that after all the trouble, this was all that was left. I could just picture Standish Henning and my former high school math teacher, Mr. Hayes, sipping hot toddies and sharing a chuckle over whether or not Matthew Arnold understood how to solve quadratic equations.

Nearly two months into the academic term, I admitted I was wrong about Standish Henning. As it turned out, he was a very funny, extremely personable man. Despite my having been the only undergraduate in the class, Professor Henning always called on me during the discussion. I answered his questions with hesitation, uncertain if what I was saying made any sense. Students much older than me cited examples of literary criticism when they answered Professor Henning's questions, whereas I, unfamiliar with their examples, stuck to interpreting the text.

One day after class, I approached Professor Henning and told him I felt very uncomfortable in his class and that I considered dropping it. He looked at me quizzically and told me I couldn't drop it, since the drop date had passed; I would receive an F if I didn't complete the course. I told him I didn't care, that I was going to flunk Math 99-100 anyway, so it really wouldn't make much difference, since my grade point average was already sunk. Then he said something that changed the course of my life.

"But, Jenifer," he said, "why would you want to get an F in a class in which you are the top student?"

I couldn't believe my ears. I figured he was flattering me. On the other hand, maybe he was trying to pick me up; I'd heard of that happening in universities. I asked him how that could be when the others in the class obviously knew so much more than I.

"They may have acquired intellectual knowledge, which you can acquire, too. You just have to read the same books. But you have something that they do not all have, and they cannot get it from reading books. You have intuitive intelligence. A lot of it, I might add. If you trust it and follow it, it will work very well for you."

The minute Professor Henning said that to me, I knew on a visceral level that what he was saying was true.

Between the moment when Sister Jonah had asked me to read my story for the eighth grade and the moment when Professor Henning pointed out that I had intuition, I had received many sincere compliments. Even though I didn't like school, I nevertheless had some minor successes and knew there were things I could do well. So what was it about those two events that so deeply impressed my memory and directed my life? It was that those two teachers recognized two strengths inside me, and when they pointed them out, I knew they were true. Sister Jonah and Standish Henning did not fill me with strength. They did not give these things to me. What was so powerful was that they recognized something that was a real part of me, a part that, once named, I could follow. Once I became aware of my strengths, I began to practice them. I started to trust my intuition. I sought out places to apply my imagination.

I stayed in the class and received a fine grade. Even after my conversation with Professor Henning, I didn't fully believe the things he said to me. I never thought I was stupid (I always felt there was something wrong with the school, not me), but it never occurred to me that I might be smart. I thought back on my high school experience and was overwhelmed with disbelief: "You mean to tell me I may have been one of the brightest kids in the class and nobody could even see that?" This realization defined a mission for my life. I would devote my energies to preventing this kind of oversight in the lives and educations of as many kids as possible. I decided to become a teacher. Where others saw weakness, I would search out strength. I became a champion of the underdog, believing with all my heart that through identifying strengths, the underdog could become top dog.

My life didn't change overnight. I struggled and fell behind and refocused on several major occasions and hundreds of smaller ones, but I always found my way back to my path. I began teaching in a public high school in Frisco, Colorado. From there I went to Izmir, Turkey, followed by Nairobi, Kenya. I received two graduate degrees—one in English from the Bread Loaf School of English at Middlebury College and one from Harvard University's Graduate School of Education. I have been a principal in four schools, including the girls' boarding school where I am currently Head of School. I mention these facts not to boast or brag, but to point out that sometimes our concepts about secondary education and what we need to do in high school to be successful in life are just wrong.

Disabled concepts can create disabled students. My abilities were disabled in a system that didn't recognize my strengths and punished me for my weaknesses. I found math difficult because I didn't understand its language. My questions were attempts to grasp this language, but the teacher was unable to understand what I was asking him. He considered me a nuisance. I didn't have a weakness in math at all. As it turns out, I have some talent for statistical analysis.

Theory, personal experience, and practical application figure equally in this book. In any effort to effect positive changes in education, *why, who,* and *how* are questions that need to be asked and answered on both an individual and a national basis. This book answers each of these questions. It is a guide for families and individuals, as well as a wake-up call for a nation.

Contents

YOUR CHILD'S STRENGTHS

INTRODUCTION

Give me a lever long enough and a fulcrum on which to place it, and I shall move the world.

—ARCHIMEDES

THE STORY OF DEVELOPING STRENGTHS IN YOUNG PEOPLE IS NOT just a *feel-good* story. It is not about mere praise and self-esteem building. It's about igniting each child's individual potential and preparing them for successful, fulfilled lives in school and beyond. This objective has implications not just for the next generation of schoolchildren, but for the future of the American economy. The prevailing zeitgeist at the opening of the twenty-first century is reflected in such books as Thomas L. Friedman's *The World Is Flat* and Dan Pink's *A Whole New Mind*. The world lies on the cusp of great global change, and in order to remain competitive, future generations of Americans will have to be more adaptable and inventive than ever. We can't rest on the assumption that we will come out on top. Today, the United States ranks nineteenth in the world in education. Forty years ago, it ranked number one. A country's economic system cannot sustain this kind of gradual decline, especially when technological progress is accelerating and most jobs of the future will require knowledge skills over labor skills. Many people, from economists to CEOs to professors, have accurately described globalism and all its challenges and opportunities, but there has been little exchange between the people responsible for educating the future workforce and those who fear there will be too few skilled people to fill the demanding jobs of the future.

In December 2006, the New Commission on the Skills of the American Workforce issued a challenge to the U.S. educational system in their publication of *Tough Choices or Tough Times*. Among other things, this publication calls for a radical change in our educational system in order to prepare our citizens to compete in the global economy. The report is clear in outlining the qualities that will be necessary in individuals to succeed in the workforce of the future. Among those qualities are the abilities to be creative and innovative. Because out-of-the-box ideas come from the combination and synthesis of several disparate elements, creative teams will be necessary in every field in the workplace of the future. These teams will need to assemble, disassemble, and reassemble in a short amount of time, requiring each person to be adaptable, cooperative, and innovative.

Those who experience repeated success will be the ones who know their strengths and can bring those strengths to the teams they join. If schools expect to develop innovative thinkers who can consistently perform in a highly fluid, furiously paced future, then it is imperative that they focus on helping students identify and practice their areas of strength before they join the workforce. It is no longer acceptable for schools to promise to deliver students to the next level and drop them off hoping they land somewhere on their feet. Future, direction, purpose, and meaning can no longer be compartmentalized assignments delegated to the guidance office.

For hundreds of years, educators have known what to do in schools. We have created program after program, and many of them have been quite good. Schools have introduced character education and career planning, invested in the arts, and educated the whole child. The reform movement and the idea of progressive education are concepts with over fifty years of history attached to them. So why have our schools been on such a decline? Why have we not been able to create a unifying concept that will sustain a national culture of high achievement for everyone? Perhaps we as a nation have not yet felt threatened enough to really change. Maybe the current implication—that if we don't begin to develop the kind of workers we need for the new economy, America will see a steady decline in quality of life—appears overstated.

If you believe that to be the case, just look around and you will see signs to the contrary. Today, Americans face mass school shootings, fluctuating global economics, dwindling social resources, and an environment stressed to near breaking points. Our nation's children will inherit these problems. They will be responsible for solving them, and the old approaches will no longer cut it. The world has changed, and it will never move backward. In order for the next generation to be successful, they will need to think differently, and that begins by knowing what their strengths are. The concept of strengths development is the unifying element that flows through all efforts at school reform. It makes sense in every arena that is focused on raising healthy, productive, and happy children.

This book attempts to not only describe a possible future but to provide an easy-to-follow road map to getting there. I wrote it with everyone's interests in mind. Most parents I know spend hundreds of hours worrying about their children but ask very few important questions about *what, how,* and *why* we do what we do in schools. Most people who have the ways and means to opt out of public school and place their children in independent schools believe they have found the answers and do not have to worry about their children's futures. Many parents of public school children think that if the testing would stop, if the teachers were better trained, or if the funding were increased, the system would be fine. Each of these notions is wrong. The effort toward change begins at the personal level, with you and your children. The time for this journey is now, because the twenty-first century will demand strength. Focusing on weakness is what leaves people behind.

This book has three parts. Part 1 describes some of the ideas and practices that contribute to children's feelings of weakness. Part 2 explains what strengths are and how and why families and schools should help children develop theirs. Part 3 offers a variety of workbook exercises that parents, teachers, or children can use to discover and develop their strengths. In the appendix, you'll find the Strengths Inventory, a questionnaire children can take to help them identify what their strengths are, as well as some worksheets, suggested resources for developing a strengths-based culture in your organization, and an outline of the Affinities Program, a four-year high school curriculum designed to create a strengths community in schools. In total, this book invites you to heed a call and to join in spreading the word about how focusing on children's strengths will change the world.

PART 1

THE WEAKNESS HABIT

You cannot run away from weakness; you must some time fight it out or perish; and if that be so, why not now, and where you stand?

—ROBERT LOUIS STEVENSON

Chapter 1

THE FACE OF WEAKNESS

I AM STANDING IN A MOST UNUSUAL PLACE AT THE MOST MIRACULOUS moment of my life. I am crying as I watch Lucy's head and then her elegant little body push into the world. My best friend, Laura, has invited me to witness the birth of her daughter. We arrive in the middle of the night, her husband, her father, and I. Lucy is finally born early in the morning, just after sunrise, and I stay at the hospital while she awakens to the world. During the initial hours of her life, I am aware of a glow in the hospital room. There is a feeling of awe that is so rich we can almost see it hanging in the air around us. Lucy is beautiful in every way. She grasps at the air, wriggles and twitches, gaining a sense of what this life feels like. I watch her as she discovers light and sound and hears her name spoken by the people who will know and love her throughout her life. Her journey has just begun. I hold her and think, "I have you here with me at this moment, when you have no fear, and you are not worried or anxious. You have failed at nothing. The only thing you have experienced from others is love." What a day! I know what will come for her. There will be mistakes and loss . . . and pain. Everyone must suffer a little to grow. You get tough, you get strong, and you learn to survive through life's challenges. However, on this day, for this precious child, there is only joy. I pass her into her father's arms and watch him kiss her fuzzy head. What can we do to keep her strong? How can we best prepare her for a life that is fulfilling and rewarding? How can she learn to be optimistic and resilient in the face of setbacks?

Every child is unique. All children come into the world bearing gifts. All have strengths and talents inside them, and yet there is the possibility that their uniqueness will go unrecognized. Lucy is no different. She will need to discover and develop her strengths in order to avoid a life of weakness. What does weakness look like? We stare weakness in the face every day and often have no idea what we are looking at or where it comes from.

Weakness is a feeling of depletion, a constant draining of energy. There are countless ways that people experience and express feelings of weakness and depletion. It can manifest as the perpetual sense that tomorrow, or next year, things are going to get better—but they don't. Being an adult without a direction or a sense of greater purpose is also a form of weakness. The face of weakness can appear as frustration, anger, isolation, or addiction. Weakness personified is a persistent and cunning thief, creeping into your life and the lives of your children masked as hope and constantly nagging, "Look at me, fix me, improve me, and then you will be happy."

Weak lives begin in childhood, yet often the damage done then is subtle and doesn't show up until later in life, when many factors and events merge together to create feelings of uncertainty, a lack of creativity, a loss of direction, and an insatiable hunger for something more. Weak lives can cause people to make poor and hasty marriage choices or rush into careers they have no taste for, or blame others when things do not go well. Weakness is a trap, but it can be escaped. Best of all, if we recognize it, we can help children break free or avoid it altogether.

The opposite of weakness is strength. Strong lives are those that are marked by a sense of purpose, connectedness, resilience, and fulfillment. So how can we foster these traits in our children?

Children are not that different from adults. They want clear and realistic goals, expectations for their futures, and systems that will allow them to arrive at those goals feeling fulfilled and strong. They also want a voice in setting those goals and expectations for their futures. When children go to a particular college, take up a new hobby, or follow a career path just to please someone else, they end up in positions of weakness, not strength.

No matter what their personalities or characteristics, children will not develop their true talents or discover their real strengths without a process of encouragement, nurturing, and sustained approval. Most people reading this book will think they already encourage, nurture, and show appropriate approval—and most of you are right—but there are things that you do and that your child's school does that unintentionally weaken children. We're unwittingly sending disapproving messages to children all the time. In general we do this through the systems we have in place, and specifically with the conversations we have, or do not have, about the expectations and requirements we have laid out for their future success. I call this focusing on the weakness.

Part 1 of this book will show you how we do this and explain why we must stop. Every week I speak with at least three parents who call me looking for answers and advice on how to help their child find both joy and success in school. After listening to hundreds of stories from anxious parents about problems their child is having, at the end of these phone calls, I can honestly tell them the one thing they want to hear: *There is nothing wrong with your child.*

But the calls just keep coming, and they all sound the same. After a while I just had to stop and ask, "What's going on out there?"

The weakening of children is rooted in the concepts and practices of the traditional school environment that are outlined in this chapter: what we teach, how we teach, and the outcomes we expect from children. The negative effects of these practices are not obvious to most parents or teachers, perhaps because the system has been in place for hundreds of years. We have taken for granted what we teach and how we teach it. Until recently, our means of teaching our children and assessing their learning seemed to work. That is changing. Despite our efforts, growing numbers of children, across a wide spectrum of abilities, are not engaged in learning and leave school without a sense of direction. Many children are flat-out failing and dropping out of school altogether. Every day, 6,000 children in the United States drop out of high school—one every twenty-nine seconds—making for 1.1 million dropouts a year.

Most parents share a growing anxiety about the schooling of their children. That is because the American educational system today is an anxiety-producing machine. The alarming message it presents is that there is not enough to go around for everyone to be successful. American schools are functioning in much the same way as our national sports teams; there are inevitable winners and losers. The "game" atmosphere of our schools suggests that there are certain rules that everyone on the team must obey, and that anyone who refuses to play by the rules is considered uncooperative and will be given a penalty card or even tossed out of the game. This is a fine and appropriate way to run a soccer match, but as we have applied the model to schools, we have failed to ask three critical questions: What if the rules are all wrong? What if we have played a flawed game from the start and, without realizing it, have thrown out some of our best players? How can we be sure that our child will not become weakened by this game? To answer these questions we must begin to look at what we teach, how we teach it, and what we expect from children. Only when we look at these three things in a new way can we see precisely what is causing the weakness and, in that, understand how our child can avoid it.

THE CONTENT WEAKNESS: WHAT WE TEACH

> *It is important that students bring a certain ragamuffin, barefoot, irreverence to their studies; they are not here to worship what is known, but to question it.*
>
> —J. BRONOWSKI, *THE ASCENT OF MAN*

We teach the same topics in our schools today that we taught over one hundred years ago. Where did these subjects come from? How did we choose what to teach? In 1892, a group of ten university academics, known as the Committee of Ten, met to discern what standards would be necessary for admission to the nation's colleges and universities. Then president of Harvard University, Charles W. Eliot chaired the committee. Along with the nine others, he set out to develop a national curriculum intended to prepare students for entry into Harvard and similar institutions of higher education. This group convened to address a growing concern that the high school curriculum catered to two kinds of students; the college bound and those for whom high school was the terminal point in education. Schools taught basic arithmetic alongside classical Latin, causing much debate over the purpose of education. Was it to prepare children for college or for the labor market? Of course, many of the same debates continue today. In 1892, Charles Eliot and his committee narrowed the scope of the curriculum by reducing the number of courses from between fifteen and twenty to six or eight, and broadened the sequence by making the study of each course occur over several years. Today, in most schools in the United States, we still follow the same regimen.

As parents, you should know which subjects the schools are teaching your children, but more important, you should ask why. Why, for example, do we arrange history courses as a march through the world's wars? Why not teach it as a march through the history of scientific invention? Why do we teach trigonometry, a subject few people will use in their lives, instead of statistics, a topic that is valuable in many professions? Why is *Romeo and Juliet* taught in ninth grade and *Macbeth* in tenth grade? Why don't we learn how we govern our local communities or where the food in our grocery stores comes from? Who determines what is important, and is the same thing important for everyone? Is what was important ten years ago still important today? Part of the reason today's children are not motivated in school is that they do not understand why they need to learn the things we teach them. How can you explain it to them if you also don't understand? Parents and teachers should ask and answer these kinds of questions together, with the understanding that there is not one easy or right answer but that without scrutiny we are not really investigating how to best prepare children for a future that will be radically different from life as we know it today.

"I hate school" means many things. Sometimes it means "I have no interest in the topics presented and nobody cares to explain why I should." Children cannot develop interest in a subject just because adults tell them they should be interested. Children become unmotivated when they don't understand the importance of what they are required to learn. And they become frustrated and anxious when they are expected to demonstrate high achievement in subjects that don't seem important—especially if they lack a natural interest or talent in that area.

Think back to your own schooling. What did you learn? If you were like me, you probably learned quadratic equations, the reasons for the Spanish Inquisition, and the past perfect tense of the foreign language you studied. As a matter of curiosity, I pulled a dusty red spiral notebook from the back of my closet to check and see if my memory served me. The red cover was faded, my name written in big block letters across the top. Instead of a dot over the letter *i* in Jenifer, I had drawn a flower. I followed my name with six exclamation points. On one page I read my homework assignments:

Thursday

SPANISH- Review demonstrative adjectives and pronouns p. 336 and relative pronouns, p. 341.

BIOLOGY- Multiple alleles & co-dominance; Read and take notes on ch. 9, p.159-166. Continue working on Review Packet.

ENGLISH- Finish reading the *Epic of Gilgamesh*, do grammar exercises.

HISTORY- Finish review questions on ways in which the Ming and early Qing Dynasties represent the high point in Chinese Society.

MATH- complete nonlinear functions.

I stared at the homework assignments realizing I could not remember anything from any of the topics. Nothing. Looking over the assignments, my back tightened. I hated *Gilgamesh*. In fact, I don't think I ever read past the first two chapters. I loathed most of the reading we had to do in high school, and because of that, I didn't complete most of it. And English was my favorite subject! What I do remember is what teachers I liked and why. I remember Mr. Huth, my favorite English teacher, and the wonderful poems we read in his class. I can still remember reading *The Heaven of Animals* by James Dickey. I read it to myself in class, and the moment I understood its meaning it hit me like a thump to my back. "Oh, oh wow! This is so cool, they are perfect, always perfect," I uttered. Mr. Huth winked at me. He actually winked at me as if I knew a profound secret that only he and I understood. I will never forget that.

Today, I have no idea what multiple alleles are. Co-dominance sounds like shared leadership to me, but I am sure we didn't study that in biology class. Perhaps if the teacher lifted the biology concepts from the textbook and applied them to a broader understanding of the world, I would have some recollection of them today. However, this didn't happen, and as soon as my classes were over, I forgot almost everything I learned. How was that supposed to help me discover my path in life?

Very few people ever specialize in careers that leverage history, algebra, or chemistry. Those who do and excel in those professions do so not because they remember the information contained on page 458 of an 884-page textbook. Instead, it is because they understand why the things they learned are important in a larger context. True learning is all about making connections between what you learn and how it makes for a better life or a better world. Without these important connections, children are not engaged in learning. When children are not engaged in learning, they stop paying attention. This is where the downward spiral into weakness begins.

Children become passionate and interested when they see real-life ways that the subjects, topics, and lessons are applied. This must happen if we are to justify learning so many subjects in school. Children, like adults, want to first understand why a topic is important to learn and then be shown how to use it. Like adults, every time a child studies a topic because he has to, he finds himself faced with a motivation problem. If you don't know why you need to know something, it is difficult to learn it and even more difficult to retain it. The first step parents and teachers can take in preventing this is to ask more questions about the relevance of what is taught in the classroom.

Once you consider these questions in dialogue with someone else, you will appreciate how difficult it is to answer them. Eventually, if you pursue this conversation and everyone doesn't walk away upset, you will arrive at the understanding that learning skills are more important than the actual topics per se, and that children can help choose the topics without compromising the need to and means of developing certain skills. Parents and teachers can ask children what they are interested in learning. They can also explain to children why it is important to study certain topics. When explained with reasons that are more significant than "to get into a good college" or "one day it will all make sense," children will begin to respect the process. These conversations are necessary. Children have a right to good and compelling reasons for studying and achieving in areas for which they hold no interest. How can we expect them to develop passions and talents if they have no choice in the things they learn? We foster weakness when we force children to sit all day absorbing content for which they will never have any use, then chastise them for not showing any interest.

The basic ideas behind Western education have their roots in Aristotelian logic, which is based on categorical thinking. We teach children that learning is the process of sorting and naming things. If it is this, then it is not that. We divide bodies of knowledge into neat subject categories such as history, science, and math. Most courses are further sliced, with the slivers packaged in precise and orderly boxes: the Revolutionary War, the Civil War, the Vietnam War, algebra, biology, art. Much tension in planning content occurs because we believe each topic must be presented discretely, with no spillover into another category. I have watched teachers as they rack their brains trying to determine what box the history of science should fit into. Schools spend months arranging and rearranging their curriculum, lining up all the pieces in a grand sequential order known as the school's "Scope and Sequence."

The assumption embedded in this sorting and labeling exercise is that there is one body of information which every child must learn and that we can divide this body of information into twelve grade levels, and then further still into five or six subject areas and 180 daily lessons a year. A lot of teacher confusion comes from trying to take topics that naturally resist categorization and force them into one of the boxes. We toss aside many great lessons because they cannot be categorized neatly. The reality is that the march though the content is not as important as the student's ability to work with that content. Children need to learn *how to* as much as *what*. Our schools need to transform into places that constantly give children the tools they will need to design their futures. The passive memorization of facts will not lead to a future in which students are ready to push beyond their limits. Today's children must learn how to work with information, and lots of it, because thanks to the Internet, everything is available to everyone, just about anywhere, twenty-four hours a day, right at the end of our fingertips. The learner has changed from passive receiver to active agent. We no longer need the teacher as a vehicle to deliver the information. Now we need the teacher to help children synthesize and assimilate it.

Over a hundred years ago, the American essayist and poet Ralph Waldo Emerson wrote, "We are students of words: we are shut up in schools, and colleges, for ten or fifteen years, and come out at last with a bag of wind, a memory of words, and do not know a thing." Emerson, a Harvard graduate, died in 1882. If Emerson were teleported from the Great Beyond into today's world, he would not understand how to go into a library and look up one of his books. That he could shop for them on Amazon.com would dumbfound him, but he would feel at home in many of the country's classrooms, and his criticism would still be relevant. Today, Emerson would find school even more frustrating because the rest of the world has become so much more complex. Knowledge alone is not enough. Children know this. They hunger for active involvement in the learning process. Even though the teachers do not intend this to happen, the passivity of their methods causes students to turn away from commitment to the classroom. Without their commitment, there is no way to fuel their passion or develop their strengths.

Teaching is one of the most complicated transactions that take place between people, and parents, teachers, and children should all be part of the conversation about it. For the development of strengths, and therefore lasting learning, to take place there must be a high level of trust, flexibility, creativity, and shared commitment. Children must be part of this dialogue, since they are the number one people in the transaction. They hold all the clues to their strengths. Parents can help by finding out which subjects will be taught and discovering where their children's interests lie. Whenever I think of bringing children into the dialogue about their learning and really listening to them, I think about my friend Janie's daughter, Marley.

When Marley Rockwell was in seventh grade, she was enthralled with a fort she built in the overgrowth in her backyard. She lived in southern Florida, where the vegetation is plump and gooey. Her new best friend, Caitlin, joined her in the fort every day one March. They were a little old for fort building, but this fort was different. From the ravine behind an apartment complex three blocks down, they pulled out two old chairs, a tarp, and some clay pots to keep in the fort. They lined the outside with shells and rocks. They made a little bookshelf out of bricks and boards on which to place their notebooks, magnifying glasses, tweezers, and binoculars. As the days inched toward spring, Marley and Caitlin spent more and more time in the fort, and my friend Janie, Marley's mother, worried about it.

"She goes out there every day immediately after school," she told me, her forehead a wavy sea of worried wrinkles.

"So what do you think, are they smoking pot out there?" I asked.

"Pot? God, no!" Janie laughed.

"Don't think they are beyond it. Kids experiment, you know, and Marley will not be the exception. If I were you, I'd check the fort carefully."

"What should I look for?" She asked.

"Matches, incense, I don't know, cigarette butts."

Marley and Caitlin were, in fact, not doing any drugs, or any other questionable activity. Instead, they were studying nature. Marley and Caitlin spent many afternoons in the fort bonding over their shared love of nature. They captured all manner of insects and catalogued them, putting their crusty bodies into small baby food jars, occasionally dissecting the larger ones. In their notebook, they wrote detailed descriptions of the vegetation around them, the way the insects moved about, and what most interested the birds. They became close friends. They shared a secret life together that was part play and part investigation—and it belonged to them alone.

"Here is her history homework assignment for the week," Janie said, thrusting an index card into my hand. "She hasn't done one stitch of it. Every day, out in that fort like a child. It is weird. I thought they were doing some kind of witch ritual out there. Did you see all those jars filled with bugs?"

I reviewed the index card:

> MONDAY- Famous Shakespeare lines, reading for understanding. The Age of Elizabeth.
>
> TUESDAY- The Age of Reason.
>
> WEDNESDAY- The Industrial Revolution–The Mill Video.
>
> HOMEWORK: Read pgs. 526-530 and take notes.
>
> THURSDAY- Finish Mill Video.
>
> HOMEWORK: Read pgs. 530-536 and take notes.
>
> FRIDAY- Industrial Revolution Test.

I laughed. Her teacher expected her to cover more ground in one week of seventh grade than I did in an entire college career.

"You know, Janie, you should let them keep the fort. You should even encourage the fort. They care about it. They are learning out there—they are developing a strong interest in nature. In the long run, they will remember the fort and not the four pages in their textbook that describe the Industrial Revolution."

"What are you suggesting? That we let her play in the fort all day and skip her classes?"

"Of course not. I am only suggesting that you not minimize her experience in the fort. Don't devalue it or threaten to take it away if she doesn't do her homework. And as far as her classes go, I am simply pointing something out, giving you something to think about. Where did you get this index card anyway?"

"It was pinned to a tree near the fort. I thought it was some kind of witch's spell. I was pretty freaked out."

"Well, if kids can actually cover and retain this much material in a week, it truly is a form of witchcraft."

THE METHOD WEAKNESS: HOW WE TEACH

> *Much education today is monumentally ineffective. All too often, we are giving young people cut flowers when we should be teaching them to grow their own plants.*
>
> —JOHN W. GARDNER

If the content of the high school curriculum is becoming obsolete, the methods we use to teach it are near fossils. What was high school like when you were there? How were your classes taught? Thirty-two years ago, I sat in a chair attached to the desk with a shiny silver tube. The trouble with these chairs is that you could not lean back in them, although some boys tried. There was a wire basket attached to the back to put our books in, but nobody ever used it for that. Some kids threw paper balls at the baskets, trying to score points. The desks were set up in rows, or sometimes, if the teacher was cool, in a semicircle. Most classes used a fat textbook that weighed between two and three pounds. I had between four and six classes a day, and each one of them assigned some kind of homework, usually an end-of-chapter series of problems that we were supposed to solve and turn in the next day. My classmates and I knew that the teacher never read the homework problems; she just walked up and down the aisle scratching a check next to our names in her grade book if she saw that we completed the work sheet. Some kids didn't really complete the homework; they just wrote some answers on the page so it looked as if they did. The teachers never really looked closely, so the kids got away with it. I thought this was awful until I became a teacher and learned that some teachers don't really keep track of the homework; they just pretend to mark a check in the book so students think they have to do the homework.

Thirty years later, classrooms look pretty much the same as they did then, except instead of green chalkboards, many classrooms now have white dry erase boards. The basic configuration of the room is still the same—desks in rows or semicircles. Some classrooms have everyone sitting at a seminar table. Fat textbooks still abound, at least for math and science . . . and history . . . and literature . . . and foreign languages. I always thought textbooks for literature were such a shame. How often do people pop a textbook in their bag and head off to the beach? How many people do you see reading textbooks on the train on the way to work? Reading habits begin early, and books can seem luscious and inviting to children, arousing their interest in reading. Textbooks? Not so much.

The schedules in today's schools are similar to the ones we had thirty years ago: discrete courses divided into separate time blocks. And the homework routine is pretty much the same: complete the problems at the end of the chapter; turn in to the teacher the next day.

Most elementary schools have a variety of hands-on, creative, and group activities. Students are encouraged to explore the classroom and the work actively with other students. By the time students get to middle school, these methods are used more infrequently, and by the time kids are in high school, it is rare to find a class in which the teacher is not standing in front of the room directing all the learning. If class discussions occur, the teacher is usually the one in total control of the questions and answers rather than students conversing with one another. The majority of high school classrooms require that students absorb rather than interact with the information provided by the teacher. Learning is assessed with small quizzes that are followed by tests. Most questions on the quizzes and tests are recall questions, which test students' short-term memory rather than their knowledge or understanding of how to work with a subject. This is why a television show like *Are You Smarter Than a 5th Grader?* can become successful. Most Americans cannot recall the simple facts they learned back in fifth grade, not because they are stupid but because our minds are not programmed to retain and instantly recall information we do not need to know in order to work or survive.

These methods do not engage children in true learning. And they certainly don't help them discover their potential or point them in the direction of their talents. When the focus is on whether a child can regurgitate content, it is off the child's thoughts or his or her true opportunities for learning.

Most teachers instruct in the style in which they learned best and teach the subjects they enjoyed learning. Few teachers were not naturally passionate about and talented in the subject they teach. Counterintuitively, this often makes them the worst teachers, for they cannot imagine what it must be like to struggle with a subject that came naturally to them and they therefore learned with ease. In their classes, they praise and reward students who learn in the same manner as they do. As a society, we accept and perpetuate a hierarchy of learning styles. We consider the methods used in today's traditional classrooms to be the pinnacle of the hierarchy. We have concluded, without any scientific evidence, that the right way, the best way, for the majority of learners to learn is the traditional method. How are we so certain that is so? In some respects, what we label as weakness in children is not a weakness at all—it is simply that the child doesn't come into the classroom sharing the talent, passion, and learning style of the teacher. The teacher's job is certainly made easier if the student comes in already loving the subject and is able to learn it as easily as the teacher did. This, however, does not make a great teacher. I once heard an educational consultant talk about independent school classrooms as the easiest teaching jobs around. He claimed that the children are preselected for success in the traditional system. He was fond of saying, "If you are going to sit on eagles' eggs, you better darn well hatch eagles."

There are as many teaching styles as there are learning styles, and this presents exciting adventure—rather than a complicated burden—for teachers and parents. True teaching talent reveals itself when the teacher struggles to engage students in the process, not giving up until he finds a way to bring about understanding and competence in the student. I think everyone should read that last sentence a few times. It says every child can and wants to learn and that it is the teacher's and the parents' responsibility to discover how to make that happen. Too often, we place the entire responsibility for learning on the child. When learning is difficult, we assume the child, rather than the teacher or the parent, has the problem. Parents are also important teachers in every child's life, and they are often unaware of the ways in which their own style prejudices the way they view their child's approach to tasks and to learning.

I remember an example of this from one of my first jobs in teaching. I ran the Middle School Talented and Gifted Program at a school in Summit County, Colorado. The program was new, and it was my job to build it up and make something of it. When I started, the talented and gifted (TAG) program consisted of nine students. I was perplexed from the beginning at the name of the program, believing that all students were somehow talented, and I was eager to discover what made these nine children different.

All of the parents contacted me about their expectations for the TAG program, and no two parents had the same requirements. Additionally, I did not see a clear connection between their goals and the respective child's goals.

One evening in mid-October, I met with the parents and their children to discuss and plan a trip to Taos, New Mexico. I created a working session for them, designed to give me an idea of the ways the parents interacted with their children. I divided the room into three stations: meals, transportation and accommodations, and activities. At each station there was a planning activity for six people, three parents and three children. Each station's activity was very different. The meal station featured enough food items for nine meals. The people at the table had to use only the food that was there to make menus for three different meals. Another station had maps, a phone book, travel books, and some pencils and paper. The task was to figure out transportation, everything from renting a vehicle to determining which routes to take, where to get gas, and where the group was going to stay each night. The third table had cutouts of magazine photographs of people participating in many activities. I cropped them very carefully so as not to suggest more than necessary. For instance, I cut out a group of people in a white-water raft but left out the background. There were scissors, glue, markers, and a long piece of white butcher paper on the table. The people who chose this station were supposed to create an artistic timeline of the events and activities the group was going to engage in during the day. If a preferred activity wasn't represented in the photos, they were free to draw it. The instructions were to fill in as much background information as possible using the supplies on the table.

When all nine students and their parents arrived, I invited them to first walk from table to table to gain a sense of what each station entailed. I told them that this would be a two-part exercise. They were free to choose a table to work at for the first half hour; however, I stipulated that the parents must go to the same table as their children. After a half hour passed, parents and kids would be free to split up and then choose any table they wished.

Only two sets of parents and children wanted to go to the same table, and they immediately went to it and waited while the other parents and children negotiated. Three children won the negotiations, while the other four ended up at the table of their parent's choosing. I walked around and observed all three stations at work. Coincidentally, the two pairs who immediately agreed on which job to do both wound up at the meal station. They worked together quickly and efficiently, taking the lead in the planning while the other family at the table watched. There were many dynamics in the room to observe, but some of the more striking ones were these: the children who were most involved were the ones who chose to join that particular table. Likewise, at the tables where the parents won the choice, they took the lead in the exercise while the child sat back and observed. At each table, someone was not participating as much as the others. After thirty minutes, I walked around and graded everyone on their participation. I handed an index card with an A on it to everyone who was actively participating and an index card with a C on it to all the inactive parents and children.

I invited them to switch tables if they wanted and to go to the activity of their choice. I told them it was okay if they were not evenly distributed and said parents and children were free to choose separate tables. Both pairs of parents and children who originally chose the meal table remained there together. Everyone else split up, and all the people who were inactive moved to a new table. After about ten minutes of explanation and negotiation to bring the new groups up to speed, everyone seemed to be participating in some way at the stations. Near the end of the session, I gave everyone an index card with an A on it. After each group presented their ideas, I asked those who had initially received Cs to share their individual experiences with the group.

"I was excited to do the map exercise," one parent explained, "so when I got stuck at the activity table, I was bummed. I am no good at art."

"I loved the meal planning," said another. "It was much easier when we had the food in front of us to picture how to reuse it. I usually take way too much food on trips."

"So you liked the visual aspect of the task?" I asked.

"Oh yeah, I don't think I would have chosen to plan meals unless the table was set up like that."

I turned back to the parent who said he was no good at art. "Mr. Henderson, if you were the teacher and you had to teach a class on any topic that you wanted to, would you ever choose to have a group work with scissors and drawings like the first table you attended?"

"God, no. That kind of creative group work drives me crazy. It feels, well, childish to me," he admitted. I turned to the people who chose to go to that table in the second round.

"So how does that make you feel?"

One child said, "Well, I think we came up with a great idea for the trip. I got a C on my card before I came to this table and I was not interested. I got an A from this table."

When teachers, or parents, for that matter, teach using only their own dominant style, some children will be energized by that style and some will be weakened. If we use only one way to teach, children may never have an opportunity to discover, let alone develop, their strengths. As this experiment shows, oftentimes, as parents and teachers, *you* make choices for children that make *you* comfortable, that accommodate *your* learning style and that allow *you* to succeed rather than your child. Children usually do not have the language to express their frustration at this with you. As I stated earlier, true teaching talent reveals itself when the teacher struggles to engage children in the process, not giving up until he finds a way to bring about the child's understanding and competence. Let's face it: there is much at stake in the process of teaching and learning, regardless of the age or level of the learner. Education of any kind is definitely not one size fits all. Many feelings of weakness are the result of a breakdown in a teaching moment, both in the schoolhouse and in the workplace. People often feel misunderstood and betrayed by their teachers and schools because their unique styles and strengths have no room to grow.

You don't have to look far to find stories about bright and talented people who are completely misunderstood in their school communities. I am drawn to the story of Thomas Edison, the inventor of the lightbulb and the phonograph. In fact, he was maybe the most prolific inventor in history, the holder of 1,093 U.S. patents. But schools nearly destroyed him. In 1855, when Edison was eight, he was enrolled in a one-room schoolhouse presided over by a man named Reverend G. B. Engle. Edison wrote that he felt his teachers didn't sympathize with him, and his own father felt he was stupid. One day, Edison overheard the teacher saying he was "addled," as in mentally defective, and he left school never to return. Today, Edison's teachers would no doubt say he fidgeted too much in class. He would be asked to "focus more," and I doubt he would have done well at all on the SAT. Fortunately, with the help of his mother, he figured out his own learning style. He wrote that she understood him and knew that his success would come from "letting him follow his own bent." I love that line. Today it means he was allowed to develop his strengths. With 1,093 patents to invent, there simply was no time to remediate his weaknesses.

THE EXPECTATION WEAKNESS: HOW WE SHOW CHILDREN CONSTANT DISAPPROVAL

> *Each man is afraid of his neighbor's disapproval—a thing which, to the general run of the human race, is more dreaded than wolves and death.*
>
> —MARK TWAIN

Parents and teachers have fallen into the trap of believing that academic accomplishment is the sole basis for achieving the well-lived life. Because of this belief, schools are set up as competitive arenas, and we have all kinds of illogical and nonverbally communicated expectations for our schools, our teachers, and our children. As in any competition, there are inevitable winners and losers, but in the high stakes grading game, no one is standing on the sidelines whispering, "It doesn't matter whether you win or lose, it's how you play the game." Losing matters. In the game of academic achievement, society punishes losers for life. At least that is how most parents and teachers act.

For children, learning within this paradigm becomes a means of ensuring emotional safety. The message children receive is that they are a disappointment if they do not learn and learn better than everyone else. Every day parents tell their kids in all kinds of ways that any display of academic weakness, in any realm, is cause for disappointment. Grounding children for poor grades, taking away all their privileges until their grades are raised, threatening to send them off to military school, and comparing their children's performance to how well they did in school are all weakening tactics.

So what do you do if your child is not studying, not making the grade or not living up to his or her potential? You first need to figure out why this is so. You will need to figure that out with the teacher and with your child, taking into consideration all the things you read in this book. One of those things is that for children, parental or teacher disappointment is one of the worst things they can experience. With so many ingredients in the recipe for a happy, successful, and fulfilling life, it is preposterous to put all the expectation for that outcome on school performance, and more specifically on your child's ability to master the content of a hundred-year-old curriculum. This dynamic drives children to desperate pursuits of success, and these pursuits can and do have adverse effects. When children overachieve, strive for perfect grades in every class, feel pressured to take all advanced-placement courses (in addition to being the captain of the debate team, editor of the school newspaper, and student council representative), we reward them with our praise and approval as though success in life means a full plate of outstanding achievement at the expense of an empty sense of authenticity. The pressure children feel to overachieve comes from a place of weakness rather than a place of strength. The message we give children when we say that they have to be outstanding at everything is that they are not good enough just being who they are.

We are not always aware of the language we use and the weakening effects it can and does have on children. They hear everything we say and absorb it even when it is not directed at them. How adults talk about children will convey the message that they either believe in them or not. A classic situation is adults overemphasizing a child's personality as though that is the variable that should be changed. How often do you hear teachers describe kids in these ways: "Allison is bright." "Charlie is a pleasure to have in class." "Karen is disruptive and unmotivated." What do these personality descriptors tell us about how children can learn and grow? Parents and teachers make a grave mistake when they believe that children's performances will improve as soon as their personalities change. *As soon as Maria learns to be a little less "out there," she will be able to focus better in school.* What better way to confound and frustrate our children than by telling them that the only way they can move ahead in school is by changing the unchangeable? You cannot turn a personality trait into a behavior by applying pressure. Take the following teacher comment as an example: *"Martin is bright and motivated. He is just above average in our class and enjoys the current unit on poetry, although at times he is confrontational in class discussion. We are working on fixing that."* Most parents would welcome this description simply due to its length and explicit attention on Martin. However, it doesn't say much that is useful. Contrast that with this version: *"Of late, while studying a unit on modern poetry, Martin has been making lively contributions to the class discussion. He uses a confrontational style, which I suggested he use in a debate for the final project on this unit."*

Education is about actions, not simple personality descriptions. The language parents and teachers use with and in front of children is critical to developing strength or focusing on weakness. Children need to know that adults believe in them even if their actions are not always strong. You can help change this. In part 2 we will explore the ways you will avoid some of these things.

As a parent or a teacher you may question some of these points, taking them to suggest that I am against academic achievement. This is not the case. I am in favor of promoting genuine learning and growth by focusing on strengths. That is the only way all kids will be able to fulfill their potential. Many children today have not yet identified what they really care about, so they run aimlessly after achievement to gain approval—approval from their parents, their peers, their schools, the college admission officers. Children should be motivated to achieve out of a true interest in learning. That is not going to happen unless they are actively engaged in lessons to which they can bring their strengths.

Parents and teachers are often clear about what they expect from children's schooling, whereas children are rarely given the opportunity to state what they hope to get out of it. Children's strengths won't develop unless they are able to participate in the conversation regarding expectations. Even if provided the opportunity, years of conditioning on the weakness path make it difficult, if not impossible, for children to know how to express their lack of connection with learning. We must understand this in order to strengthen the relationship needed for true learning to take place. Consider this statement of expectation that a history teacher wrote on a high school course syllabus presented to students at the beginning of the year:

> Expectations:
>
> The most basic expectation of this course is that you take an active approach to learning. What does this mean? Fundamentally, it involves an internal drive to pursue and ensure an understanding of material; a penchant for thinking about information and arguments that you encounter; a willingness to ask questions and look for possible answers; a sense of genuine personal investment in the endeavor. At a tangible level, you must be comfortable reading on a regular basis, be able to organize your efforts and material, and be willing to participate in class discussion. In sum, success in this course will depend on the extent to which you invest in the process of learning and act on your intellectual curiosity.

I read those expectations several times. Initially, they seemed noble. Who wouldn't want their students to demonstrate these things? Then I read the paragraph from a child's perspective. The teacher describes the *most basic* thing he expects and then lays out exactly what that entails. Expectations are serious for children. Nowhere in the course syllabus does it state what the teacher's role is in helping the child meet these expectations. What if I just need to take and pass this course? What if I am good at the subject and can do well, but do not have a genuine personal investment in this course? The problem children face is that all teachers want their students to be as passionate about their subject as they are. Teachers unknowingly reward the students who are and penalize the ones who are not. This desire on the teacher's part sets up an across-the-board expectation that students are motivated, engaged, and passionate about every subject. Teachers, operating within the narrow scope of their own department, usually do not consider a child's total experience in school. (This is clear when children end up with three major tests on the same day.) Back in the home, parents review a scorecard; we call it the report card, which parents tend to read like a stock portfolio. The grades that are up are good and must remain closely monitored. The ones that are down are in need of immediate attention. They signal trouble—let's fix them right away before we lose our investment.

For children, this reporting to expectations without any input or discussion about their strengths, what they may have a passion for, is demoralizing. It is rare that we invite children to give input or ask them what they love to do, want to do, or what they believe is possible. Many parents and teachers think that mere exposure to the content and completion of the work will result in the "internal drive," "genuine personal investment," and "comfort level" needed to engage a child's intellectual curiosity. These admirable goals cannot be achieved when learning becomes a chore for children or when both partners in the relationship are not committed to meeting the other's expectations. All children, whether or not they can articulate it, have the expectation that their teachers and parents will play an active role in shaping and defining their futures. They expect that parents and teachers will help them find futures in which their actions will make a difference and their work will be meaningful. To children, you don't live up to their expectations when you fail to involve them or assess their interests. Students are disappointed when parents and teachers fail to live up to this most basic expectation, and this disappointment can cause them to become emotionally disconnected from school.

They might still get good grades, but they have reduced their chances for strong and meaningful futures. Many children who are emotionally disconnected cannot hide their attitudes. Bad attitudes lead to underachievement. It is a vicious cycle we are in, and parents support this cycle without recognizing it.

You may be seeing my points but feeling frustrated because you want what is best for your child but wonder how you can change if the system won't change. There is a way out from under this weakness, and the entire system doesn't have to change first. This is the beginning, and it starts with you and the way you see your child and his education. Every important movement, be it the civil rights movement, the women's movement, or the environmental movement, began with one person changing her point of view. You are doing something important now. You are opening your mind to see why, in general, awakening to strengths is so important and, specifically, why this awareness is necessary to your child's education.

As is, the current win-lose, right-wrong model of education is entirely a model of scarcity. This model has everyone from the most academically talented to the most challenged believing that there is one road to success—and that all the on-ramps to that road are backed up for miles. This is all wrong. You can feel in your gut that it is wrong. This approach sends children the message that if they are not superhuman, they are weak and without inherent worth. Participating on the swim team or doing well in physics doesn't define who a child is or is able to become. Children cannot keep standing on tiptoe straining to grasp some ever-elusive magical combination of socially accepted activities that will give them the golden ticket to a successful and meaningful future. Parents today appear to be in the process of branding their children as if they were some marketplace product. They package them and present them to the world as if their résumés of achievements and activities are their identities and the foundation of their personalities. This is why children are anxious. They want to be more than a list of achievements and scores.

We must really start believing in the inherent worth of each child if we are to have any hope for their healthy future. If we could do this, school could become a journey, an exploration, rather than an evaluation that lasts eighteen years. Think about it—sixteen years of someone telling you what is right and what is wrong about you. And throughout, you've never had an ounce of input into the discussion. Imagine if this were happening to you in your workplace; imagine if you never set any of the goals or expectations, and you never had the opportunity to disagree. We could never fathom success in such a repressive environment for ourselves, so why do we think it is healthy for our children?

Chapter 2

STANDARDIZATION AND THE WEAKENING OF THE INDIVIDUAL

Standardization of our educational systems is apt to stamp out individualism and defeat the very ends of education by leveling the product down rather than up.

—HARVEY CUSHING, 1928

REMEMBER CABBAGE PATCH KIDS? IN 1983, THERE WAS SUCH A demand for them around Christmastime that parents were making the evening news for having fistfights in stores over the remaining few dolls on the shelves. These were soft-bodied dolls with plastic heads, and the sales gimmick was that they could be "adopted" by kids. The other thing that made these dolls so wildly popular was that no two dolls were alike. In order to be mass-produced, computers generated millions of subtle differences among the dolls. No two dolls had the same face, clothes, or coloring. It is incredibly ironic that the Cabbage Patch craze occurred the same year the National Commission on Excellence in Education published *A Nation at Risk: The Imperative for Educational Reform.* The Cabbage Patch Kids mania revealed a mass craving for individuality while *A Nation at Risk* spelled out a national agenda for standardization.

A Nation at Risk brought into widespread use the term *at risk* to describe all manner of children and behaviors. The report itself was a scathing condemnation of the state of education in the United States. The first paragraph, reprinted below, gives insight into the report's contents:

> Our Nation is at risk. Our once unchallenged preeminence in commerce, industry, science, and technological innovation is being overtaken by competitors throughout the world. This report is concerned with only one of the many causes and dimensions of the problem, but it is the one that undergirds American prosperity, security, and civility. We report to the American people that while we can take justifiable pride in what our schools and colleges have historically accomplished and contributed to the United States and the well-being of its people, the educational foundations of our society are presently being eroded by a rising tide of mediocrity that threatens our very future as a Nation and a people.

One of many false assumptions the report helped promulgate is that heightened competition between students in classrooms would translate into a nation that is able to compete in a global economy. After declaring that America has lost its competitive edge, the document goes on to say, "Our society and its educational institutions seem to have lost sight of the basic purposes of schooling, and of the high expectations and disciplined effort needed to attain them."

Unfortunately, the report spells out a means for schools and students to achieve renewed greatness that has nothing to do with identifying their talents or developing their strengths. *A Nation at Risk* was a weakness-based document, one that has instilled fear and anxiety in the American people, thus doing more harm than good.

Despite the lack of data or evidence proving that America was actually falling behind in the world economy, the commission nevertheless zeroed in on the following areas as ones demanding national public attention, based on comparisons to achievement in other nations and declining test scores in the United States:

- Achievement of high school students' standardized tests
- College Board Scholastic Aptitude Test (SAT)
- College Board Achievement Tests
- Time spent on homework (suggested more of it)
- Increase in number of remedial mathematics courses in public four-year colleges (Hey, Math 99-100!)

The commission's conclusions seemed right to many Americans because Americans are obsessed with comparisons. This is not the way of the rest of the world. British-born leadership expert and best-selling author and speaker Marcus Buckingham points out one significant difference between American and British culture by noting that England is not a highly competitive nation. He jokingly refers to England as the AVIS of nations; their motto is "We try harder," but they rarely win anything. He says, "Contrast that with the U.S.—you guys are the most competitive nation you could possibly imagine. How do I know this? Because you measure everything. Just look at your sports pages. Competitors love scores and metrics, because if you can measure it, you can compare it, and if you can compare it, you can compete. And if you can compete, you can win."

A Nation at Risk made many recommendations that were aimed at helping America become a nation of "winners" again. Here's a sampling:

- Do away with course electives and student choice in the high school curriculum.
- Develop a New Basics Curriculum that places study in the performing and fine arts as a complement to the Basic Curriculum.
- Raise the requirements for admission to college.
- Apply standardized achievement tests at every major transition level in school, with special attention given to the transition between high school and college.
- Standardize the use of textbooks in schools and make them more rigorous.
- Assign more homework.

Not one of these recommendations has lasted as federal policy except the call for mass standardized achievement tests. This standardized testing mandate reemerged on January 8, 2002, as the federal Elementary and Secondary Education Act called No Child Left Behind (NCLB). Although the name of the act suggests a worthy goal for our nation, tragically the legislation exacerbated rather than solved the real problems that cause many children to be left behind. Informed by the same weakness and fear-based paradigm as *A Nation at Risk,* NCLB has forced schools to narrow instruction to what is tested. In most states, reading and math test scores are the sole determinant of a student's progress. This approach is damaging to children in that they are coached to pass a test rather than to learn a rich curriculum that would prepare them for life in the twenty-first century. Testing in early grades interferes with instructional time that should be spent on teaching reading, writing, and problem solving. This crucial time cannot be regained. It is the time when children's brains are most receptive to learning new concepts—the time when they learn how to learn.

How many of us actually believe that any standardized tests can accurately reflect a child's intelligence and competence? Or that one metric is capable of classifying all children? Such assumptions defy almost everything we have come to understand about how children develop. Teachers and parents know this. When they have a chance to step back and reflect on their children, few will accept that any test score can define their child. The time our teachers spend preparing children for these tests is further evidence of a system that is trapped in it own weaknesses. Here is one story that shows how preparing for tests can get in the way of real learning.

KILLING THE LOVE OF LEARNING

Last March, my friend Laura suddenly had to take her toddler to the emergency room to get stitches. She called and asked if I would pick up her fourth-grade son, Jeffrey, and his three carpool mates from school. Of course, I agreed, and at 2:40 p.m., they emerged from the school. After I introduced myself and they tossed their backpacks into the "wayback," Jeffrey proudly claimed "shotgun" and sat up front with me. He struggled to pull the shoulder strap across his body, and once snapped in, he leaned over to push the heated seat button even though the temperature was in the sixties. "Cool!" he exclaimed, and turned around to see if his classmates were paying attention.

Cara, Travis, and Franklin sat buckled in across the backseat of my station wagon as I slowly pulled away from the school.

"So what did you all do in school today?" I asked, spying them through the rearview mirror. Cara's eyes met mine, and she waved.

"We got ready for tests," Travis said in an oddly sarcastic way for a young boy.

"What does that mean?" I asked.

"It means we have to practice taking tests and we have to practice accelerated reading prompts and we have to practice filling in the bubbles." Travis's voice was cynical as he described all this to me in singsong.

"You're just mad because you didn't get a certificate," Cara admonished.

Travis bit back: "Who cares? Those are dumb."

"What kind of certificate are you talking about?" I asked, trying to manage the tone of the conversation.

"For getting high accelerated reader scores," Jeffrey told me.

"What are those?" I asked, straining to see the name on the street sign that had faded so much I couldn't read it.

"You read a book and then take a test on the computer, and if you get a bunch right, you get a high score, and every week the highest scores get certificates," Cara explained proudly.

"It's stupid," moaned Travis.

"What books do you like to read?" I asked.

"I like a book called *B Is for Betsy,*" Cara announced.

"*B Is for Betsy.*" Travis mocked her.

"Travis, be nice. What books do you like?" I asked him.

"I hate reading," he announced.

"Oh, that is too bad. Why do you hate reading?"

"Hey, turn here, this is my street!" shrieked Franklin.

I had to go two more blocks to turn back around and get to his street. I stopped the car, got out, and pulled his backpack from the pile. As I handed it to him—it must have weighed twenty pounds—he said: "You didn't ask me, but I used to like reading. I read all the Lemony Snickett books. My favorite was the *The Penultimate Peril.* I thought you'd like to know because Lemony Snickett went to a boarding school, and Jeffrey says you do, too. Anyway, I don't really like to read so much anymore. I feel like we have to read fast and like there are only some things in the book that matter, the things on the test, and I can't think about the story as much as I used to because I am trying to guess what will be on the test. Thanks for the ride, Mrs. Fox." Franklin hoisted his backpack onto his right shoulder. I watched him as he scuttled down his driveway and slipped in the back door. Back in the car, Cara and Jeffrey were giggling.

"What's so funny?" I asked them.

"What was Frankie saying?" asked Jeffrey with a devilish grin.

"Did he tell you he is the lowest reading scorer in the whole class?" Cara snickered.

"Franklin the flunky, I bet he stays back a grade." Travis mocked.

"You kids be quiet, I think he's a nice boy, and I want you to be kinder to him."

"But he always has check marks beside his name," Cara said whiningly.

"Check marks?"

"Yeah, if you do something bad, the teacher puts your name up on the board, and if you do it a lot, she puts checks beside it so everyone can see."

"So what kind of things does he do?" I asked, genuinely curious.

"He always talks without raising his hand first."

"Sometimes he daydreams too much."

"He laughs when the teacher wants us to be serious."

"I see," I said, and drove the rest of the way in silence.

Unfortunately, this is an increasingly familiar theme for children across the United States. As more pressure is placed on doing well on tests, more children lose interest in learning because they are unable to connect the reasons for learning to anything meaningful in their own lives. Test scores do not intrinsically motivate children.

STANDARDIZATION VERSUS INDIVIDUALITY

Standardized test scores have the power to make or break a child. Today, children are being failed or denied access to advanced-degree programs and specialized schools, or even refused a high school diploma based on a single standardized test.

Recently, a father called my office and asked whether he should pay for his daughter to take another SAT prep class. She was only in tenth grade, so I asked him how many she had already taken. He told me that she had completed two courses, each costing over five hundred dollars, and she was still getting poor scores on the practice tests. His daughter spent almost three weeks of her summer in the SAT prep courses. Her anxiety was building, and he didn't know what to do. I asked him what he wanted for his daughter. He said he was concerned she might not get into college, and that would ruin her future. Every year it seems parents start worrying earlier about their child's ability to get into college. My advice to him? Save his money, stop worrying, and give his daughter a little more time to be an adolescent. Sometimes parents worry so much about the future for their children that they make a mess of today. Once children leave childhood, they can never return. Childhood affords them the time to be creative dreamers. In the end, these qualities will help them get into college as much as a good score on the SAT.

Most parents know the fuss over standardized testing is emotionally damaging for their children, but what many may not realize is that it is also educationally unsound. While there are some good reasons for using standardized testing, many more factors make it an inadequate tool with which to formulate the educational policies of our nation. Most educators know this. Among teachers, the following items are common knowledge:

- It is a common misconception that what is taught in a classroom and what is tested are the same thing. Unfortunately, what students are tested on doesn't always match up with the instructional content and objectives of the classroom.
- Most standardized tests are multiple-choice. Multiple-choice tests most often test knowledge at the recall level. Recall is a function of memory. Even at their very best, multiple-choice formats limit the demonstration of problem solving and critical and creative thinking.
- High-stakes standardized testing has negative emotional effects on students and teachers. After doing poorly on a test, low-achieving students often become disillusioned and less motivated, which leads to a decreased desire to learn and starts a downward spiral that is very hard to halt.
- Being "test savvy" and being well educated are not the same thing. If someone is test savvy, he understands the strategies that help him do well on the test. These include little tricks such as skipping the questions on timed tests that will take up a lot of time and answering all the questions you know right away because you can always go back to the more difficult ones and they are worth the same amount of points. It is easy for teachers to raise test scores by teaching these strategies. However, if teaching test savviness achieves the needed gains in test scores, what are the tests really measuring?

Apparently, American children in the year 1983 were on to something entirely different from the Commission on Excellence in Education. Children craved Cabbage Patch dolls. They craved them precisely because each one of them was unique. The children of the eighties deeply and intuitively valued individuality. Unfortunately, schools bought the recommendations in A *Nation at Risk* wholesale. The rules of the new standardization were clear— sharpen the competition, narrow the definition of success, and map out one educational road upon which all children would become travelers, barricading all alternative routes. Individuality, a founding tenet of our country, went a long way for the sale of Cabbage Patch Kids. Had our education system responded to the same desire, today our schools might be places where differentiated instruction based on strengths and curriculum materials build the creative thinking and problem-solving skills needed for success.

Individuality by definition resists standardization. If the educational system is ever to truly embrace the unquestionable rewards of individualized instruction, we must devise new methods for measuring achievement. This challenge will demand a national refocusing. People will have to learn to rely on different types of evidence that measure individual achievement and satisfaction. This is going to require a major paradigm shift, but just like every other important shift in outdated, conventional thinking, the process begins with the individual. We can make things better for future generations, and for our own futures, if we begin instilling a positive, strengths-based focus in the youth of America.

Chapter 3

THE HIGH COST OF A BRAND-NAME COLLEGE

What you know you can't explain, but you feel it. You've felt it your entire life, that there's something wrong with the world. You don't know what it is, but it's there, like a splinter in your mind, driving you mad.

—THE MATRIX

APPLYING TO COLLEGE AND GETTING INTO THE "GOOD SCHOOLS" has become an intensely competitive process during which many children are so fixated on getting in, they don't fully consider why it is they are even going to college. Anxiety around college admission seems to be the driving force trapping parents and children in a damaging cycle of weakness in most educational experiences leading up to college.

Annually since 1983, *U.S. News & World Report* magazine has ranked America's 100 Best Colleges. This publication has changed the way parents and students choose institutions of higher education, leading them to believe that the value of a college degree is only as good as its brand name. For the past twenty-five years, this annual ranking system has almost guaranteed that SAT scores are considered the most important factor in college admission. In reality, SAT scores remain a notoriously poor measure of both student ability and likelihood of success in college.

Early last spring, I had a conversation with the associate dean of admissions at a nearby university, and it drove these points home. The story starts with a beleaguered parent at our school. She was beside herself with worry that her daughter Maggie, a diligent, socially adept student with a great talent for dancing, was not going to be accepted to college. She had good grades throughout high school, and her teachers considered her a good student. Maggie had impressed me many times with her utter confidence on stage. She performed in many school musicals and on the competitive dance team. She felt motivated by dance, and she worked hard to become good enough to build her life around it. Like many students, Maggie bombed standardized tests. She had a poor memory and suffered from all too common test anxiety. Like many young women, she performed better on the ACT than on the SAT.

Everyone was proud of Maggie after she returned from her dance audition at a small liberal arts college in a nearby state. She had chosen the college specifically for its very selective dance program. Over sixty-five students had auditioned for the program, and Maggie was one of sixteen who were chosen. When her mother called me frantically one day and asked me to please contact the college's admissions office to see if they were going to admit her or not, my first reaction was one of nonchalance. Of course they would admit her, I thought. She has good grades, and she was selected for the dance program. I advised Maggie's mother to do what most colleges want and have Maggie herself contact the school to advocate for her own admission. I explained that admission officials looked for that kind of self-motivation. Another week passed, and our school's college counselor stopped me in the dining hall.

"Maggie hasn't heard from any of the schools she applied for yet, and her mother is getting really anxious. Can you call her?"

Because I wanted to call with good news, I first called the admissions office to find out what was going on. Tania, the admissions person in charge of Maggie's application, was warm and friendly but told me that she felt it would be very difficult for their admissions team to admit Maggie because of her low SAT scores.

"But what about her grades?" I asked.

"We are just worried she won't be able to handle her other courses."

"What gives you that idea? She's an excellent student here."

"Yes, but you are a performing arts school, so she hasn't been prepared for college," she said assuredly.

"No, I think you misunderstand. We are a college preparatory school; she dances a lot here, but we have a rigorous college program. Have you looked at the transcript?"

I went on to explain that while Maggie may not be able to earn all As or Bs in college, she would be a good student, a solid student motivated to succeed, one who would by no means flunk out of school. The admissions officer told me she would take this information to the dean, but that I shouldn't get my hopes up.

I was in disbelief. Who did those people think they were? I called Maggie's mom and vowed to fight this.

"Be careful," she cautioned me.

The next day I placed another call to the admissions office. I again told the officer that Maggie was a right choice for admission, and she told me again that she would bring the information to the committee, but that her SAT scores were most likely going to prevent her admission. You can imagine my frustration. Before I could go on to explain why they should overlook the scores and admit her anyway, she interrupted the conversation.

"If she had mailed in *only* her ACT scores, she probably could have gotten in without being sent to committee."

I quickly rifled the green college file the college counselor's assistant had left on my chair that morning. I found the right paper and saw that her ACT scores were not that much better than her SAT scores. I asked her about this.

"I don't understand," I said. "Her ACT scores are only slightly better than her SAT scores. I told you, she doesn't do well on tests, any standardized tests."

She told me that ACT scores don't count. I asked her what she meant by "count."

"You know," the admissions officer explained, "for the ranking data."

I listened while she explained that they had to submit all the SAT scores of students who were admitted in the freshman class to *U.S. News & World Report* for the 2006 rankings, and that Maggie's scores would bring down the average and negatively affect the university's ranking. She told me that since the publication doesn't use ACT scores in the ranking, colleges were able to overlook those if they were low. I thanked Tania for her honesty and asked to speak with the dean. Despite Maggie's mother's caution the previous morning that I be careful, I gave the dean an earful when I got her on the phone. This was a young woman's future we were dealing with, not some ranking. I couldn't let this pathetic prioritizing go unchallenged.

In the mad rush to make their school seem more desirable, the admissions office was driven to deny admission to the very type of student who would actually contribute the most to the community and make the institution better.

Maggie, by the way, was admitted to the program. Midway through her freshman year, she came back to visit us and reported that she was maintaining a 3.5 grade point average. She was as happy as could be.

In June 2007, the *New York Times* ran an article announcing that Sarah Lawrence, Barnard, Kenyon, and several other small liberal arts college presidents have opted out of the *U.S. News & World Report* ranking issue. These presidents recognize that colleges and universities are as diverse as the students are. The most important question a student can ask is what the differences are between the schools she is interested in and how they will benefit her future. Many students make poor choices based on the ratings and find themselves in environments that are not a good match for their personal preferences or their goals. This leads to failure and disappointment in the early years of college, and some students don't recognize this failure as a poor choice. Instead, they see it as a sign of their weakness. Many kids who drop out of college after their first year might have stayed in if they had better guidance in finding the *right* school instead of the *best* school. For years, heads of independent schools have banded together, refusing to provide statistics for the edition that ranks high schools, thus making it virtually impossible for *U.S. News & World Report* to publish a ranking of independent high schools. Increasing numbers of educators believe that the ranking of schools does children more harm than good. Parents, one hopes, will also see that each child has different requirements and that "different" doesn't have to mean "better than" or "worse than."

Weakness comes when we rush headlong into the pursuit of achievements that have nothing to do with our real desires. Such achievements do not activate our essential strengths and leave us feeling empty and depleted. Empty achievements, those that lack a connection to an inner sense of meaning and purpose, are pushing unprecedented numbers of college students into campus mental health offices with complaints of depression and anxiety. In a 2004 report by the American College Health Association, 40 percent of college men and 50 percent of college women surveyed said they had experienced depression so severe at some point in time that they could "barely function"; 14.9 percent said they had been medically diagnosed with clinical depression. In the same survey, 60 percent of students reported "feeling things were hopeless" one or more times during the previous school year.

This anxiety starts developing as early as middle school, when parents and teachers begin to warn children that if they don't get good grades, they will not get into college. These kinds of threats make getting good grades and high scores more important to children than learning. When "getting in" becomes a matter of family pride, children will do anything to get good grades, including cheat. Children cheat in school when they do not feel invested, committed to, and motivated by learning. Earning good grades and pleasing parents and teachers are not effective motivators for true learning. Good grades alone do not help students discover their strengths, and the emphasis on getting good grades just to get into a school has caused cheating in high school to become a national epidemic. The results of the twenty-ninth Who's Who Among American High School Students poll found that 80 percent of the country's best students cheated to get to the top of their class; 54 percent of middle school students said they had cheated on an exam within twelve months of the poll. Ask any middle or high school student to tell you how many of his peers cheat at some point during school just to get by, and he'll most likely say that everyone cheats.

Now, consider this in relation to a young man named George. George understood there was a path he needed to get on in order to meet the expectations set by his parents and teachers: earn good grades, get into a top-name college, land a lucrative job, marry, have children, and live happily ever after. But George was unaware of what really mattered to him. He had no idea what he really wanted to do with his life or who he really was, and he lacked an understanding of his true strengths. Like his classmates, he learned to play the cheating game.

EVERYONE'S CHEATING TO GET IN

> *Treachery is more often the effect of weakness than of a formed design.*
>
> —FRANÇOIS, DUC DE LA ROCHEFOUCAULD

When I arrived as the principal of George's high school in southwestern Florida, the honor code was a sore spot in a highly competitive school culture. The code mandated that anyone who knew of a student who cheated was equally as culpable as the cheater if he did not report his knowledge to the school administration. These types of codes are standard practice in many schools today. I find they function as Band-Aids at best, masking what is inherently a larger problem in the school culture. The policing of values usually signals underlying trouble.

If you truly believe in kids, you must believe that they are not inherently bad and that they cheat for a reason. I began to investigate this assumption, looking for the reasons behind why so many students felt compelled to cheat. I began by asking students what they believed constituted cheating. Most students agreed that cheating was only truly cheating if you were caught. Their rationale was that since cheating to get by had become the norm, the negative definition must only apply to those caught in the act.

I tested this response on a cross section of students—boys and girls, as well as students across every grade level—and almost all shared this belief. Our inclination at these responses is to become horrified and simply deduce that moral values among adolescents today have vanished for good. However, I fundamentally believe in my students, so I decided to mine them for more information. I asked students why they felt they needed to cheat—not whether it was good, bad, right, or wrong, just why they felt the need. They responded with three reasons: first, because it was so easy; second, because nobody really cared about what was being learned anyway; and third, because their futures depended on it. I found the third response most telling. It told me that they believed the content of their courses was so inconsequential that it rendered cheating acceptable, yet, they nonetheless hoped for and believed in a future that was worth everything to them. I asked further questions to better understand this.

"So, let's talk about your future. Do you envision continuing to cheat in your future?"

A few said yes, they might cheat in college. But not one of them believed they would continue to cheat in their jobs. In fact, a few students were offended that I would even ask about the possibility of their cheating in the workplace. For them, the first real connection with who they really are would not occur until they were out of school and at work in a job. They felt their job would be something that was theirs and therefore deserving of their respect. What this response means is that they didn't consider their high school education their own. They felt no sense of personal investment in it. It was just a game they had to play to get to the next level in life. Some children felt that college would be more their own, whereas others didn't feel they would experience anything that validated their personal uniqueness until they got their own job.

To most students, cheating is just a school game. There are two rules: don't get caught and don't snitch on anyone.

"Do you cheat in all your subjects?" I asked them.

"Just the boring ones or the ones where you don't understand what is going on," they admitted.

Yet, there were exceptions to the rule.

"Sometimes, if I know the teacher really cares about me, then even if the class is really boring, I won't cheat."

We do need to teach children that cheating—for any reason and regardless of whether they're caught—is wrong. To be truly effective, we must first acknowledge that a culture of cheating has cropped up in response to an educational system which unintentionally tells young people that where they are going matters more than why they are on the journey. If all cheating suddenly stopped tomorrow, we would still have a system in which kids are turned off to learning because it is seen as a weakness-based pursuit done for the approval of others. When students are engaged in discovering strengths, they are motivated to work toward goals that develop them. Strengths are like a compass; without them, people just get lost in life. With them, children end up reaching their goals—both academically and otherwise—because they feel ownership and pride in their work. Unfortunately, George didn't understand how to follow his strengths, and he ended up in a life that was less fulfilling than he'd hoped.

George left high school to attend a small liberal arts college in Florida. One afternoon, about three weeks from the time he was finishing up his junior year at college, he appeared at my office door.

"Hey, Ms. Fox, remember me?"

"Why, George, of course I remember you. It's so good to see you. How is college life treating you?" I asked, pushing aside my paperwork and gesturing for him to come in and take a seat. He looked tanned and healthy, as if he'd been spending most of his time outdoors.

"College is . . . well, it's okay," he said.

"Just okay?" I asked, sensing there was something more he wished to talk about with me.

"I just wish I had read more in high school."

"What do you mean? I recall you took AP English your senior year—wasn't there a hefty reading list in that course?"

"Oh, that?" he replied with a guilty smirk. "I didn't read any of those books. Isn't that funny? I got an A in the class and a three on the exam, and I didn't even read one book."

"How do you cheat on an AP exam?" I asked, astonished.

"No, you can't cheat on the AP. I just listened to the teacher tell me what the books were about in her lectures," he boasted.

"So, what else is going on with you?" I asked, feeling ill at ease.

"Oh, just trying to figure out what I want to major in," he said unenthusiastically.

"Well, what makes you feel excited?" I asked.

He looked at me quizzically.

I rephrased my question. "What do you like doing so much that you actually look forward to it?"

"Nothing in school," he replied.

"Well, what is it outside of school then?" I asked.

"I guess I really like playing league soccer," he said. "But it's not like I'm going to get paid for that."

"What exactly do you like about it?" I probed.

"What do you mean?"

"I mean do you like the strategy of the game or being part of a team?"

"Oh, I like both of those."

"Which do you like more?" I asked.

"I guess I like being part of a team—and being outdoors. I love being outside; that's one of the huge benefits about living in Florida." His face was animated for the first time since we had begun our conversation.

"Then you'd better focus on figuring out what kind of a job you can do that allows you to work outdoors and on a team," I said.

"Sounds good, but I got my sights set on making a lot of money, so I'll probably have my dad help me find a job."

"Doing what?" I asked him.

"Who cares so long as I can make some good cash?"

I felt there was nothing I could do to convince George that he would reap the rewards of life if he followed the path of his strengths. Unfortunately, we frequently convince our children and ourselves that making money is mutually exclusive from doing the things we love. Those who know their strengths and use them most of the time will say they discover happiness in doing things that are energizing and meaningful. There are enough of those things to go around. It just takes some creativity to figure out what they are and how to apply them to a student's career goals.

The last time I heard about George was from Bess, a former colleague who still works at the school where I met George. Small town news travels fast. She told me he was working in an office selling insurance and spent a lot of time hanging out in local bars with his old high school buddies. She heard he'd changed jobs a few times and believed his boss fired him from the last one when he caught him at the beach on an afternoon when he had called in sick. I felt guilty when I heard that news. Somehow, his school had profoundly let him down. Still, to most people, George was a success. After all, he did well in school and he graduated from a well-reputed college. If he could land one high-paying job, he could land another. But I knew in my heart that George was not playing to his strengths most of the time in his job, and in that respect, the little extra something that makes life magic was just out of his reach. Although I cannot take responsibility for the decisions people make, I do know that we can do more to ensure students learn as much about themselves and their strengths as they can before they leave school. In school, you could argue that George was cheating the system or, more pointedly, that the system was cheating him. In transferring the tendency to cheat to the work world, George ended up cheating himself.

The system cheats students by failing to provide them with learning experiences that will engage their sense of uniqueness, inspire their creativity, and bolster their ability to solve real-life problems. We cheat our students out of real opportunities for growth and insight when we fail to connect their learning experiences to what they already know about themselves and their lives. When this connection is not made, students see the entire process as a game that they are forced to play. In order for them to take school seriously, children need to understand how their learning experiences will enhance and advance their lives.

Chapter 4

LEARNING DISABILITIES FOR DUMMIES

If a man does not keep pace with his companions, perhaps it is because he hears a different drummer. Let him step to the music which he hears, however measured or far away.

—HENRY DAVID THOREAU

IN FEBRUARY 2001, THE *NEW YORK TIMES* PUBLISHED A MEMORABLE article about a scientific study by a group of psychologists. The group claimed to have done an "exhaustive" review of *Winnie-the-Pooh* literature and then catalogued and diagnosed a range of clinical, personality, and psychological disorders among the major characters in the *Winnie-the-Pooh* books. Their study, called the *Pathology in the Hundred Acre Wood: A Neurodevelopmental Perspective on A. A. Milne,* was one in which the authors describe the various deficiencies of each character. Pooh, for example, has impulsivity issues signaling ADHD, which is compounded by his addiction to honey. For him, they prescribe Ritalin and adherence to the Zone diet. Piglet, they contend, is beset by generalized anxiety disorder and may benefit from a low dose of paroxetine. Owl, though bright, is dyslexic; no drugs are able to help him. Christopher Robin spends too much time playing "make-believe," perhaps signaling some future malfunction, and the scientists noted the total lack of adult supervision in the Hundred Acre Wood. "That could be a problem," they said, suggesting the child could be "at risk." Finally, they turn to Rabbit, noting that while he hasn't any diagnosable symptoms, his tendency to be extraordinarily self-important could be a problem. They believe he exhibits "an overriding need to organize others into new groupings, with himself always at the top of the reporting structure."

The study was a great joke, highlighting our increasing tendency to label each other and focus on weaknesses rather than strengths. An amazing number of people didn't get it. They complained research "shouldn't be used for stuff like this." Other people got it but didn't think it was funny. "These things are much too serious to be joked about," they said. The joke is in the madness of it all. We have created in real life a storybook world that is as crazy as the study done on the Hundred Acre Wood. Most of the labels we ascribe to children overlook what is right about children. We prefer to concentrate on labeling weaknesses. The problem is that eventually the label begins to inform the child, rather than the other way around. The British philosopher G. K. Chesterton wrote, "Madness is the preference for the symbol over that which it represents." As we rush with increased energy to apply labels to our children, the labels become more than mere words. As we accept and identify more deeply with the labels, they begin to become symbolic and generate a meaning of their own. The total effect of this is a reality that puts more stock in weaknesses than in strengths. A label is a description of "what is." A child is the definition of "what can be." Teachers and parents must begin to change the focus from labeling weakness to proclaiming strengths.

The growing industry around labeling and treating children with *specific learning disabilities* should be everyone's concern. It is difficult to know just how many young people are labeled as having a learning disability, but estimates are that one in every five children is referred to educational testing at some time in his or her pre-K–12th-grade career. Those numbers are alarmingly high. I write this chapter as the head of an independent school that celebrates girls who have been diagnosed with learning disabilities, so I know firsthand that these kids have more strengths and positive qualities than they do weaknesses. In this chapter, I address the most commonly diagnosed learning disability—*specific learning disability*—which is a term defined by the U.S. government to determine who is eligible to receive funding for special educational services. A specific learning disability, usually abbreviated to LD, means there is an observed discrepancy in one of more of the basic processes involved in understanding or in using language (spoken or written). This appears as an imperfect ability to listen, think, speak, read, write, spell, or to perform mathematical calculations. *These* problems are *not* primarily due to visual, hearing, or motor handicaps; neither are they due to mental retardation, emotional disturbance, or the result of environmental, cultural, or economic disadvantage. A child is considered to have an LD if his achievement in one or more of the above areas is not on par with what educators determine to be the ability level of his age group. I have been on both sides of the argument over whether we should label these learning struggles as "disabilities," and the argument is difficult to make from either perspective. (I will later explain why that is.)

In this chapter I'll reveal some basic facts that will enable you to see why I believe that the "learning-disabled paradigm," with its half-baked solutions for helping children who struggle in school, is the epitome of the weakness myth. I think it is important to state up front that I am not suggesting that the students who are labeled LD do not struggle—they clearly do, and suffer as a result. And I am all for helping kids catch up and learn what they need to know to get ahead in life, but the way in which we do that—with a sole focus on the weakness of the students—is only half the equation. If we are going to remediate weaknesses, we must have an equal commitment to building strengths. To do so will require embracing the philosophies related in this book and then backing them in Congress with the same energy that we enforce No Child Left Behind and with the same vigor with which we federally fund the remediation of weaknesses. This is one of the most powerful ways in which we can help struggling students succeed.

Furthermore, as you will see, we don't help children succeed when we place all the blame for the learning problems on them. This is how the learning disability paradigm operates. We begin by assuming that the struggle in school is all the student's fault when there are many factors that can contribute to a child having difficulty in school. Contrary to popular belief, most learning disabilities, those diagnosed as specific learning disabilities, are *not,* by definition, due to abnormalities of the brain. When referring to specific learning disabilities, the definition does *not* include Asperger's syndrome or autism. Aside from these known medical conditions, hundreds of thousands of children are being diagnosed with LDs every year. They have high IQ's and show success in other realms of life where learning is involved, just not in school or academic settings. In order to understand what is happening with these children, we must at least consider the following:

- If an adolescent is left home alone most afternoons, with no one to talk to her or help her solve problems or learn how to interact, the child may become delayed in social or intellectual development.
- If teachers have a learning style that is at odds with the child's style (such as a highly visually oriented adult and an energetic child who learns by doing, not by seeing), the mismatch may appear to be a learning disability in the child.
- If a child is fed a constant diet of junk food and gets little exercise, he may be unable to concentrate in school.
- If early instruction in reading and math was poor, a student who cannot catch up may become so frustrated that he gives up.
- If ever-increasing numbers of middle and high school students are being diagnosed with LD, then the weaknesses in our antiquated school systems must be reviewed as contributing factors.

As you have no doubt witnessed, there is a lot of emotion and confusion surrounding the topic of learning disabilities. If, as a parent, you see any signs of difference or "slowness" in your child, you may wonder, is my child okay? How will I know? How will the teachers know? If you have a child who struggles in school, you have already felt the confusion. Since you were first confronted with the idea that your child was not keeping up, you have no doubt felt as if you are on a roller-coaster ride. Between the conversations with family members, who each offer different advice, and the special meetings at the school with the teachers, who although well intentioned don't seem to understand what you are going through, you've probably felt the emotional fatigue caused by not knowing exactly what's going on and apprehension about figuring it all out.

In a likely scenario, on the school's recommendation, you've been to the doctor, although on your way there you wondered if it was necessary. You've considered a psychologist, and all the while questioned whether anything was wrong with your child. All parents who have children who seem unhappy or have slipping grades have a moment when they worry that something may be deeply wrong. And all parents have moments when they question this impression. There is good reason for all the uncertainty and seesawing feelings.

The first good reason is that your child—whether born of your own flesh and blood or lovingly adopted—standing in front of you struggling was not so long ago a perfect blank slate onto which you projected all your hopes and dreams for the future. Then a moment comes in which you realize things are not going as well as planned. The one thing that all parents share in this experience is that once you realize things are going off course, it is extremely difficult, seemingly impossible, to figure out why. Moreover, while you are looking for answers, time keeps marching on. School doesn't stop and wait while you try to figure it out. Your child doesn't stop and wait. Your boss doesn't call you into the office and say, "Kerry, I know you are having trouble figuring out what is going on with your daughter. Why don't you take a few days' paid leave to sort it all out." Even if your boss did say that, this is not a problem that can be sorted out in a short time.

Allison is a thirteen-year-old student in the eighth grade. Her grades have recently begun to fall in several subjects, and for the first time in her life she says she hates to go to school. In elementary school, Allison was inquisitive and enjoyed learning. After she entered middle school, her parents began to notice changes in her attitude. These changes bothered her parents, but they chalked them up to adolescence. When she visited her grandmother's home for the holidays, Allison's mother confided in her mother that she was worried about Allison.

"Don't worry. She'll grow out of it. It's just a phase," her mother advised.

However, Allison didn't grow out of it, and now in eighth grade, she returns home from school and barely says a word to anyone. She spends all her time in her room sitting at her computer, logged into *myspace* with earphones stuck in her ears listening to music. When her mother asks her what she is doing, Allison rolls her eyes and says, "Homework." Allison is irritable and often complains that she hates school. Concerned, Allison's parents take her to a child psychologist who runs a battery of tests on her. She is given the Wechsler Intelligence Scale, an IQ test for children, and something called Woodcock-Johnson Psycho-Educational Battery (WJPEB).

The WJPEB includes educational achievement testing and cognitive ability testing. Dr. Woodcock also produced the Woodcock Reading Mastery Test. Today, the current test series is called the Woodcock-Johnson Psycho-Educational Battery—Revised (WJ-R), which is an educational achievement test that includes the Test of Cognitive Abilities. Allison's parents find these tests difficult to understand but are told not to worry. Allison's parents are told that according to the evaluations, Allison has a learning disability. Initially they are shocked. They feel shame and, at the same time, an odd sense of relief. They do not understand the psychologist's explanation of the test but are instructed to take the report to Allison's school, where, they are assured, they'll receive help.

When Allison's parents discuss their concerns about their daughter's lack of progress with her teacher, they are reassured that she is making progress and they are told to be patient. They think that patience is not the issue; they are worried about what kind of future Allison will have. This is really their main concern. They are being ushered into the jargon-laden, unfamiliar world of learning disabilities. It appears to be a label-driven world—one that focuses exclusively on the remediation of weakness, one that actually may harm Allison as much as it may help her. It seems harsh. It feels wrong. How did we all get here?

In 1977, when the Education for All Handicapped Children Act (EHA) was passed, it is safe to say that no one could imagine the ways in which this act would alter the course of education in the United States. This landmark law, whose twenty-fifth anniversary was celebrated in 2002, is currently enacted as the Individuals with Disabilities Education Act (IDEA).

With the passage of this act in 1977 came the classification "specific learning disability" as a category of special education. Thirty years ago the world was a very different place. In 1978, there were 796,000 students receiving federal funding for special education. That number was an aggregate of all forms of disabilities, including mental retardation, physical impairment, and autism. By 2005, there were 2,831,000 students receiving special education funding. That number has continued to grow, with the bulk of the funding serving students with "specific learning disabilities." In fact, the number of children receiving special education funding for mental retardation and physical handicaps has actually declined over the past ten years. The 2005 Digest of Education Statistics reported over a 300 percent rise in the number of children diagnosed with "specific learning disabilities" since the inception of the Education for Handicapped Children Act. No other category of disability has come anywhere near that kind of increase.

For parents, a great deal of the emotion and confusion around the label *learning disability* today stems from the ambiguity in the definition and the brief history of this phenomenon. Most of the students today who have documentation of a learning disability, and work with Individualized Education Plans (IEPs), do not appear to have anything wrong with them. When I was a girl, no students in my public high school were referred to as *learning disabled.* All the disabled kids were either mentally retarded or physically handicapped. That is still the association many adults have with the word *disabled,* which is not uncommon given the relatively short history of the use of the term. This misassociation is important insofar as it becomes a sticking point for many people and thus an unnecessary source of tension for parents whose child has been labeled learning disabled.

WHY SOME CALL IT A *DISABILITY* AND OTHERS PREFER *DIFFERENCE*

The seemingly simple statement that is the title of this section is the cause of much debate and a lot of emotion in families as well as in educational and political arenas. For the most staunch advocates of children with diagnosed learning disabilities, the terms *disability* and *difference* are not interchangeable, and for good reason. The labels lend legitimacy to the fact that their children do not learn in the same manner in which the school teaches. For many parents, this label was and continues to be a public victory, as they are guaranteed, at least under the law, equal access to educational methods that suit their child's learning needs. This is a matter of civil rights for parents and their children. By identifying students as learning disabled, parents exercise their rights to receive federal funding to provide a different kind of education for their children—ostensibly one that will enable them to be more successful. But when does a different way of learning and thinking become a *difficulty* with learning or a *disability*? The point at which we consider a different way of learning a disability is when the person has difficulty in settings where other people are learning with much more ease. Many people prefer to use the term *learning* ***difference,*** believing it to be a more accurate way to describe someone who by all other outward appearances is "normal."

In the public school system, *differences* do not receive funding. Family after family I have spoken with reported that the diagnosis of a disability was the first step toward being able to learn effectively. One of the reasons this seems to be the case is that it provides the individuals and their families an explanation. They are finally assuaged that their child's difficulties are not just willful personality weaknesses. Usually up until that point, we labeled the child lazy, disorganized, and uncooperative—a willful combination of weaknesses that would be controlled if the child would simply "try harder," "focus," or "get it together." The term *learning disabled* gives families hope that there will be an opportunity to thrive, for what is **dis**abled can surely become **en**abled. This is a far better diagnosis than living with the idea that you are destined to be permanently stupid, or dumb, or slow.

Still, the term *disabled* does not sit well with most parents I know, and in many cases, especially in independent schools, this label actually does the opposite of what it was intended to do: it hinders students from receiving the kind of teaching that will truly engage them in learning.

For many parents, having the term *disabled* applied to their child is more debilitating to them than their child's struggling through school with low grades. These parents may find it difficult to disassociate the classification with their early-life experience with the word *handicapped*. As one man described his daughter to me, "Of course she doesn't have a learning disability. She's just a little slow."

Both groups of parents are on the same side. They both want the same thing: meaningful learning experiences for their children—experiences that will allow them to successfully engage in life and all life has to offer. The problem is that the plan for addressing learning struggles in this country is to focus entirely on what these children can't do and not at all on what they can do. Remediation of weaknesses is only half the equation.

Almost daily we hear of a child (or in recent times an adult) who has a learning disability. Currently, there is no agreed-upon or precise definition for a specific learning disability. Physicians assert that people with learning disabilities have a disorder in one or more of the basic psychological processes involved in learning. There are usually two things that doctors and teachers refer to when speaking about learning disabilities: processing and discrepancy.

First, psychologists suggest that having a learning disability means that a person's brain "processes" information differently than most other students. Although teachers and doctors cannot actually see into the brain to determine if this is true, a number of tests and controlled activities are used to make this evaluation.

Second, for a person to be classified as *learning disabled,* a large *discrepancy* must be in place. This discrepancy is defined as a sizable difference between a student's ability (as indicated in various tests) and her achievement (as indicated in her schoolwork). A learning disability is not simply underachievement. If it were, every student who was not performing to his potential would be considered learning disabled. It is presumed that a *processing function* is what is causing the discrepancy between a person's ability and his achievement, and it is the combination of those two phenomena that creates the learning disability.

Usually learning disabilities are associated with visual and auditory processing functions. A great deal of information in the classroom and at home is presented visually and verbally, so children who process information differently or more slowly in either of these two modes is considered to be at a disadvantage. Given the ever-growing numbers of children with the learning disabled diagnosis, one may question whether the processing methods we believe are the norm are any longer the norm—or if they ever really were. Albert Einstein did not speak until he was three years old. He found it nearly impossible to express himself in writing and was poor in math. There are many examples of other famous people with learning disabilities—Magic Johnson and Tom Cruise, to name two. We hold these examples as reminders that perhaps there is not something wrong with people who process differently. Maybe it is not a weakness at all; maybe it is a clue to what might become fertile ground for the sprouting of a great strength. People with learning disabilities do not have low intelligence; in fact, many have average or above-average intelligence, and some are even double-labeled as gifted and talented.

I have a relatively high IQ as measured by standard intelligence tests. But I scored extremely low on the achievement tests I needed to take to enter college, which is why I was placed in the remedial math class. Had I been tested for a learning disability in high school, it is likely I would have been so diagnosed. I believe that in the educational system I was in throughout high school, I was disabled. I have not overcome, or been cured of, my "disability." I am simply no longer operating in that learning system. Today, I am reading a book called *Teaching Mathematics Meaningfully: Solutions for Reaching Struggling Learners* by David H. Allsopp, Maggie M. Kyger, and Lou Ann H. Lovin. I picked up the book because I wanted to give the math teachers in my school a good resource for understanding ways to teach students who struggle in math. Math weaknesses have always perplexed me. I am forever searching for someone who understands that math makes sense to me when taught in narrative form. I need to know the story of math, and when I struggle with the concepts, I have to discuss in detail the processes I am going through. This is not disabled, it is just different. In

Teaching Mathematics Meaningfully, I finally discovered people who understand the need to teach differently.

So much remediation is just more of the same method, only in a smaller room with fewer people. Tutoring doesn't work if the methods don't change. Excessive tutoring without any change in methodology will only serve to further weaken a child's sense of motivation. Parents often say to me, "I have spent thousands of dollars on all kinds of tutors, and he still doesn't get it." I always ask the parents what the tutor is doing differently than the classroom teacher, and it is rare that parents have any idea. Usually tutors are classroom teachers. If the method didn't work in the whole class setting, what makes us believe it will work one-on-one? What is clear to me now is that during my primary education, I needed to understand the "big ideas in math" and the "big ideas for doing math" before I could tackle a problem. I also needed further scaffolding that would take me from concrete problems to abstract ones. I actually needed to spend much more time on math. As a child, I could not articulate these needs. As an adult, I scan through all the math and science books and feel there is a whole universe of wonderful things to learn that I missed. In the end, there just is not time for everyone to learn and understand everything. And this is okay and as it should be. It is too bad that in getting to that understanding, we have to inflict weakness and shame on children.

There is no question that the students who say they struggle actually do struggle or that they are, in fact, disabled in our current system. But exactly what constitutes a "large" discrepancy between ability and achievement, and consequently a learning disability, is decided by each state individually. There is no uniformity among states in this determination, and, according to my observations, there appears to be a lack of rigor in the diagnostic process. Every set of diagnostic testing that I have seen at the high school level is different.

A learning disability in one state may not be one in another. So why, if this isn't even precise, are thousands of people rushing to pediatricians to get their children diagnosed for learning disabilities? It sounds crazy, doesn't it? As a nation, we are rushing to classify our children using a system that is in many respects arbitrary. And it's not as if we are rushing to impose labels that make our children seem more attractive or more desirable. In fact, we appear eager to apply labels that can be inherently stigmatizing to them.

CAUSES OF LEARNING DISABILITIES

Currently, there are no known causes for learning disabilities. Recent brain research using magnetic resonance imaging (MRI) has linked the origins of dyslexia to the brain, but we have yet to determine with certainty what causes the garden-variety learning disability we have been seeing crop up in schools across the country. In almost every book, article, research study, Web page, and film I have ever seen on learning disabilities, the problem always resides in the child, and the prescriptions almost always call for a change in the child, the medication of the child, or a new or different understanding of the child. Every approach, it seems, suggests that the child is the one with the weakness.

As a result, dozens of illogical conclusions are drawn about teaching kids for whom the traditional system is a challenge. Here is one that is particularly curious: many children with learning disabilities are told they cannot learn a foreign language because they have a language-based learning disability. Except that they did learn a language. They learned how to think, speak, write, and listen in their native language. So why not another language? Schools tend to teach foreign languages very differently from the way we learn our native language. The concentration on grammar baffles me. I have no idea what the grammatical rules of the English language are. I always tuned out in English class when we got to that part. It was boring and felt useless to me. Had I been in an English class that devoted a lot of time to grammar, I probably would have failed. And were I to have repeatedly failed in English class, I would have turned off and stopped learning. Luckily, that was not my experience, and I have a master's degree in English. Not being able to conjugate a verb does not seem to prevent me from expressing myself well through writing. Not all kids need to learn the respective rules of grammar in order to learn a foreign language. And not all kids learn in the same way. Of course kids with learning disabilities can learn foreign languages; we just have to figure out how to teach them. That is our responsibility.

We seldom discuss the possibility that learning problems have their roots in a variety of places other than in the child's brain. We don't hear about a "teaching disability," a "parenting disability," a "school disability," or a "federal policy disability." I don't deny that there is something very wrong that is grossly challenging the thousands of young people who are diagnosed every day with learning disabilities. I not only believe in their challenges, but I also think it is imperative that we address them. The reality is that many students who have been diagnosed with learning disabilities are extremely good learners outside the classroom. Many students with learning disabilities are very skillful in other areas, such as in the performing arts. A girl with a math disability may be exceptional at designing clothing. I know a young man who struggles in reading but who is the most socially skilled person I know. He speaks eloquently, acts onstage, and is a leader in his school even though he reads three grades behind grade level. One girl I know has invented several ways to put stage flats together to create different scenes in a play, yet she cannot pass her biology exam. Somewhere along the line it was determined that if students don't perform at a high level in all content areas, the areas in which their performance is weak should deem them to be considered disabled. Somewhere along the line it was determined that success means that every student be perfectly well rounded in all subject areas.

A blind person is disabled in the *seeing* world. In the comfort of a dark auditorium, listening to a symphony, that same person is not disabled with regard to his or her ability to understand, appreciate, and experience the performance. In fact, it could be argued that the senses of some blind people will be heightened in this situation even more than those of sighted people.

A hearing-impaired person would have a hearing disability in the same situation and would not be able to experience the event with the same result as the other audience members. However, in another setting, that same person might outperform the others. For example, someone with a hearing disability may be an expert photographer. The label *disability* has as much to do with the setting and the requirements of the setting as it does with the person. The setting most responsible for the proliferation of the term *learning disability* is the traditional school. If all public and private schools are working off the same model of teaching and learning, a student will be disabled in every school that uses that model. The manifestation of the disability may vary somewhat depending on whether the school has small or large classes, tons of money or no money, or chooses to read one book instead of another. Therefore, schools most willing to depart from the traditional methods used to teach and assess performance will do the greatest service in addressing the issue of learning disabilities. Those schools will create programs that meet students where they are and take them where they have faith they can go.

IS IT A MEDICAL CONCERN?

Children arrive in school today with all kinds of prescription medications to quell what parents and doctors believe are the effects of learning disabilities. But are learning disabilities diseases? Medications are prescribed for ADD, ADHD, and other physical conditions that often accompany learning disabilities, but these learning disabilities in and of themselves are not relieved by medications.

The number of psychiatric drug prescriptions for children has more than doubled since 1996, according to a study by Dr. Julie Zito of the University of Maryland. As a society, we insist on administering medications to children—medications we hope will settle them down or dispel their moodiness so they can better focus on the parcels of academic information we present to them as being so important and necessary to their future success. This growing tendency is more than misguided. It is tragic. Only recently have we begun to question seriously the rapid rise in the medicating of our young people.

My first encounter with a child on medication for ADD was at a school in Colorado, where I was the high school principal.

Colleen's parents came in to talk with me one day about the comments on her report card and how they related to her average grades. One comment read, "Colleen needs to focus more in class and spend less time socializing with her peers." Another said, "Colleen tends to distract the other students during quiet study time, thus her participation grade is low." I listened while Colleen's parents described a recent visit to their pediatrician. She had prescribed Ritalin to help Colleen focus in class and, as a result, one hoped, to get better grades. They asked if I would get the teachers together and let them know this so we could all monitor her behavior. I agreed to the request and didn't tell them I thought they were making a big mistake. I am not a doctor, but what they described to me did not strike me as a medical condition.

I will always remember the day I sat in the conference room with Colleen's six teachers. Half the teachers were outraged. She was doing quite well in their classes, and they worried that this would change her. The other half was hopeful. "She really needs to settle down," they said.

One month later, we sat in the same room and had a similar conversation about Colleen. Half the teachers were delighted. She was focused, turning in much better assignments, and no longer bothering the other students. The other half was saddened. She had lost [illegible] smiled, and they missed the funny way she said hel[illegible] cerned that her skin looked dull and her hair was n[illegible] seemed irritable. Was this good for her health? Her par[illegible] was safe, and they were pleased with the grades. Safe? S[illegible] making sure she was as healthy as possible? Colleen may hav[illegible] better grades, but something about her was gone. It has been ov[illegible] since I've seen Colleen. I still wonder if she got that brilliant lit[illegible] back.

It is time to stop focusing on symptoms as if they were the [illegible] Medications may help in getting children to conform to a prescribed be[illegible] ior, but at what cost? And are we certain that these are the behaviors th[illegible] will allow them to discover their strengths and will ensure them success in the future?

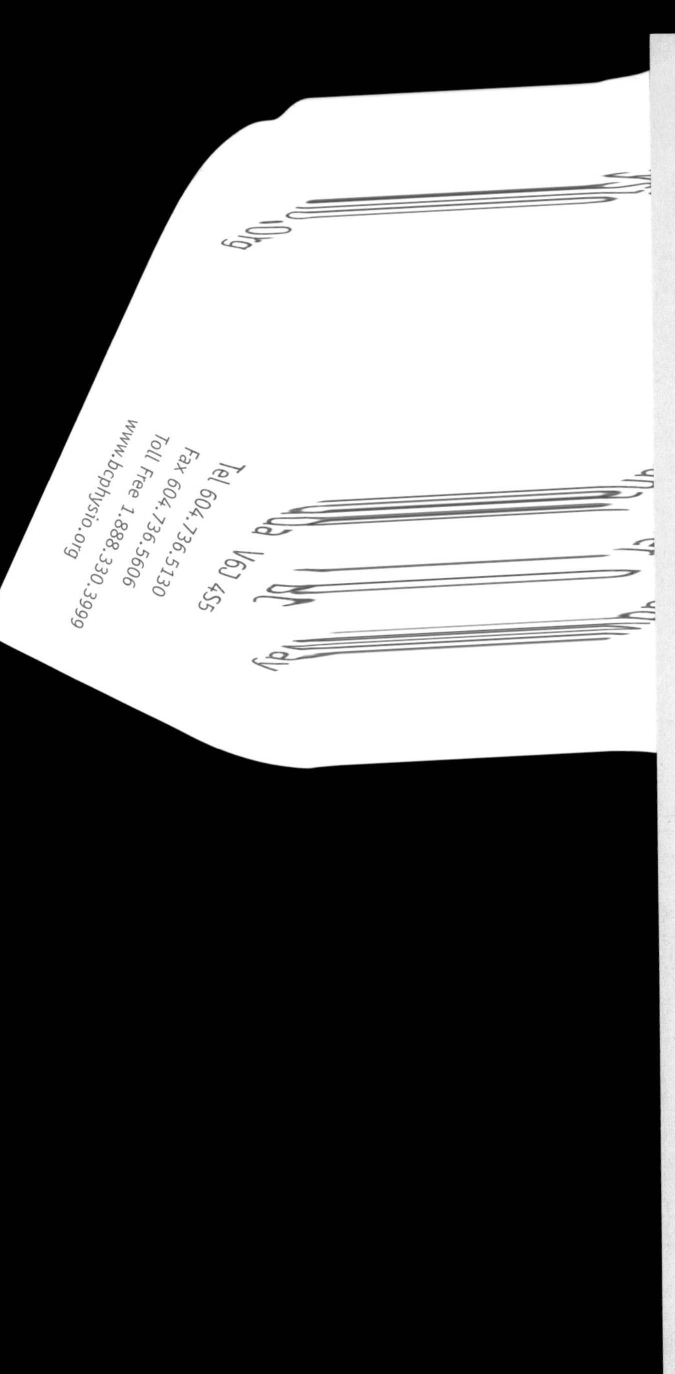

Chapter 5

THE MYTH OF ADOLESCENT REBELLION

Children are born as individuals. If we fail to see that, if we see them as clay to be molded in any shape we like, the tougher ones will fight back and end up spiteful and wild, while the less strong will lose that uniqueness they were born with.

—MELVIN KONNER

IT BEARS REPEATING THAT MOST CHILDREN FIND SCHOOL BORING when their strengths are not engaged in class. In this case, boring is just another word for irrelevant. Kids thrive on relevance; it is the first thread in the vast tapestry of meaning that defines their purpose for living. Here is where we often sell teens short. We may think that if something doesn't relate to their life, chances are they just don't care that much about whatever it is. But that isn't the case. The truth is that young people care very much for big ideas. They wonder about the meaning of life and death; they yearn to make a real difference in the world. They crave attention from adults who will take them seriously and who do not laugh at them or mock their attempts at significance, even if those attempts appear immature. The classes teenagers are most turned on to are the ones in which the teachers treat them like fully formed people with profound and important ideas. Many adults miss this important point. They see adolescents as self-indulgent and preoccupied with seemingly unimportant activities. Many adults are even afraid of teens. Kids can detect this fear a mile away, and it insults them. They don't naturally see adults as the enemy, but they react strongly to a sideways look, a judgmental sneer, or disapproving body language. This is one form of "rebellion." It usually happens in the safety of a group. Get the rebellious child away from the crowd, and usually all the wind falls from his sails.

We tend to believe the myth that adolescents are innately rebellious. Adults press excessively on teens to conform, and the harder they are pressed, the more they rebel. The kids who rebel most are those who have been pressed the longest, the hardest, and from a variety of different angles. Conflict erupts when adults challenge teens on their appearance and their mannerisms as they search for identities to claim as their own.

The story of adolescent rebellion is as old as time, but that does not make the story true. The rebellion story is always full of disappointment and pain, and it can be expressed by means of slamming doors, angry exchanges, sarcasm, family betrayal, alcohol, drugs, and, sometimes, death.

In order to change the outcome to one that portrays happier, more successful, healthier adolescents, we must change the way we view what they do and the way we listen to what they say. Adults must wake up from the divisiveness of the rebellion myth and instead *empathize* with the adolescent experience.

THE NEED FOR ATTENTION

When I was a teen, just after my father remarried, I crawled into his apartment through a window while he was away for the weekend. I stole a silver-and-turquoise bracelet from my stepmother. Then I wore it the next time I saw my father. I did not consciously put the bracelet on and think, *I'll show him.* (Which isn't to say that on some level I didn't do it on purpose. Of course I did.) He spotted the bracelet on me and told me to give it back. He was quite angry, and rightly so. He lost trust in me and was hugely disappointed, and that was fair. I think about this incident often because working for so long with teens, you encounter the full spectrum of behaviors in consistent patterns. Many children steal things. When girls steal, it is rarely because they desire the things they are taking. Most girls who do this also desire to be caught. Looking back, I realize I didn't want the bracelet at all. On some level my act of rebellion was complexly symbolic. After I matured, I was able to reflect back on this humiliating event and understand my motivations, which explain rather than justify the action. I felt my stepmother had stolen something from me—my father's attention. Therefore, I stole something in return, her bracelet. I wore the bracelet so my father would notice and pay attention to me. Even if it was negative attention, it was what I craved.

Like all teens, I wanted to be noticed, but in a way very different from before. Like all teens, I yearned to be recognized as someone unique and different from the child for whom my parents took credit. I wanted the adults in my life to see that I was special—not in some prima donna–like way (although that is how this craving sometimes comes across) but in an "it's my world, too" kind of way. The subtext of a lot of teen behavior is "let me into your world, and when you do, let me surprise you like a new friend." Of course, children cannot do it all on their own right away, but you will help them by letting them be different and separate from you and still accepting and even delighting in who they are becoming. This may be difficult for you, because in their attempt to be someone other than you, they will sometimes go to maddening extremes. The harder you press, the further they go.

REBELLION AS SEEN THROUGH A STRENGTHS LENS

There is a great example of a teenager in the midst of a an identity crisis in the film *Little Miss Sunshine*. Dwayne, an offbeat teen, has taken a vow of silence in the hopes that this test of his own determination will magically help him get into the Air Force Academy. When his uncle asks him who he hangs out with, he writes, "I hate everybody." Dwayne is sullen and has a five-foot drawing of Friedrich Nietzsche hanging in his room. We're meant to see him as a typically surly and antisocial teen. Of his demeanor his father says, "Nine months of silence shows discipline. Dwayne has a dream. It may not be your dream or my dream, but it is his dream." Dwayne's family recognizes that he acts odd, even spiteful, but they don't challenge his choices, and this keeps him from acting out. Later in the film, Dwayne learns that he is color-blind, which precludes his acceptance into the academy. He freaks out and starts yelling at his parents, saying, "You're not my family! I don't want to be your family! I hate you, you are losers!" Nobody takes this personally or tries to quiet him, and later he apologizes, saying he didn't mean it. Dwayne, like most teens, is a nice boy underneath his facade. His parents resist giving advice, and they never suggest he be anyone but the person he is struggling to become. Whatever their quirks and shortcomings may be, Dwayne's parents get it right when they view his actions through a strengths lens, looking for the good and pointing out his best qualities. Near the end of the movie, Dwayne makes a declaration of his strength when he says, "If I want to fly, I'll find a way to fly. You do what you love. Forget the rest."

To hear young people differently, we must first see them differently. I am able to look at most acts of rebellion and see a positive and healthy desire that was turned on its ear. When adults look closely, they will see how fresh and original—how open to discovering life's meaning—young people really are.

CONNECTING TO SOMETHING BIGGER

Adolescence is the purest and most primed time in human development for reaching out and touching the unknown. Adolescent hormones flow not only through the body, causing it to physically grow and change, but also through the brain, offering adolescents their first unadulterated opportunity to merge their emotions, cognitive abilities, and physical activities into a comprehension of the vast possibilities of life. Up until the onslaught of these hormones, children grow with various societal and cultural influences but without an organized sense of self. In their adolescent years, kids become aware of themselves as separate and powerful people who have choices in their development. This can be exhilarating at times and overwhelming at others. Hormones awaken and release for the first time the deeply encoded messages about life and death, purpose and meaning, love and rage. Adolescents live in a state of heightened awareness, searching for something bigger than they are to mirror their yearning for significance. They look to adults to be that something bigger, to grab hold of them and pull them up out of the general clamor. They long to know that the world wants them and that life has, in fact, been waiting for their arrival. This is not a rebellion, it is a strengths awakening. I look back on my own youth and recall many moments when my thoughts and ideas seemed profound. Children have deep experiences all the time, and yet parents may not even be aware of what is going on with them.

I remember the summer of my sophomore year in high school. I slept over at my friend Colleen's house, and around four in the morning we woke to someone throwing stones at the bedroom window. It was Zach, Colleen's boyfriend, and his friend Kyle. We quickly threw on our clothes, tiptoed down the hallway past Colleen's younger sister's bedroom, slipped out the kitchen door, and met them in the backyard. "You ever seen the sun rise?" Zach asked. None of us had, and I distinctly remember thinking, "This is going to be the first time in my life I see the sun rise." I remember thinking that because it was one of the first times in my life I was aware of my ability to collect my own unique experiences. The four of us mounted bicycles and headed toward the beach to watch the sun rise over Lake Michigan. It was the height of summer, and I felt electric as I rode down the middle of the deserted street.

"Look, no hands." Colleen pedaled without touching the handlebars; she flapped her arms like wings. I was dizzy with the feeling of freedom to the point that I glanced over at Kyle, whom I barely knew, and wondered if I was in love with him. A moment later, I laughed out loud at how preposterous that thought was and decided he must be in love with me. We stashed our bikes in the bushes, climbed the fence, and bounced down the trail to the beach, where we lay in the sand and looked up at the stars.

"The sun is gonna rise in about an hour," Zach told us. He was lying next to Colleen, holding her hand. Overhead, I saw more stars than I had ever seen.

"Each star's a sun," Kyle said. "And each sun could possibly have planets with life on them."

"What do you think that life's like?" Zach asked.

"I doubt that's true," Colleen whispered. "I think we're alone in the universe, and that's the whole point."

"What would be the point of that?" I asked.

"The point would be that it is up to us to figure it all out," Colleen replied.

We carried on with conversation for the next half hour, until we noticed a bright orange glow creeping across the horizon.

"It's coming, see?" Zach pointed to the horizon and sat up abruptly. The four of us sat there in a row and watched as the sky turned from black to orange, and the sun peeked up from the horizon. The sky gradually lightened as the sun rose, and it was like nothing I had ever seen before. "I can't believe this happens every day and it's so amazing and we're like totally unaware of it."

"And just think," Kyle said to me, "while we're seeing this, other people in some other part of the world are sitting on some beach watching it set." I thought of that and felt a jolt of excitement.

When the sun was up and we were completely exposed to the daylight, we scrambled quickly up the path toward our bikes. At the top of the path, as we began to mount the fence, a security guard showed up.

"It is illegal for you kids to be in there. I called the police. They'll be here shortly."

We received a strict warning. I was grounded for two weekends and not allowed to sleep over at Colleen's again. I spent several hours listening to a lecture about how dangerous it was to go out at night and how dishonest it was to sneak around like that. I agreed, felt ashamed, took my "medicine," and went to my room. Lying on my bed, all I could think of was watching that sunrise, and how disappointed I was that we'd been caught. I could have sworn that if we hadn't been caught, Kyle may have tried to kiss me.

A STORY OF THEIR OWN

Children coming of age in the world do not have the experience or sophistication required to communicate the particulars of their deep internal drive toward meaning. This is the most crucial time for them to be engaged in guided self-discovery. Parents and teachers can help students grow by acknowledging this time as an important and positive chapter in their lives. However, conventional wisdom does not think highly of this experience. Many adults scoff at and reject young people's behaviors as part of a phase they will soon grow out of. For example, adolescents have an intense interest, some might say an obsession, in music and the latest fashions. They latch onto new ideas en masse, engendering crazes or fads. Adolescents are more attracted and open to a variety of unconventional relationship configurations, much more so than any other age group. These things are symbolic. They become a newfound language for teens, allowing them to connect their inner experiences with a growing awareness that they are becoming someone who has a future full of potential for great meaning. For the first time in their lives, adolescents are capable of using metaphor to link their inner understanding to the world around them. The metaphors they use for this linking are their modes of self-expression: their clothing, their appearance, their music, and their relationships.

Adolescent expression is emotional, and the energy in these emotions can attach to either positive or negative symbols. Because adolescents are still immature and have little experience with the symbols that enable them to express their newfound significance, their attempts to express themselves often appear scattershot and erratic. Often, it appears, this is what turns adults off to them. A closer look reveals something different from what the conventional wisdom has conditioned us to see: adolescents are wildly enthralled with their lives—good, bad, or otherwise. This is why they gallivant about the way they do, stuffing themselves in cars with the music turned up so loud that everyone can sing at the top of their lungs without the kids sitting next to them hearing their voices. This is what has them scrawling out heaps of discombobulated verse about death and love. They love anything extreme, mysterious, and out of the ordinary. This is why many of them cite Edgar Allan Poe as their favorite poet.

Adolescents seek out powerful experiences to provide them with profound memories. They string their memories together, forming a narrative to write the first story of their lives. This is very important because once they have a story to tell, they are able to fill that story with meaning. They are not content to have mundane or uneventful stories. These stories become reflections of their identities. This is why the high school prom is such a big deal, and sweet sixteen parties grow with meaning that is disproportionate to the actual milestone. This is what causes them to work after school at the video store or delivering pizzas for six weeks, scraping together as much money as they can just to blow it all in one night on a concert and refer to it later as the best time of their entire lives.

They want others to validate their meaning and worth, which causes them to do things like stay up all night whispering into their cell phones to the same person to whom they are under the covers sending instant messages. They want their individuality to matter, which is why they put their entire lives, their desires and passions, their likes and dislikes up on *myspace* for the whole world to see. They need to rehearse their new selves, and this lets them believe it is okay to stage a scene in a restaurant when out to dinner with the family. The seeming insanity in which adolescents are involved is a form of infatuation. To them it can be devastating if life is an unfaithful or indifferent lover. Adolescents, unskilled at handling the newfound significance brewing inside them, are willing to risk anything for that sustained feeling of passion.

Positive, productive, and meaningful futures depend on our ability as parents and teachers to link this powerful cascade of emotions to adolescents' inner strengths, and then direct those strengths toward participation in positive experiences. When parents and teachers fail to recognize this, they are not listening to adolescents. Adolescents are pleading to be noticed; they are calling out for adults to express unconditional belief in them. Adults do not intend to do and say most of the things that end up entrapping children in a mind-set of weakness. We act from our own models, and for the most part, we see many people overcome the negative experiences they have in life. It is important for children to experience struggle and failure. However, given another way to view life, another way to teach children, another way to raise them, why not give these alternative approaches a try? Instead of being motivated by what we see as weaknesses and deficiencies, why not reorient our thinking—in our homes and in our classrooms—toward discovering and developing strengths?

It is a crisp October day, and I am babysitting for my friend Laura's daughter Lucy. Curious, I pick up and read *Winnie-the-Pooh.* It has been too long. What I find in the book is very different from what the psychologists found in their study of the Hundred Acre Wood. I find that the community described in *Winnie-the-Pooh* is actually the ultimate learning community. It represents the ideal. To begin with, there is a high degree of intellectual curiosity. Everyone has questions and is motivated to find the answers. Learning is very active and experimental. Every question leads to some sort of adventure, an "expotition," as they call it, which means expedition, but nobody can spell, and it doesn't seem to matter much that they can't.

So Pooh experiments with the physics of hot air balloons and the physics of flotation and so on in his never-ending search for honey. In the community of the Hundred Acre Wood, almost no learning experience is undertaken alone. Someone usually joins in willingly, either just for companionship or to volunteer his unique strengths to the project. Everyone is aware of the strengths and weaknesses of his fellow learners and has a genuine appreciation for the strengths. Pooh has a terrible memory; he can't even remember a simple rhyme. But he more than makes up for it in his capacity for empathy, and everyone knows it. Everyone is tremendously supportive of each other's efforts, even in failure. When, for example, Pooh realizes that he has been tracking in circles through the forest and he can't remember what he was looking for—*Was a woozle or a wizzle?*—he berates himself: "I have been foolish and deluded," he says, "and I am a Bear of no brain at all." To which Christopher Robin replies soothingly, "You are the best bear in all the world."

I close the book and look at Lucy; she is still innocent and untouched by the world beyond her home. Now she is smiling and laughing all the time. Still, I wonder about her future. Will her differences be appreciated and nurtured, or will she have a learning disability? Will she feel pressure to sacrifice cultivating her true interests to focus on getting into the "right" school? Will she be judged and valued according to numbers and grades assigned to her, or will she have the wonderful opportunity to experience life with a focus on her strengths?

The next two parts of the book show you what you can do to ensure that your child—or the children you teach—will reap the lifelong rewards of a focus on strengths. Everyone who has a role in raising children has an important part to play in releasing their strengths. When you look at a child, you can either see her strengths or her weaknesses. The choice is yours. When you begin to focus on the strengths, you will rediscover the same feelings of wonder, positive anticipation, and hope that you felt the day your child was born, or when she first walked into your classroom. Look for the strengths—they are right there waiting for you to notice and applaud them.

PART 2

A STRENGTHS AWAKENING

Our real problem, then, is not our strength today; it is rather the vital necessity of action today to ensure our strength tomorrow.

—DWIGHT EISENHOWER

What you don't want to be is a not very special, not very specialized, not very anchored, or not very adaptable person in a fungible job. . . . In a flatter world, you really do not want to be mediocre.

—THOMAS L. FRIEDMAN

IMAGINE WAKING UP ONE DAY AND HAVING EVERYONE YOU ENCOUNTER understand the ways in which you are unique and extraordinary. What if everyone viewed the things you did as needed contributions, and rather than looking for what is wrong with you, people pointed out what is right with you? If that happened, you would be supercharged. You would feel free and released from the burden of having to defend yourself. You would be psyched to jump out of bed and get to work. You would feel, well, strong. Wouldn't it be nice if just one day of your life could be like that? It can be, and it doesn't have to come from someone else. The Strengths Movement is about getting *you* to change your thinking in order to experience the sense of purpose and fulfillment that comes from living life from your strengths rather than your weaknesses. And one of the most important reasons for you to change your way of thinking is so you can guide your child's thinking about his unique strengths. This is the best gift you can give your child. It is what every child deserves.

Some things endure; they are *sticky* in an important way. Other things breeze into the world, cause a momentary stir, and dissipate as soon as our attention is diverted. Hula Hoops, super-low-rise jeans, Tupperware parties—those are fads. The women's movement, preserving the environment, and the Strengths Movement in schools—these are societal advances upon which our future depends. They are not fads. They will endure even if the whole world ignores them. People will keep circling back to the ideas and causes that are universal and timeless and demand our attention.

Simply put, strengths are the things that we do that make us feel energized and alive when we do them. Every single person has strengths. Children's innate strengths are like live wires connecting their unique inner qualities to their promise as adults. Those wires have life's most potent energy flowing through them, and we as adults have the power to amp up or damper down the energy flow. When the energy is turned up and strengths are developed to their fullest, people's passions light up. Life becomes meaningful and enjoyable even in the face of conflict. Strengths are what push people to that place. They are the things that keep our curiosity engaged, that step out ahead of us and beg us to follow. They are what we would do if money, prestige, and responsibility were inconsequential. Our strengths speak to us with a persistent, urging voice that begs for us to take notice, to unleash them, and in doing so, we put our best selves forward—not just in school, but on the job and in our relationships with others.

For most children, we have unintentionally created a world of limits. In order to change this, we must change the way we think about raising children. We must begin to nurture their strengths from a very early age. To do this we will need to retrain our minds and theirs to see people's strengths rather than their weaknesses. This involves commitment—commitment to knowing that inside every human being there is something valuable and worthwhile and that this needs to be realized and released into the world. When limits are placed on this belief, children swell up and become bloated by their unexpressed sense of purpose. This leads to many ill effects—frustration, anger, depression, reckless abandon, or, the worst effect, complacency toward life. Children do not start out in these weakened states. They begin with the knowledge that on some level they are special.

This is more than a simple prescriptive book on parenting or education—it's really about changing the way we think. There will be people who want to argue against and criticize these concepts. They can do that if they wish, but they will only be delaying the inevitable. The world is calling for our schools to change, and for this to happen, we must do things differently. It's plain common sense that we will not get new results from sticking to the same old methods. Naturally, the ideas and suggestions about how to bring about strengths will seem different—they are. Any amount of real change might seem uncomfortable to begin with, and the activities in this book are no exception. But the result is worth it, and once you begin, you will find the process rewarding—even fun.

The time for a national strengths awakening is now. The world is not going to wait for us to change the way we raise and educate children. We will need the strengths of future generations to solve problems that threaten to undermine the well-being of society as a whole.

There are many U.S. high schools that employ wonderfully, creative practices and programs that promote individualization. And organizations such as the Coalition for Essential Schools, the Bill and Melinda Gates Foundation, the Big Picture, the George Lucas Foundation, and Harvard University's Project Zero, among many others, are all invested in creating school environments in which students are engaged in meaningful learning. There are thousands and thousands of dedicated teachers employing very creative methods in classrooms, often under very difficult circumstances. A national school reform movement is bubbling. Future-thinking schools will be of even greater benefit to students when they include programs that intentionally focus on student strength development. Many fabulous teachers in good schools have adopted the strengths-based philosophy, using all kinds of useful activities and tools, but there is still no comprehensive, documented program with systematic activities for creating a whole-school strength environment that includes a multi-year curriculum. The Affinities Program, described in the appendix of this book, leads the way as the Positive Psychology Movement advances into elementary and secondary schools. Yet that is still not enough. For any real and enduring change to happen, parents must join teachers. To this end, in part 3 I have broadened the concepts from the Affinities Program into a workbook that every parent and teacher can begin using both at home and in the classroom.

Every day more people realize that focusing on strengths is the answer to creating a life that is truly worth living. We all stake our futures, our health, our livelihoods on the promise of the accomplishments and decisions of the next generation. They will need to develop their strengths to care for us as much as they will need them to care for themselves. Children cannot do this alone. They need adults—parents and teachers, especially—to guide, teach, and serve as their role models. Strengths are for everyone, and the sooner people realize we must overturn the deficit model, the better off we'll be. What follows are the tools needed to accomplish the task.

Chapter 6

YOUR THREE TYPES OF STRENGTHS

Our observation of nature must be diligent, our reflection profound, and our experiments exact. We rarely see these three means combined; and for this reason, creative geniuses are not common.

—DENIS DIDEROT

THERE ARE SEVERAL DIMENSIONS THAT EVOLVE SIMULTANEOUSLY in children, all of which contribute to their overall growth and development. These dimensions include academic learning; physical and emotional growth; socialization; and character and moral development. Research shows that children excel when they develop self-awareness of their strengths in these categories. To create a practical system for identifying and developing strengths, I combined these developmental areas to form a strength triad: Activity Strengths, Learning Strengths, and Relationship Strengths. Together, they cover what educators commonly refer to as the head, the heart, and the hands (although I have changed the analogy of the hands to feet because Activity Strengths are what get people moving forward). Although these strengths work together, a person must first identify them separately in order to put them to maximum use. Many people use a variety of tests to help describe their strengths. The themes and descriptions that they get from these tests can be useful, even fun, but they do not necessarily point the way toward initiating new behaviors, and as we will see later on in this section, new behaviors are essential to changing your focus from weaknesses to strengths.

In part 3 you will find a variety of activities that will help you and your children begin the process of identifying the three types of strengths described in this chapter. The activities are for parents and teachers to use at home and in school. The important thing to remember as you read about children's strengths is that there are no shortcuts to figuring out what strengths are; every child's strengths must be drawn out. This happens *with,* not *to,* children. As the poet Khalil Gibran wrote in his poem entitled "On Children," "Your children are not your children. / They come through you but not from you, / And though they are with you yet they belong not to you. / You may give them your love but not your thoughts, / For they have their own thoughts."

Knowing your own strengths will help your children understand theirs. You can go on this strengths-finding journey together. There is something in it for both of you. When you join your child in discovering strengths, you become an important role model, which children need to develop trust in the process. For you, this journey is an opportunity to rediscover your true nature, something children are closer to than adults. You have very likely lived a whole life dodging judgment and disapproval. Or you have taken it on the chin and moved on anyway. You have sold yourself to the "real world," where people believe that criticism can be constructive and praise can only yield unfettered egoism. You may have long ago forgotten your interests, set aside that dream you chased, graduated from college, and took the first job that presented itself to you. Now you get up, go to work, come home, squeeze time in for responsibilities and obligations—which now include your family and friends and attention to your health—counting the days until you can get to that two-week vacation that you have circled in red on your calendar. Changing to a new way of seeing things will be more difficult for you than for your children. However, this is your chance. Do it with them, learn from them—learn how to explore, discover, and know the sense of wonder you left behind years ago (the day someone started to tell you what you should not do, and who you should or shouldn't be).

Finding your strengths and exploring those of your child will open you up to the things you do that make you feel alive. You will teach your child how to live a full life by living one yourself. Your example will be the most powerful teacher.

Activity, Learning, and Relationship Strengths cover a lot of ground. In the following sections, I describe them as discrete and separate categories, but when you have developed a habit of thinking about your strengths, you will see these categories merge, giving you a new outlook on life. Now let's take a look at each one.

ACTIVITY STRENGTHS

The quality of life is determined by its activities.

—ARISTOTLE

An Activity Strength is simply something you are both good at and feel good doing. This is not to be confused with something you are simply good at doing. You may be very good at cleaning your house, but it might not particularly energize you or make you feel good while doing it.

Activity Strengths are

- verbs,
- innate (i.e., no one can give them to you or take them away),
- things that can be transferred to a variety of activities,
- used to engage talents, and
- specific and precise.

They

- combine with other strengths, and
- make you feel good and strong when you are using them.

There are as many examples of Activity Strengths as there are specific activities in which someone can engage. Two of my activity strengths are *designing marketing materials* and *brainstorming ideas about new educational programs*. These activities engage my talents, help me perform well in my job, and bring me pleasure. Children may have Activity Strengths that include participating on a sports team in the role of manager or working on problems that involve comparisons. These strengths are specific and precise rather than broad and all-encompassing. Here is a somewhat offbeat example from a young student of mine: Amelia's strength is in noticing and collecting things that others may discard as useless. This statement is specific, but the beauty of it is that it can be potentially transferred and used in a variety of activities, from science to antiques dealing.

For the moment, Amelia collects Altoid tins and little trinkets—the odd little things that are sold in the checkout lane in dollar stores. She stashes these things in her closet and is not exactly sure why. She just knows that finding and collecting these things is an activity that energizes her. She says, "Why would anyone want to throw away something as useful as a little tin box?" While shopping, she will notice a few small things that are unlike the rest of the items in the store. One day she pointed out a rack of tiny staplers in an office supply store, not the kind designed to be carried in a briefcase or pencil box, but even smaller. They didn't seem to have any use at all, and Amelia was drawn to them, even enchanted by them. Neither she nor I had ever seen anything like them, ever, anywhere. Amelia is also deeply interested in art. Combining her interest in art with her strength in collecting and noticing obscure objects may unleash for her a wave of talent. In a furniture design class, she used collected items to create an amazingly abstract chest of drawers. Her passion for the miniature also informs her practice of drawing Japanese-style anime. These are only first steps. How she will ultimately put this strength to use in her future remains to be seen. Nevertheless, the first step—identification—has taken place.

As you can see from this example, there is no strict, finite pool of predetermined strengths. There are as many possible strengths as there are activities, and figuring out what yours are will take self-examination. At first glance this may appear difficult. And it is. Discovering strengths takes practice, and that is what all the exercises in part 3 are for: practicing. At the end of part 3, after you have done the investigative work, you can take an *un*test called the Strengths Inventory. The inventory is more general than specific and gives names to wide-ranging themes related to people's strengths. It is a tool for conversation about strengths rather than a test to help you discover what they are. I call it an *un*test because it helps you name what you have already discovered to be true about yourself. Discovering your strengths is precise and individual. Talking about them with others can be general and thematic, and the Strengths Inventory is designed to help stir that conversation.

My friend Paul has always had an interest in movies. What he likes most about movies is his ability to pick out signs and symbols. The mental activity of searching for signs and symbols and using those to interpret a narrative is what he identifies as his strength, and he is very good at it. He transfers this understanding to a variety of other activities. In fact, that is what he did when he decided to become a private investigator. In the movies, we refer to these signs as literary devices. In the crime world, they are clues and evidence. Paul feels engaged when applying his strength to both of these activities, and both activities can be used to give his life purpose.

Focusing on Activity Strengths doesn't mean that you pay attention only to what you are already good at doing. Just because you have a strength in an activity doesn't mean you are talented or skilled in that activity. When you identify your strengths, you are then responsible for working at them to turn them into your skills and talents. You aren't going to turn your weaknesses into talents or skills. It is your strengths that you will have the most success with in life. There is more about this in the chapters ahead.

Remember the description of Rabbit from the Hundred Acre Wood study? The psychologists anticipated problems for him because he considered himself extraordinarily self-important. They cited his weakness as his constant need to organize the other members of the woods into new groupings in which he always placed himself at the top. If you view this character from a strengths lens, you will see that Rabbit is a leader. He has strength in motivating others, and therefore he is constantly finding ways to be involved in that Activity Strength. In order for him to rise in the group as a leader, he needs to view himself as important and so will the others in the woods. Real people are the same. We discover our Activity Strengths by examining what we like to do best and getting an idea of how we can use those strengths to make a contribution.

LEARNING STRENGTHS

You don't get harmony when everybody sings the same note.

—DOUG FLOYD, NEWS EDITOR AND AUTHOR

Infants' brains are wired for rapid and complex knowledge assimilation. From the start, children come into the world ready to learn. The first thing they master, without any formal instruction, is the highly symbolic and complex system of their native language. In this process, they actually learn two languages, verbal and nonverbal, both of which use symbols as means for making the abstract concrete. Over a lifetime children encounter a variety of symbolic systems across a wide range of disciplines, and their minds develop all sorts of ways to absorb, make sense of, and interact with these systems. This is what learning is.

Everyone learns in a unique way, with a unique combination of Learning Strengths. Over the past twenty-five years there has been a lot of research into the way people learn. This research evolved from a long line of educational history and learning theory, which extends as far back as China in the fifth century BC.

Most parents, and even many teachers, do not understand the roots of the teaching methods used in today's classrooms. There is not one clear and agreed upon way to teach any subject. Almost every teacher has a hand in creating his own methods and makes daily decisions about how to carry out a lesson. Sometimes these methods are grounded in a theory or a practice that the school has adopted, sometimes not. A brief history of educational theory will help you see the foundation that underlies modern-day methods of teaching and learning. While this history is by no means exhaustive, it offers a glimpse into the major movements that have influenced the variety of educational models, both good and bad, found in today's schools and classrooms. It may make you wonder why it is so difficult to change things.

THIRTEEN MOMENTS IN HISTORY: A BRIEF HISTORY OF EDUCATIONAL THEORY

Chinese Roots

The history of education is naturally a multidisciplinary study that combines philosophy (what is important for people to learn), psychology (how our personalities and social systems affect our learning), and science (how the brain actually functions). Educational theory has a history that can be traced back to the fifth century BC, when Confucius developed a method of study in which students read examples of problems and then worked hypothetically to solve them. This evolved into the modern-day practice known as the case study, which is becoming widely accepted in business but has its greatest application in the study of law. Another prominent fifth-century thinker was the philosopher Lao-tzu who wrote, "If you tell me, I will listen. If you show me, I will see. But if you let me experience, I will learn." This is perhaps the first recorded learning theory, demonstrating that the concept of experiential learning has been around for a very long time.

Greek Pillars

Socrates and his most prominent student, Plato, entered the educational history scene around 300 BC. Socrates involved his students in the learning process by asking them engaging and thought-provoking questions. Today we refer to this approach as the Socratic method. The process assumes that the answers are within a student, and if he wrestles with them, he will jog his mind and the mind of his classmates into understanding by searching for the answers. Plato took this idea a step further when he developed a theory and a practice known as the dialectic. Plato posited that real learning happened in the exchange between students, not just the individual probing for answers to questions, but in a dialogue about the questions. This theory led to the founding of the first known university, the Academy, in Athens around 385 BC. Plato also believed that all knowledge is innate and it is through various experiences that we release this knowledge. In addition, around this time Aristotle emerged as the first known advocate of the "whole-person" approach to education. He believed that education should involve the mind, body, and soul (head, heart, hands) and that in order to nurture each aspect we must use play, physical training, music, debate, and the study of science and philosophy. Aristotle was therefore the first person to make the history books that divided learning into separate categories intended to nurture different parts of our growth.

Empty Bucket

When schools became organized (around the tenth century), the methods of Socrates and Lao-tzu were laid to rest in exchange for a method that maintained that students are "empty vessels" and that the teacher can "pour" knowledge into them. Learning happened through transmitting content from teacher to students. This approach to learning is called pedagogy and infers that the teacher is responsible for all decisions about learning because the teacher is the one who knows best. This is the method still used by most classrooms today.

Blank Slate

John Locke, the English philosopher who lived in the late 1600s, advanced the hypothesis that people learn primarily from external input. In An *Essay Concerning Human Understanding* (1690), he asserted that at birth a child is a blank slate and empty of ideas. We acquire knowledge, he argued, from the information that our senses take in about the objects in the world. Locke believed that individuals acquire knowledge most easily when they first consider simple ideas and then gradually combine them to form ones that are more complex. Much of today's curricula is organized around this concept.

Father of the Progressive Movement

John Dewey is considered the leading progressive educator of the twentieth century, although his ideas reach back to fifth-century BC China and the Greeks. Dewey believed that two essential components in education are the experience of the learner and critical inquiry. He emphasized hands-on learning and opposed blank-slate and empty-bucket methods in teaching. His ideas prompted a drastic change in the U.S. educational systems beginning in the twentieth century.

Dewey's theory that education must engage with and expand experience has continued to be a significant theory informing current educational research. Dewey criticized educational methods that simply amused and entertained students, a practice commonly referred to by progressive educators as the "sage-on-the-stage" syndrome. He also believed that education should fulfill and enrich the current lives of students as well as prepare them for the future.

Gestalt Principles

In 1912, the German psychologist Max Wertheimer founded Gestalt psychology, based on the idea that everything is an integrated whole. In education, this introduced the concept that rote memorization is not as effective a learning tool as problem solving. In the former, the learner learns facts without understanding them. Such learning is stifling and easily forgotten. In the Gestalt model, students are introduced to the underlying principles embedded in all the concepts they study. They go deeper into the content to see how it integrates with other content. This type of learning comes from within the individual and is not imposed by the teacher. Information learned this way is generalized and therefore remembered for a long time.

Developmental Stages

Jean Piaget was a Swiss psychologist who lived to see a number of developments in educational history during his lifetime, from 1896 until 1980, and his teachings still influence the field of educational philosophy and child development. Piaget stressed a holistic approach to education. He believed that children construct understanding through many channels: reading, listening, exploring, and experiencing their environment.

A Piagetian-inspired curriculum emphasizes a child-centered educational philosophy or what we call "teaching the whole child." He is considered the father of constructivism. Constructivism is a theory of learning that says that children learn in stages and that these stages are closely aligned with a child's age. This idea is combined with the cognitive developmental theory that suggests that children cannot be filled with information they are not ready for. Instead, people must "construct" their own knowledge through experience, building on existing knowledge and beliefs, and cannot grasp the next level of thinking until they've mastered the step before it. Piaget's theories about developmental stages spawned many educational movements in the early 1900s, many of which are still in existence today. Two of the more famous schools are described below.

Montessori Method

Maria Montessori, like Piaget, saw children as natural learners. In 1907, the Italian physician-philosopher-educator opened her first school in Rome. Her method developed to expand Piaget's developmental theory by assigning age ranges to a child's learning stages, from birth to adolescence. She believed that children had three-year periods of sensitive development, and she grouped them in age groups, accordingly: birth to age 3; age 3 to age 6; age 6 to age 9; and age 9 to age 12. Like the Greeks, Montessori saw children as competent beings, and her instructional methods encouraged maximal decision-making. She also believed that the environment children learn in makes a significant contribution to their ability to learn. She was the first to introduce children's furniture into the classroom.

Waldorf Education Picks Up on Piaget's Concepts

In 1919, Austrian-Swiss philosopher and educator Rudolf Steiner founded a progressive school for the workers at the Waldorf-Astoria cigarette factory in Germany. Although the school was shut down during World War II, it regained acceptance afterward, and more such schools followed worldwide. Like Montessori, a Waldorf education's curriculum follows a pedagogical model of child development. Steiner's model divides childhood into seven-year developmental stages rather than three-year ones, each having its own learning requirements. Waldorf education subscribes to the Aristotelian notion of educating the whole child and emphasizes education that inspires creative and imaginative development in addition to the analytic development that most contemporary schools prefer. Waldorf aims to integrate practical, artistic, and intellectual approaches into the teaching of all subjects.

Under the Right Conditions, We Can Learn Anything

In the 1950s, American psychologist-educator-inventor-poet B. F. Skinner established his own philosophy of science, which he called Radical Behaviorism, and advanced his theory of "operant conditioning." *Conditioning* is the scientific term for learning, and *operant* refers to the concept that people perform actions that change their environments—for better or worse. Each environmental change gives a person feedback. When the feedback is positive, it reinforces the behavior and increases the likelihood it will be repeated. If the feedback is negative, it will decrease the chances the behavior will reoccur. Skinner believed that when behavior was positively reinforced, it was apt to be repeated. This led to the practice of positive reinforcement and introduced to teaching the concept of punishments and rewards. He also believed that the reinforcement must be immediate. This approach led to the idea that through the use of behavioral objectives (descriptions of what a person is being asked to do) and immediate, positive feedback, everyone should be able to learn anything and everything. This philosophy permeates much of our curriculum today and is partly responsible for the idea that given the right amount of learning in a small enough dose, everyone can master the entire curriculum.

Bloom's Taxonomy

In 1956, American educational psychologist Benjamin Bloom published his *Taxonomy of Educational Objectives*. Building on Skinner's theories, the taxonomy identifies a ladder of mental steps that a learner goes through to reach full understanding of a concept. The taxonomy begins with simple concept definitions and works its way up to the student's ability to synthesize and evaluate the concepts. This taxonomy is widely used today as a way for teachers to build lesson plans ensuring that learners are moving past rote memorization and toward synthesis of information, thus enabling them to reach the highest cognitive level possible. The taxonomy proved to be extremely valuable in the specification and analysis of student goals and outcomes and the need to design classes to attain them. This approach provides teachers a way to match what they want the student to learn with the plan they have for teaching.

Multiple Intelligences

Howard Gardner is a professor of cognition and education at Harvard University and co-director of Harvard's Project Zero. He is widely known for his theory of multiple intelligences, introduced in his book *Frames of Mind* (1983). In his book, Gardner proposes a novel notion: that "intelligence" should be formally measured in more ways than simply through the widely accepted logical-linguistic IQ-type formalized tests used in most school systems. *Frames* was very well received by those in the educational arena.

Gardner suggests that everyone has elements of each of the intelligences, and we use them depending on our preferences and the kind of tasks we are called to do. This viewpoint is in direct contrast to many of the language and logic theorists who believe that there is only one kind of intelligence, that we either have a lot of it or not that much, and that there is virtually very little that we can do about it.

In *Frames,* Gardner theorized eight basic intelligences:

- Linguistic-verbal (spoken and written words)
- Logical-mathematical (reasoning and problem solving)
- Visual-spatial (seeing and imagining)
- Bodily-kinesthetic (body, movement)
- Musical-rhythmic (sound and patterning)
- Interpersonal (interaction with others)
- Intrapersonal (feelings, values, attitudes)
- Naturalist (classifications, categories, and hierarchies)

All Kinds of Minds

Recent advancements in neurology have led to newer theories about neurodevelopment—how our brains work. A pioneer in this field of thought is Dr. Mel Levine, a developmental pediatrician at the University of North Carolina whose neurodevelopment constructs were first conceptualized in the early to mid-1980s. Levine identifies the eight constructs of neurodevelopment as follows:

- Attention (what we focus on)
- Memory (there are many kinds of memory, including long-term and short-term memory and active-working memory)
- Temporal sequential (how we sequence things in time)
- Spatial ordering (how we arrange, space, and perceive objects)
- Language (how we take in and put out verbal information)
- Motor skills (how our body interacts with the learning environment, both the small things like holding a pen and writing and the large things like running)
- Social cognition (how we interact with others)
- Higher order cognition (how we solve complex problems, evaluate and innovate)

The simple beauty of these constructs is that every person develops a unique combination of all eight, with different areas representing strengths and challenges for each person. This is a bit like Dr. Gardner's work; however, Levine changes the focus from generalized intelligences to specific learning tasks. Dr. Levine has developed a system for profiling student strengths and weaknesses according to the constructs. This profile is shared with the student in a process known as demystification. During a demystification, students are 'let in" on the information about how they learn. The teacher acts as a partner in helping the student figure out what works best, rather than simply telling the student. This encourages students to become self-advocates for their own learning. As a person comes to understand his profile, the learning process becomes more manageable—areas of strength are highlighted and better utilized. This philosophy of uncovering learning profiles and making them accessible to the person steers away from labels such as "deficit" and "disorder" and focuses instead on individual styles.

As you can see from this brief history of educational philosophy, there have been educators since the beginning of civilization who have advocated active, experiential learning that takes the individual learner into account. Since the 1970s, there have been many educational theorists and psychologists positing frameworks for different learning styles and personality types. Two researchers, Calvin Taylor and J. P. Guilford, proposed "multiple-talent" approaches that were precursors to Howard Gardner's models. The talented and gifted movement embraced both these models to identify gifted students. Learning-style inventories are common and have identified as many as thirty-four different learning styles. The most popular framework divides learners into twenty-four categories in five domains: four environmental, four emotional, six sociological, seven physical, and three psychological. The Strengths Inventory in part 3 is modeled after this approach. You can see how these inventories have served to advance people's understanding that learning is an individualized activity. The biggest mistake schools make is teaching as if everyone learns the same way.

Arielle is a talented dancer. She is quickly able to recall and repeat the combinations her dance teacher shows her. However, in her biology class, she doesn't do well on tests unless she has previously had hands-on activities that illustrate the concepts. Once Arielle realizes this about herself, she can tell others how she learns. As Arielle goes through life, she will learn the most when she asks if she can try things out for herself. Others students need different approaches. Some people process new information best with a visual aid. Knowing this, they will either ask for visual aids or make them for themselves.

Children thrive when they understand the many ways in which they are strong and smart. In order for children to live productive, meaningful lives, they must be aware of their individual Learning Strengths and have the language to communicate them to others. How many students fail in school simply because the teacher can't figure out how they learn? Similarly, many adults fail in the work world because they are not able to articulate how they learn on the job, and their bosses do not know how to make the simple adjustments that would spur growth. Failure in our society is too frequently the terrible consequence of an inability to effectively communicate about learning needs.

As we've seen, Howard Gardner and other multiple-intelligence proponents suggest that all children have multiple intelligences, but not all in equal proportion. There are dominant types. Some children will be in love with words and gravitate to reading and writing. These are the lucky ones because most educational systems favor these kinds of learners. Other children think in pictures, whereas others learn the most through social interaction. It is uncommon for teachers to recognize that social interaction (interpersonal intelligence) is a form of intelligence. Children with this kind of intelligence may love to role-play, plan events, and work in groups. They may be the ones who mediate feuds, run for student council, and get others to cooperate. Like me, you can probably think of dozens of careers that depend on these skills for success.

A HAMMER TO THE HEAD

One Friday afternoon, I was hoping I could leave school early. My family was arriving in San Francisco from Wisconsin, and I was looking forward to getting in a late-afternoon hike with them in the national park. Just as I was stuffing my appointment book and a pile of unopened mail into my handbag, I heard Miss Judy, the fifth-grade teacher, arrive in the outer office.

"Here, Timmy, you sit in that chair and wait for me. I'm going to speak first with Miss Fox, and then we'll try to find your mother in the pickup line."

I knew who she was with—he was the only Timmy in the school. You could not miss him; he was an especially attractive little boy with bright red hair. Before I knew it, I felt the hike slipping away, and in its place Miss Judy was standing in front of my desk, bobbing and weaving her head in that fed-up *Jerry Springer Show* kind of way, while frantically whispering to me so Timmy couldn't hear her.

"It's the fifth time I have spoken to him about this. I think we need to bring the mother in now," she hissed.

From where I sat, I could see Timmy's legs dangling a few inches above the floor. I noticed him nervously rubbing one red tennis shoe over another and figured that, despite the effort at discretion, he could hear his teacher's frustration. I put my hand up, signaling Miss Judy to be silent for a moment. I nodded toward the doorway, suggesting Timmy could hear us. I buzzed my assistant and asked if she would be so kind as to walk Timmy to the library and have him show her what kind of books he liked to read.

"I am just so frustrated by Timmy," Judy continued. "He seems bright enough, but then every time I give the children instructions, he is staring out the window. I am trying to teach the children to listen respectfully to one another, and he just daydreams while they talk."

"Do the other kids like Timmy?" I asked.

"Yes, they do, and that is part of the problem. They all pay a lot of attention to him when he is talking and they all seem to like him a lot. He has no trouble paying attention to them during recess!"

"What was it that caused you to come in here with him today?" I asked.

"Well, I was giving some important instructions, and Timmy was doodling on his notebook. I asked him to stop and he did, but then he just stared out the window. When I called for him to pay attention, he became very angry. He actually made a snide remark under his breath."

"What did he say?" I asked.

"He called me a jerk. It was under his breath, but I heard him, and a couple of the other kids did, too."

I resisted the urge to smile and instead sat for close to thirty minutes listening to Judy's concerns and thoughts. Once, I glanced at my watch and realized I was now going to miss the afternoon hike. Although on the surface I agreed to everything Judy wanted to do, I had a nagging feeling that there was something not quite right about her plan. I felt she was taking the jerk comment much too personally. I told her to call Timmy's mother and set up an appointment immediately following winter break.

I spent the next ten days of winter break with my family. There were several times during the week that I attempted to engage my father in serious conversation about my work. Every time I became passionate about what I was saying, I noticed his face haze over. His eyes would begin to wander, and he'd begin rubbing his left ear. It was as if he had left California and had instead tuned into some distant, far more exciting planet. I decided to let the conversation drop.

I mentioned this behavior to my brother and sister, and they agreed they had both seen it many times. "It's like he isn't listening to a word we say. Do you think he is like that with his clients?"

A few days after winter break, I returned to my office at school to discover an envelope on my desk that read, "Jenifer Fox, <u>CONFIDENTIAL</u>." My heart started pumping in that way that tells you something is bad just before you actually confirm it to be so. I closed my door, sat down at my desk, and tore open the envelope. It was an anonymous letter. Long and vivid in its details, the letter purported to speak for "a lot of us." As in, "A lot of us feel that you are making too many changes, too quickly." "A lot of us feel you spend too much time in your office and not enough time in our classrooms." "A lot of us think you are not a good listener. You seem to daydream, get a faraway look on your face when we are talking, and generally seem disinterested in what we are saying. Sometimes you look at your watch while we are talking." That was the comment I read several times over. Not a good listener? Excuse me? I listened to everything they said, most of the time in a reflective, nonjudgmental way. How could they think I wasn't listening? I was very hurt. I knew that Miss Judy was largely behind the writing of the letter, which really burned me up, since I often spent so much time listening to her concerns. "Jerk," I thought to myself as I was driving home that evening.

When I shared the evaluation with my husband, he laughed when I got to the part about listening.

"You know, honey, that is true. You may be listening, but you don't seem to be . . . just like your father," he said. The minute he said that, it hit me like a hammer to my head: "But I *am* listening," I told Nick.

"I know you are, but—"

"But I can't always look at the person talking because then I can't think about what they are saying. I need to look away to listen, or I need to write things down in order to process what is being said."

"Just like your father," said Nick.

I thought about this for a moment and then it became clear to me.

"Just like Timmy!" I exclaimed.

"Timmy?"

"The kid at school who always gets in trouble for seeming to not pay attention, the one who called Miss Judy a jerk."

Timmy is a visual learner. This makes it difficult for him to take in information when he is just listening to it. Oftentimes, he needs to look away in order to concentrate. An animated face, arm gestures—these visuals are at times distracting. Doodling in a notebook while someone is talking helps Timmy—and me—(and, I suppose, my father also) to listen better, although it appears as if we are not listening.

Everyone's learning style is different, and sometimes we misjudge people based on how their styles differ from our expectations. In schools, this seems to happen most commonly with learners who have a marked kinesthetic (physical) learning strength, especially in subject areas that contain little or no practical activity or movement. An auditory learner may be talking to another student during a teacher-led class. Talking things through may be the way she checks whether she understands what is being presented. The teacher, however, may see this behavior as disruptive and disrespectful. It is very important to know your own learning strengths and to be able to explain them to others.

In the case of the teachers in San Francisco, I took great care to explain my listening style, and I made sure I did not apologize for it. I asked them to accommodate me and not take it personally. I will never know whether they were able to do so, as I still look away during important explanations because I am a good listener, and I know looking away helps me commit to the activity. Now I let people know what to expect. When your child figures out what his learning strengths are, this kind of self-advocacy will help him.

RELATIONSHIP STRENGTHS

> *You cannot dream yourself into a character; you must hammer and forge yourself one.*
>
> —JAMES A. FROUDE

We connect to others through an intricate web of relationships, and they need our input to thrive. The energy we apply to our relationships either sustains or drains them. This is true in our most intimate relationships with family and friends as well as our casual ones with the local store clerk or mail carrier. Relationship Strengths are the things you do for and with other people that make you feel strong and good about the relationship. They are the application of character virtues. Character virtues are qualities such as trustworthiness, forgiveness, loyalty, consideration, thankfulness, flexibility, and dependability. They also include such skills as being a good listener and showing empathy. These characteristics can be developed and used to enrich our relationships. We can make conscious decisions to focus on a handful of these, choosing the ones that are most natural and make us feel the strongest. We use our Relationship Strengths to inform our interactions with other people.

I am more energized and better at acting courageously in my relationships than I am with exercising patience. By identifying this and sharing this insight with the people I am in relationships with, I can begin to use my strengths to help establish clear relationship expectations. Identifying this does not give me license to be impatient, nor does it mean I shouldn't try to develop as many character virtues as possible. However, we cannot be perfect. We can become better people with more meaningful relationships when we discover the Relationship Strengths that we really desire to focus on. It is rare that children learn they can have a choice in developing and utilizing strengths to enrich their relationships.

My husband, Nick, has "fixing things for other people" as one of his Relationship Strengths. He feels totally fulfilled when he can repair something for someone. I make that distinction because he also has "fixing things" as an Activity Strength, but it is the "for someone" that changes that from an Activity to a Relationship Strength. When he fixes the motor on his sailboat, he is engaged in Activity Strength, but when he repairs the clasp on my necklace, he is engaged in Relationship Strength. This is an important distinction. There are a few different character virtues at work in this Relationship Strength, generosity and thoughtfulness to name two, but they are not specific enough to describe the real strength. The way you apply generosity in your relationships may look very different from the way someone else does. As in the identification of your Activity Strengths, the more precise and specific you are, the better.

Nick is also energized by a roomful of people. The particular Relationship Strengths he brings to social situations is his ability to tell a funny story. Everyone likes having Nick around because he has a knack for making people feel good in the moment. On the other hand, he is not especially good at communication between visits. Chatting on the phone and sending letters and casual e-mails are draining to him. He sustains his relationships in person. People feel the generosity of his presence, and that is more than enough to keep the relationships going.

I, on the other hand, have entirely different Relationship Strengths. I survive the party. However, when we return home, I follow up in a personal way with the people whose relationships I value. One of my Relationship Strengths is giving personal, meaningful gifts. Once I gave my mother-in-law a book full of letters from all the women friends in her life. I scanned all the letters and photographs, printed them on the same paper, and bound the collection in hardcover. The book ended up totaling about a hundred pages. Another time I gave my entire extended family a video of my grandmother's last birthday. I feel strong and proud when I give personal things to others that make them feel connected to me. I can pump that strength through my entire web of relationships and watch it work for each one. This works well because I am not always available for many important people in my life. I have moved around a lot, so I am not even physically that close. When I give personal gifts—a book I read, a poem I wrote, a shell I carried one afternoon on a beach—the gift glows in that person's life for a long time, connecting them to me in my absence or enhancing the connection when I am around.

We can teach students to identify Relationship Strengths, and then we can engage them in practicing and reflecting on them. Children engaged in discovering Relationship Strengths will better understand how they can form and refine the contributions they make to others. This practice will allow them to be more effective in both their personal and professional relationships and reap greater rewards from them.

Meaningful relationships create meaningful lives, yet it is rare that schools actually teach students skills to promote long-term success in their relationships. Children need to learn how to choose friends. As they socialize on the playground, in cafeterias, and through the hallways, children are left to figure much of it out on their own. Adults are usually called in only when there is a problem. Recent books—such as Dan Kindlon and Michael Thompson's *Raising Cain: Protecting the Emotional Life of Boys* and Rosalind Wiseman's *Queen Bees and Wannabes*—address the social jungles in our schools. They are wise and practical books that describe the negative aspects that are already present in the social worlds of children. Schools that become explicitly strengths-based will focus on showing children that they have the power not only to protect themselves from negative interaction but also to turn these interactions around.

BFFs

The sun was barely up when I came charging out of my house on a Saturday morning last September, wearing my coat over my pajamas. I live on campus, about ten yards from my office, so I thought there was a good chance of scooting over to retrieve some paperwork before anyone was around to notice that I had not yet showered or dressed.

Once in the office, my phone rang, and without thinking I picked it up.

"This is Jenifer Fox," I said.

"Oh, Ms. Fox, I am so glad I got you. I saw you go into Main from my dorm window. I hope it's all right to call you."

"Who is this?" I asked.

"It's Chelsea—I need to talk to you. Can I come over now?"

"Right now?"

"Yes, it is urgent."

"Is everything okay?"

"No, nothing is okay—nothing." She burst out sobbing.

Chelsea appeared at my office door within three minutes, her eyes red, her skin blotchy, and her hair a snarled mess. Clearly, she had been up all night.

"Thanks so much for seeing me," she sniffled. "Why do you have your coat on? It's really warm out." She paused, looking me over, and then said, "I don't think I've ever seen you without earrings on."

I handed her a box of tissues as she sat on the couch suspiciously eyeing my slippers.

"So what's the big emergency?" I asked.

"You know how Lisa and I are, like, BFFs?"

"Best friends? No, I didn't know that."

I held my tongue. The girls had been at school together for only two weeks and it seemed too soon to have a best friend.

"Well, last night we were instant messaging this guy I know from back home—and she doesn't know him, he's my friend—well, once I went out with him, but that was dumb. So, Lisa waits for me to go the bathroom, and when I do, she takes his number from my phone and then later she calls him back and tells him all these things about me."

"What kind of things?" I ask.

"You know, *things*."

"Like what?"

"She told him that some of the other girls don't like me," she said, and then began crying again.

"Why would she do that?"

"I dunno, I guess she was trying to get him to like her more than me and—so, we are not friends anymore. I actually can't stand her now." She pulled a long stream of tissues from the box and let out a long sigh.

"Well, you have only been back at school for two weeks, and Lisa is brand-new this year, so it isn't possible that Lisa is really your "best friend." It may even be too early for you to consider her a friend. But there is something between you two because it drew you to one another from the start, right?"

"Yeah, I think she liked my music collection—we like the same bands."

"Okay, whatever drew her to you to begin with is still there. Now you need to decide whether or not you want to put in the energy to turn your acquaintance into a friendship and determine what the expectations for that are. If you want, I can talk to your dorm parent about sitting down with you girls and talking this through, okay?"

"Okay." She stood up and tossed the damp wad of tissues into the wastebasket.

"Thanks, Ms. Fox."

"You're welcome, Chelsea."

"Do you think I could ask you one more favor?"

"What's that?"

"Can I get a picture of you with my cell phone? Nobody's going to believe I saw you over here in your pajamas."

There was no photo taken.

Chelsea's relationship strength is sharing. Her virtues are friendliness, caring, and trust. She feels good when she shares herself with people, yet she will also need to learn how to manage that strength so it continues to work for her and not against her. In her case, the same technology that helps her stay in touch with friends also provides the means to undermine carefully built relationships. Given the vast networking capabilities of the Internet, Chelsea's understanding of what constitutes appropriate and timely sharing will play a huge role in her success or failure at building healthy lasting relationships.

So much time and energy is wasted for children when they feel hurt because they don't understand some simple relationship concepts that we can teach them. An important concept that many children fail to recognize is the difference between *liking* someone and *being friends* with someone. The first step in any friendship is the initial attraction. The reality is that not everyone your child is attracted to feels reciprocal attraction. This is often the first arena in which children experience pain in relationships. The main problem with this is that when someone a child likes does not return the attention, she immediately believes it is because there is something inherently wrong with her personality. Attraction is not static or based solely on personality traits. It is a form of energy between people. Sometimes that energy simply doesn't exist, and it doesn't mean there is anything wrong with the people involved.

Knowledge of this and other important concepts about friendship will provide the foundation for developing Relationship Strengths. Once Relationship Strengths become part of a child's knowledge about themselves, adults can guide children to be proactive in all their relationships. You can sit down with children and create a list of the expectations they have for their friendships. This list will include what they expect from others as well as what others can expect from them. For example, for some people, being on time for engagements is very important, and lateness is a sign of disrespect. If you can let others know up front that in order to be friends, you expect promptness, so they will know that violating this expectation is hurtful to the relationship. Other people don't mind if you arrive late. All your friendships and relationships will benefit from clearly stated expectations. I cannot be a good friend to someone who expects that I will call on the phone once a week. However, that doesn't mean there is not something else I can offer that person as a friend.

We cannot be everything to all people. Different relationships can fulfill different roles in children's lives, and this is something children can learn rather than having to wander through it all alone. Identifying Relationship Strengths will clarify these expectations and will help with these negotiations. In part 3 there is an activity for developing *Friendship Statements* that outline expectations and align them with Relationship Strengths.

Specific relationship skills will become imperative for success in the future. Rapid bonding and express-lane trust will be necessary for people to come together quickly and work synergistically on projects with firm deadlines. In his future-thinking book *A Whole New Mind,* author Daniel H. Pink describes the qualities that will reap the biggest rewards in the future as being "high touch." He says, "High touch involves the ability to empathize, to understand the subtleties of human interaction, to find joy in one's self and elicit it in others, and to stretch beyond the quotidian, in pursuit of purpose and meaning."

As the world speeds up, we don't want our children to lose the important values and virtues that make life fulfilling and worth living. By developing Relationship Strengths, children become committed to retaining the important character qualities that make their relationships rewarding and valuable. In part 3 you will discover ways to do this.

Chapter 7

SETTING THE STAGE FOR DISCOVERY AND DEVELOPMENT

Making mental connections is our most crucial learning tool, the essence of human intelligence; to forge links; to go beyond the given; to see patterns, relationships, context.

—MARILYN FERGUSON

THERE ARE SIX CHILDREN IN MY FAMILY, AND NO TWO OF US ARE alike. We each have different interests, abilities, quirks, and styles. We all share a few qualities, like a healthy sense of humor and a competitive drive, but in most ways we are very different. I am slightly introverted, whereas my brother Stephen is a classic extrovert. Bill enjoys history and fact-finding, while Martha prefers creative and artistic endeavors. Our parents are even more different than we are. One day my sister, Martha, and I sat down and listed the strengths of everyone in our family, and we came up with two entirely different lists. This happened because when we view other people, it is very difficult to see them through an unbiased lens. We tend to see others much in the same way we view ourselves. This is what makes it impossible for you to tell your child what his strengths are. You may come close to identifying them, but he must tell *you* what they are, rather than the reverse. Your job is to guide your child, no matter what his age, toward recognition and understanding of his strengths.

As I said earlier, this is not an easy task. Getting to know anyone as an individual can be time consuming. Helping someone to know himself is even more difficult, especially since this activity is not the norm. Discovering strengths is a skill that must be developed, and as with any other skill, it takes practice. There aren't any shortcuts. Between work, social commitments, and personal obligations, who has time to devote to such an exhausting task? Believe it or not, this task *can* be done, and in the long run it will save you hours, perhaps even years, of dealing with the potentially negative fallout of parenting someone who has no idea what his strengths are. The discovery process is an ongoing journey of questions, observations, and impressions. The ideal time for a child to begin this journey is around the age of ten or twelve, but anyone can begin at any time. Before age ten, parents and teachers can lay the foundation with a variety of activities that will make discovering strengths easier once your child is old enough to begin his personal journey. We will explore these activities in a later section.

HOW DO CHILDREN DISCOVER THEIR STRENGTHS?

The real process of strengths discovery begins with self-reflection. When both children and adults begin to reflect regularly on the things they do that make them feel strong, they develop a new way of thinking. Thinking about strengths becomes part of your daily life and eventually part of your future—it becomes a habit.

There is a lot of noise in our heads. We cannot discover our strengths without being able to focus on what we are doing and how it makes us feel. This will entail quieting the mind and beginning to observe how you respond to activities and interactions. The more you guide children into this activity, the better they will become at it. The more you work with your child on recognizing and thinking about strengths, the more habit forming that kind of thinking will become. Currently, our minds are programmed to see the negative and the weaknesses in people. It is easy, and seemingly natural, to see what needs "fixing" in another person. If our minds can also be trained to take on this altered viewpoint, they can also be retrained to see the strength. This retraining will take work. The younger the child is, the easier this will be, as their minds are less entrenched in negative thinking.

Strengths are not simple preferences. They are not just items to pick and choose from a list of options. We are not looking for the "strength of the week" or a slogan. Discovering strengths is a lifelong commitment. It begins with asking questions about preferences, but it eventually turns into a way to think about life as a positive journey over which you have control. So strengths are not preferences, because preferences change depending on the options. Twenty years ago a child could not name computer design as an Activity Strength because there was no such activity available to the general public. Likewise, people did not have strength in digital photography any more than they did in designing avatars. Strengths lie *underneath* the preferences and desires. Your child's strengths will interact with new and different choices throughout life, but her innate strengths will not change.

Similarly, strengths may be used in the service of talents, but they are not talents in and of themselves. For example, I may have a talent for cooking, and everyone who eats my dinners may remark, "Wow, you are a talented cook," but that talent is not a strength if I don't enjoy myself while I cook. Talents alone do not lead to lives and careers that people are passionate about. As we talk with children about what they love and feel strong about, we need to be careful not to discuss our own aspirations or desires to mold and form them. Remain open. No one can tell you what your strengths are, and you cannot tell your children what their strengths are. They must tell you as a result of their own thinking processes.

Like most people, there are many things I enjoy doing, and in a few of these things I possess natural talent. By combining the things I like to do with the things I have a talent for, I was able to find a job that allows me to play to my strengths at work most of the time. Still, I need more than that to sustain long-term success in my job and life. I attribute my ability to be successful to my having identified my particular Learning, Relationship, and Activity Strengths and knowing how to put them to work for my benefit and the benefit of others. As an adult, that self-knowledge is somewhat hard to come by. How do we cultivate it in our children?

To get children to begin thinking about strengths parents can:

- **encourage** children to sit quietly and focus on some deep breaths to still their minds,
- **ask** questions about preferences and feelings,
- **listen** closely to the detail children use to talk about their activities and preferences, and
- **observe** how they respond and interact in a variety of settings.

STILLING THE MIND

To a mind that is still, the whole universe surrenders.

—CHUANG-TZU

Just before bedtime on Tuesday, Greg receives an instant message from his girlfriend, Maria, telling him she is "dropping him" because now she is "going with" Matt, the new kid who came into the sixth grade after the winter break. Greg gets up on Wednesday morning hurt and angry. He is late, and his mother pummels him with reminders as he is trying to find his books. "Remember your soccer jersey, and don't forget, Dad is picking you up early. Did you make your bed?" Greg tries to recall whether there is a history test today, or maybe it's Thursday? Maria and Matt are both in that class. What is he going to do? Late for school, Greg leaves the house without his math book, skips breakfast, and by history class, his blood sugar is so low he can barely function.

This is a typical scenario that could be true of any student in the classroom. Between interpersonal dramas, overbooked activities, heavy homework schedules, or the stress of college applications, plus the myriad distractions of cell phones, instant messaging, and other time-filling technology, children's days are just as busy and chaotic as their parents'. The chaos is compounded when there are family problems in the home. How can we expect children to be able to think about their strengths under these conditions? In Greg's case, the only way he is going to make his day right is by calling on his strengths.

Parents and teachers should assume they are starting out each day with children who are preoccupied, overstressed, and anxious and that it will be up to them to acknowledge this and help out. Children of all ages can be encouraged to sit quietly, close their eyes, clear their minds, and take a few deep breaths, focusing only on their breathing. Tell them they are becoming quiet so they can think about their strengths and concentrate on how they feel in their present activities. This will take a few minutes, but a few minutes at intervals throughout the day is better than never having any focus and clarity. At first glance, this exercise may seem New Agey, but it is not. The pace of life has changed so much that exercises like this are now necessary, not outside the mainstream. Children will do almost anything you ask of them if you frame it as a gift for them and involve them in the discussion about how and why they are doing something.

If you want to get children to focus on strengths, you have to teach them to focus and still their minds. That is the first step. It can happen in school or at home. You can make it part of their routine. When you do, everyone will benefit.

ASKING SPECIFIC QUESTIONS

Once a child's mind is focused, you can begin developing the reflective habit that will allow thinking about strength to become second nature. This habit demands not only reflection but also dialogue and conversation. Children will need to start seeing the activities that give them charges of positive energy, and then they will need to identify that feeling in seemingly unrelated activities across many arenas. The searching out of these rushes of positive energy, these "aha" moments, begins by asking children to notice when they feel especially interested and engaged in an activity. Next, it moves to a dialogue that begins with asking questions. You need to ask many questions, giving your child choices without giving advice or answers. This process is the same for discovering all three kinds of strengths.

Here is an example of the type of questioning that can take place after your child completes a family chore like doing the dishes.

"Rachel, great job doing the dishes. Tell me, is there any part of doing the dishes that you enjoy more than any other part?"

"I prefer to be washing the dishes instead of putting them away or drying them. I hate drying the dishes."

"Why do you think you enjoy washing them?"

"I like the water. And the suds. I think the suds are kind of fun."

"Do you like water in general, or just with the dishes?"

"I don't like cleaning the bathtub, if that's what you're asking."

"I'm not sure what I am asking, I am just exploring how you feel when you do different activities. Are there other times you like using water in a task?"

"Sure, I love washing the car."

"So if you worked in a restaurant, what would you rather do—wash dishes or bus tables?"

"That's easy, wash dishes."

Although this type of conversation may not in and of itself lead to the discovery of strengths, by having these inquiring talks about simple things, you can begin to direct your children toward examining how they feel about doing specific activities. You will know when the time is right to dig a little. Start simple and ask questions that give alternatives. Do you like this more than that? Follow that question up with two "why" questions:

"When you go shopping, which do you like buying more, food or household products?"

"Household products."

"Why?"

"Because they last longer than food."

"Why is that important?"

"It's not important. I just feel like I have to buy them less often, and so when I do buy them, I feel like I am saving time."

After a couple of "why" questions, try repeating the last thing said.

"So you like doing things that save you time."

"Yes, I love efficiency."

Everyone knows that you cannot script conversations with kids. Bill Cosby and Art Linkletter built great TV shows on the unpredictability of these interactions. However, you *can* steer your talks in the direction of seeking out your child's inner motivations. These conversations can start very young, and as children progress developmentally, they will become increasingly able to consciously reflect on their actions. If younger children are at a loss for words, they can be coaxed to make choices by looking at pictures of people representing various feelings and then asked to point to a photo of how a certain activity makes them feel. Part 3 will show you how to do this.

The more children are engaged in the process of self-reflection as an activity led by an adult asking them questions, the more they train their minds to spend time on thoughts that are exploratory and creative rather than learning to be argumentative and defensive. This habit can change children's lives in a variety of positive ways. It will lead them to be more proactive in all areas of their lives. They will choose friends that strengthen them, will gravitate toward jobs that are fulfilling, and will make decisions that will better put them in control of their lives.

LISTENING FOR YOUR CHILD'S STRENGTHS

One question we ought to ask ourselves every day is "How well do I know what drives my child's interests?" When we listen closely to children, at any age, we will hear clues about the things that matter most to them. Their strengths can be discovered inside these clues if we practice listening carefully. One of your goals as a parent or a teacher should be to develop a listening relationship with children. Not only does listening to children's thoughts and opinions give clues to strengths, it engenders trust.

Parents and teachers make assumptions about children all the time. We rarely take the time to listen and get to know who the children in our lives really are because we believe that as adults we are supposed to have all the answers—it is your job to tell your child things, not the other way around. Think for a moment how it feels when you are in relationships with people who never ask you about you. We have all been involved in one-sided relationships in which the other person does all the talking and makes all the plans and never once stops to consider what you may be thinking or what you might prefer. Those relationships are not all that fulfilling or rewarding. There is little room in them for mutual growth. Why would children feel any different from adults in these kinds of relationships? You know how when children get to be a certain age their entire focus becomes their friends? The opinions of their friends are much more important than yours because many of their friends have expressed more of an interest in their individuality than you have. By the time a child becomes a teenager, he has skillfully learned how to tune out you and your advice giving.

Some adults think they are listening to kids when they are not really listening. Teachers and parents must listen empathetically to children. Most of us grew up not being listened to and not having our feelings recognized, so we have few truly empathetic role models. But if you really want to help children discover their strengths, it is important to learn how to listen in ways that validate their feelings and to begin doing it as early as you can. This is important because most children aren't skilled at expressing themselves, and so they need all the help they can get from us. More than anything else, they desire to be understood. One of the biggest mistakes adults make with teenagers is to interject advice and autobiography into all their conversations with them. How often do we hear ourselves saying, "When I was your age, . . ." or "You need to get a job. All you do is lie around the house." Children don't want advice any more than they want pity. Most of the time, children don't even need much of a response. They simply want to be heard and acknowledged. Here is a recent conversation I heard between a teacher and a student when the student failed to turn in her homework.

"Molly, why didn't you do your homework?"

"I did do it, I just can't find it."

"You are going to have to get organized. You won't be able to last in college if you can't figure out how to get your assignments in and follow through on your obligations." Molly rolls her eyes and sighs. The teacher feels disrespected.

"You know, Molly, I hated to do homework, too, but I did it because I wanted to be able to graduate and get a good job. You want that for your future, don't you?"

"Whatever." Molly walks away sullenly, and the teacher doesn't understand what has gotten into kids these days.

The teacher in the above example had good intentions, but his communication is ineffective. Teens in particular want people to understand them, not immediately try to fix them. When adults jump to the fixing stage before they understand the problem, young people become disengaged in the relationship. When this happens repeatedly, kids stop trusting adults because intrinsic to trust is the idea that each person in the relationship has a basic understanding of the other. Adults cannot hope to understand young people when they fail to listen to them. Consider this alternate version of the last example.

"Molly, I see you don't have your homework."

"I finished it, but I don't know where I put it."

"You sound frustrated about that."

"Yes, I spent so much time on it, and now I won't even get credit for it."

"I hear you saying that you spend a lot of time on the homework in this class."

"Hours. It's like forever. And, like, no offense, but this isn't my favorite class."

"You feel conflicted because this is a class you don't enjoy, but you have to spend hours on it anyway."

"Yeah, that is a huge problem for me. There is so much reading, and I can never get it done."

"You wish you could read the things in this class more quickly?"

"I guess I don't understand what we read, and then I take a long time on it."

The kind of listening and conversation described above will help both teachers and parents better understand kids. It shouldn't surprise you that these tactics work not only with children; they are equally as effective when talking to spouses, parents, coworkers, and friends. That said, this advice is not easy for anyone to follow. It is not easy for adults, and it is more difficult still when dealing with an irritable child. The patience demanded of both teachers and parents in the reflective listening process feels counterintuitive when the person being listened to is upset and saying things that seem irrational or poorly thought out. Reflective listening, though difficult, is nonetheless the single best tool for getting young people to open up and reveal their true feelings. When this happens, you will see that the young people in your life truly are asking for your advice. However, they don't want it until they trust that you understand them and believe in them. Once that threshold is met, the pursuit of strengths becomes genuine for young people and not just another piece of adult advice.

The Sweet Spot

Katherine and her sister both began their education at a small progressive school, considered by many to be an oasis within the general frenzy of the Manhattan educational system. The school worked well for Katherine's sister, and she was able to find success. Although the school was a good match for her temperament, Katherine was never able to figure out her specific Learning Strengths. Although her teachers and peers were all extremely accepting of her, she began to feel overwhelmed by the things she did not understand. When her teachers could not figure out her Learning Strengths, they blamed Katherine, saying she was the one with the deficit. Katherine felt personal strength in activities in the areas of art, emotions, and spirituality, but academic success in math was the key element her school determined necessary for success. Additionally, while Katherine had many areas of academic interest, she did not demonstrate her understanding in the same way that most students in her school did.

Her parents began to investigate alternative programs in New York City, and after a time, they sadly concluded that in order to educate Katherine there would be unavoidable trade-offs: skills remediation at the expense of rich content and direct instruction in lieu of collaborative learning.

In short, Katherine would have to go through school enduring a learning-disabled identity. Katherine's parents longed for a school that would help her move beyond her stunted academic identity and inspire her to figure out who she was in the world. As they put it, "This is her life we are talking about."

Katherine's parents called me one March morning to talk about whether we would consider her for admission to the Purnell School.

Katherine arrived at the interview wearing sunglasses even though it was a cloudy day. When I asked her if she would remove her glasses, she did so reluctantly, revealing eyes that were red and puffy. "I have allergies," she said, not looking up. Katherine sat beside her mother on the couch in my office and quietly stroked Buddy, my border collie. Buddy is a charming character, and a perfect companion for an insecure girl. I sat in an armchair beside the couch, pretending to write some notes on a pad, allowing her time to get comfortable.

"So why do you think you want to come here?" I gently asked.

"I dunno," she muttered, avoiding eye contact.

"Katherine is extremely talented in the arts. She loves to draw and sing, don't you, Katherine? Tell her about your singing," her mother said urgingly.

Katherine rolled her eyes at her mother and let out a little "I am so embarrassed by you" sigh. Her mother pursed her lips and clutched her purse in her lap. "She really has a talent for singing if she would put her mind to it," her mother assured me. I nodded and then asked if she wouldn't mind stepping out of the room to allow me a moment alone with Katherine. She hesitantly agreed, and as she closed the door, she shot her daughter a look that said, "Don't say anything to blow this."

"You must hate school," I said, unintentionally startling her. "It's okay. School is actually pretty boring." I then paused until she looked up at me again, this time with a glimmer of interest.

"Really," I said, "all you do is sit all day and the teacher thinks you don't know anything, and if you even seem confused, they take it personally, right?"

She smiled.

"What do you hate the most?" I asked. "It's okay. I hated math."

"Chemistry," she replied.

"I see. So what is it about chemistry you hate?"

"It's boring," she said.

"What is boring about it? I mean, do you even understand it? Because it is okay if you don't."

"Nope. I don't really get it," she answered honestly. Buddy stretched out, pushed his legs into her, and yawned.

"He's bored most of the time, and he probably doesn't understand a word we are saying, and you know what? It's because he really doesn't care. All he cares about is fetching a ball. He is great at fetching a ball," I told her.

When I said "ball," Buddy's ears pricked up, and he suddenly sat up, ready to go. Katherine laughed to see that he knew the word *ball.*

"That's his strength," I told her. "What's yours?"

"My strength?" she asked.

"Yes, that thing you do that pricks up your ears. That one thing that gets you up off the couch and excites you like he's excited now."

"I don't know." She shrugged. I waited.

"I guess I really like tennis," she offered. She sat up straight, looked me in the eye, and reluctantly smiled.

"That's funny," I said, motioning to Buddy. "You two like the same thing!" She laughed.

"So tell me about the tennis."

"What about it?" she asked.

"What is it about it that you really like? I mean, what part of the game really gets you excited?"

"Well, there was this one tennis coach I had," she began after a few beats, "and he said, 'Don't return the ball until it finds that one place between where it goes up in the air and where it comes down.' He called that the sweet spot, said it was all about gravity. He told me to watch for that and to look for the second where it sat, you know, kind of still in the air. He said that is when I should hit it. So that's what I did, and it worked, and then I got good at hitting it."

"So is that what you like about it? That very moment or the actual hitting of the ball?"

She looked at me as if something important had just dawned on her.

"That very moment."

"The sweet spot? Is that what you like?" She nodded quickly, and her grin stretched from ear to ear.

"Yeah, that's it," she said excitedly.

"Oh, I see . . . Well, Katherine, I believe you when you say you don't like chemistry, but I certainly think you can find something to like about physics. They'll just need to let you play the game."

Katherine ended up coming to Purnell. She joined the tennis team. She struggled in chemistry and math, and she hated English. One day in her junior year, I ran across her in the hallway, where she and another girl sat holding a meterstick and a couple of dollar bills.

"What are you doing with the money?" I asked them.

"Oh, Ms. Fox, this is so cool. We're testing reaction time. You know, we're looking at the distance a thing will fall in a gravitational field. Isn't that tight? You wanna be part of our experiment? It won't take long."

"Yeah, sure, that would be tight," I said, making them giggle.

Katherine folded the dollar bill lengthwise and instructed me to place my thumb and forefinger opposite George Washington's portrait.

"Ok, so that's how you have to catch it, just the way you are holding it now."

While her partner held the meterstick, Katherine positioned the dollar bill above my head, then dropped it. I watched as closely as I have ever watched anything before, and for a nanosecond I thought I saw the instant where it hung dead in the air—the sweet spot. I caught the dollar bill the way she'd instructed me. In a flash, the meterstick was up alongside me measuring, and Katherine was frantically punching the buttons on her calculator.

"It's all about gravity and reaction time," she beamed. "Oh, and Ms. Fox, you can keep the dollar if you want. You're probably going to need it more than me."

Strengths are more than the bits and pieces and slices and slivers of compartmentalized topics that a teacher tells a child she must master in one particular way to be successful. Strengths are individual epiphanies that open doors to further understanding about what turns one on to life. Schools need to become places that help children identify these things for themselves and encourage parents to join their efforts.

OBSERVING YOUR CHILD'S STRENGTHS

Hunting—that is what you are doing when you observe children for insight into their strengths. You are not playing the role of an inventor; rather, you are searching for something that is already there. To be successful in your search, you will have to look here, there, and everywhere—even in places you would not expect to find strengths. Observation is not a passive act; it is a scientific endeavor that involves creativity. It involves coming up with alternative conclusions to the first thing you see in your child—and these alternatives are often hiding in plain sight.

Looking for Clues

Remember Marley, my friend Janie's daughter, the one with the fort? Last spring Marley called me and asked if she could stop by for a visit. She and several of her college friends were gathering in New York City before heading off together to "A Semester at Sea." Her mother, whom I had not seen in years, gave her my phone number and told her to try to drop in on me. Always the obedient child (she never did smoke any pot or cigarettes), she rang me up one Indian summer day in mid-September.

Just after noon my doorbell rang, and I opened the door to a happy reunion with Marley. She was all grown up, with a giant purple backpack strapped to her back and two friends, Thatcher and Kate, standing beside her. They had come to spend the night before catching a late-afternoon flight out of Newark to California, where they would board a boat and spend months at sea studying the ocean.

After dinner, Marley offered to help me do the dishes while her friends went off in search of allergy medicine. We passed wet, sudsy dishes between us, stacking the dishwasher as I blithely asked her, "So, Marley, do you remember that fort you used to have in your yard?"

She laughed. "Remember it? It almost killed my mom. She hated that thing, thought I was some kind of freak for hanging out there. Do you know she actually thought I was smoking pot out there? I was in like seventh grade!"

"Hmm, I guess I didn't realize how worried she really was," I lied. "So what happened?"

"Well, we had this pretty big tropical storm, and that was the end of that."

"I'm sorry," I said, thinking for a moment that I may have had something to do with the demise of the fort.

"Oh, it doesn't matter," she said. "I found another place to hang out and, come to think of it, that is how I ended up on this trip."

"Really? What is that?"

"Well, I have this other friend, Christine. Her dad had an old boat he kept on Anna Maria Island, and it needed a lot of fixing up. So we spent a whole winter cleaning it up and getting it in shape. We used to hang out there after school, studying and reading. I became really interested in marine science after that."

I felt then that Marley had let me in on a simple secret. I thought about her comments for a while before asking, "Marley, how would you feel about going up in space?" She was moving behind me, gathering the pots from the stove. I heard her stop as though she'd frozen. The room swelled with a beautiful silence. I paused there with her, and then she sang, "Well, don't you know it, that would be my idea of the greatest thing a person could possibly do," she said. She went on to talk about her ambition to study at NASA in the next few years.

"But, Jen, how did you know I was interested in this?" she asked.

"It was a crazy guess," I said. "I mean, it is clear you are very interested in studying the natural world—first your yard, now the ocean. And it is clear that you enjoy having a base of some kind to study from—like the fort and the boat. You don't seem to be put off by small spaces you can share with friends. I just thought that the ultimate joining of those two strengths might be in a rocket ship in space."

"That is so freaky you said that. I wasn't sure why, but you are right . . . you are right. How did you ever know this?" she asked.

I was surprised that she was so excited. I knew that whether or not she ever made it into space, she would continue to do work that involved both science and the intimacy of discovering things in small spaces with people she enjoyed. Just knowing that would help her find meaningful work. "I don't know, Marley. I guess I am just good at looking for clues," I said, pouring the thick green liquid dishwasher soap into the little cup before twisting it shut.

"Yeah, so I heard. Clues, like matches and incense?" she asked, and winked at me.

You will begin to recognize your children's personalities as soon as they begin to communicate with you. Your job—from your child's birth until around age twelve—is to notice the unique qualities in your sons and daughters and celebrate those qualities. Your child's schools should be engaged in the same "noticing" process. The things you observe may or may not turn out to be strengths. Parents and teachers can seed the strength garden through recognizing innate tendencies in a child's personality without trying to change or squelch them.

Think about the most rambunctious and loud child you know. This person may appear rude and off-putting to quieter, less verbal types. By the time he enters school he will probably have received thousands of messages aimed at curbing his behavior. One can bet that few of these messages are validating and most are critical. Developing strengths does not give people license to act inappropriately or rudely, but telling someone all the time what they ought *not* to do—especially when that thing is a central part of what makes them feel enlivened—is not going to help them discover how to put that quality to use in ways that are productive. Children who are easily verbally excited need channeling, not outright extinguishing. That is what parents and teachers of young children can do—notice their personalities, the dominant aspects as well as the quirky smaller things, and channel behaviors toward positive and appropriate uses of those traits. That is where children will discover their strengths when they are ready. There is more about how to do this with very young children later in this section.

Many parents have asked me if they should tell their children what their strengths are. If you do that, you will come up with the same results you would get if you tried to tell them who to be friends with or who to fall in love with. Your children's strengths are not for you to choose. What you can do is provide them with a variety of rich and rewarding activities so they are able to explore how they feel while doing varied tasks. But it is a mistake to believe that just because you engage them in certain activities at a young age, they will develop a passion for those activities. Sometimes, forcing children into too many activities will actually dampen rather than ignite strength. We all know someone who was forced into piano lessons and, much to a parent's disappointment, refused to practice. It is that interchange of expectation and disappointment that knocks a child off his strength path at an early age. There is nothing more debilitating for a child than having a parent feel disappointed that he is not living up to expectation about strengths. Examples of this are abundant—the father whose son doesn't make the football team; the little girl who didn't really care about gymnastics, even though she won state champion; the doctor who wants nothing more than for her daughter to grow up and become a doctor, too.

These days, with parents increasingly pushing their kids to excel and focus earlier, the consequences for children are worrisome. Your child's strength path is her own. Take notice of her uniqueness and the things she naturally gravitates toward and allow her to explore those in ways that feel positive and comfortable to her.

STRENGTHS CHASING AND STRENGTHS EPIPHANIES

When I was a child, my mother referred to my stomach as my tummy. My tummy was round, in the middle of my body, and sometimes it hurt. My heart, on the other hand, was the thing in my chest that was shaped like a tulip; portrayed on valentines, its purpose was to produce love. As I grew up, not only did the names of these organs change, but my understanding of their purpose in my body also changed. A time came when I was able to understand that the heart pumped blood, not love, and another important time came when I was able to understand why we used the heart to symbolize our feelings of love. The symbolic understanding of the heart is subjective and open to interpretation. Some may say that the heart is used to symbolize love because without the heart, we cannot live, and without life, there is no love. Another may suggest that the purpose of life is to love others, so the heart, as the organ that most determines whether we live or die, is the place to position the locus of love. A third idea may be that when we feel deep emotion, such as love, we physically feel it in our chests, near our heart, and a fourth person may say it is all those theories combined.

Thinking about strengths is rather like thinking about anything else in a deep and analytic way. A person begins with an observation and then posits a theory. The first observations may be rudimentary and completely informed by the culture of the home and the culture of the school, as in the way you first learned about the heart. You may look at your child and decide he has strength for reading because he reads a lot. Upon deeper inspection, though, you will discover that he likes to read certain kinds of books, and it is in the specific kinds of book that there will be a deeper clue or clearer insight into his strength. Each time you peel a layer off a preference, you arrive a bit closer to the core of a strength. This is called strengths chasing. It is called this because discovering strengths is a very active process. It is seldom automatic. Often it calls for breaking an observation into separate parts and then regrouping it. Analyzing, hunting, combining, and finally changing your mind about what you observe a strength to be—that is the process involved in truly finding strengths. When this kind of thinking results in a new idea or insight about your strengths, it is called a strengths epiphany. The important thing to recognize here is that your child needs to come to an epiphany on his own. You can lead him with your questions, but you cannot have it for him. Your job is to redirect the child's attention. You can also model this by doing it yourself and giving your child examples of your own discoveries. Role modeling in this way will be one of the most powerful tools you can use in helping your child develop strengths.

A strengths epiphany is the result of deliberate questioning and thinking about strengths. Questions are what spark the search for strengths—they become the strengths chasers. Who, what, why, how, when, where questions are not enough. Real strengths chasers break even those questions down into more specific parts: what if? what for? what else? what other uses? what other possibilities? These questions are what lead to new insights. This process is like trying to catch a ladybug. It crawls away so quickly, and its shape makes it almost impossible to grab. Then, when you finally get it onto your hand to have a good look at it, it spreads its wings—which you didn't even know it had—and flies away. That is what having a strengths epiphany is like—it turns what you think to be true about yourself into something "more true"—and when you see it, you can then release it to the world.

Chasing a Big Dream

Adrienne was a vivacious and creative young girl who was eager to try everything. She had a difficult time making up her mind about what she wanted to zero in on, which wasn't necessarily bad. School is a place to try out many things, and it is through engaging in many activities that a child will begin to see how her real strengths—even if she hasn't named them yet—transfer from one area of study to another. Adrienne, like many young people, took a liking to filmmaking. Filmmaking is one of those multilayered activities that can attract a wide variety of strengths. Adrienne made several very creative films in the project class I taught one spring, so when, a year later, I asked her to tell me about her deepest interest, it was a surprise to me that she announced "History" with punctuated certainty.

Hmmm.

"Oh, so what is it about history that you like?" I asked her, a wee bit deflated that she transferred her interest from my course to another.

She looked at me, face full of energy, eyes wide, smile sparkling, and said, "I love studying epics. So, I guess I really love literature, too, if it is about the epic." She was gushing, and I was hooked. There is no better way to catch my attention than for someone to tell me something she loves and be very specific about what it is.

"Really?" I said, left eyebrow arching, head tilting slightly to the right, inviting explanation as if I were offering a kitty a sardine.

"I love the way an epic will span such a large geographic area, how one theme can touch a nation, how everyone can rally around basic human elements. I love the scope and the swoop of it."

"The 'swoop' of it?" I asked her, laughing.

"Yes, yes, and that is what I want to do with film," she suddenly offered. It was as if she had a bouquet of flowers behind her back the whole time, and when I was finally most deserving, she pulled them out and presented them to me.

"You want to make epic films?" I asked.

"Yes!" she said.

I am not one to quash dreams, but I am one to make sure that young people see alternatives so they don't bargain away their strengths on a singular dream. Strengths can jump from plan A to plan B to plan C and bring equal satisfaction. The goal of strengths chasing is to chase down the understanding until it sheds itself of all its fickle preferences and desires and lets you pin it down in a very precise way that allows you to see how it can be applied to a variety of situations, activities, and experiences. This takes a lot of time and a great deal of thought. It takes a commitment to recognizing it as it changes forms and travels across a variety of activities. Its name may change several times, in the way your tummy changes to your stomach and your tummy ache changes to a need for comfort.

I thought about Adrienne's desire to make epic films and then asked her, "What is it about making epic films that you would say is your strength?" I didn't expect her to answer that question with such certainty and assurance, but she replied, "I can see the artistic in the big or expansive thing and make it accessible and meaningful to people." This conversation happened quite by accident in a roomful of people, with several adults who came to visit the school. I looked around—everyone listening was stunned. Her comment hung in the air, and we all listened to it ring true. Adrienne had developed a clear and focused understanding of one of her strengths, and when she named it, she felt proud and unique and we all felt the power of her understanding. Adrienne chased after her strengths to arrive at a strengths epiphany. If Adrienne never made an epic film, she would no doubt find some other way to translate the big, expansive thing into something artistic for people. With her wide range of interests, she was sure to engage this strength one way or another in the future.

Before you can guide your child to strengths chasing, try it yourself. When you start diligently observing and examining your experiences, you alter the way you think about yourself and your life. You have a strengths epiphany each time you are able to recognize and name a new activity that energizes and excites you. The more strengths epiphanies you have, the more you begin to observe yourself, because these epiphanies feel good. The more you begin to observe how you are feeling in each of the areas of strength, the more strengths epiphanies you have. As you identify strengths and follow them through your activities, you will see that your understanding of them changes. A person can have many different strengths, or just a few. It all depends on how your mind works and how you categorize and experience the world. Strengths provide more meaning to your relationships, activities, and learning situations because you begin to make connections between everything in your life. Previously separate and compartmentalized activities integrate into a coherent whole as you begin to see how the same strength works across multiple activities in a variety of arenas.

A Horse Is a Horse, or Is It?

Many girls I work with are in love with horses, and living in horse country, this is a perfect place for them to nurture their passion. Not having grown up with horses, and being a bit afraid of the thought of riding an animal so large, I was curious about why girls loved horses so much. Each girl I asked responded with a different answer that gave insight into her strength. During the course of one of these conversations, one girl arrived at a strengths epiphany, which made her giddy. Here is a synopsis of that conversation. (Notice how I chase this strength down to its essence.)

"So, Angie, what is it you love about horses?"

"Well, they are such big and beautiful animals. I love big animals."

"Why are you drawn to horses and not, say, giraffes or elephants?"

"Oh, I like horses because you can ride a horse."

"People ride elephants. How come not an elephant?"

"I don't think you could get an elephant to jump."

"So is it the jumping you love?"

"No, I love horses because at first they don't do what you want them to do."

"What do you mean?" I asked her.

"Well, at first the horse doesn't know you, and he is trying to figure you out. You have to stay with him until he trusts you."

"Do you think you are good at getting him to trust you?"

"Oh, yes. I think horses trust me pretty quickly, at least until I get on top of them."

"Then what happens?"

"Then they kind of freak out a little again, and you really have to work with them."

"So what does that feel like?"

"It feels like a challenge," she said confidently.

"So you like challenges."

"Only ones I know I can conquer."

"So is a strength of yours conquering challenges?" I asked.

"Nope. It is more about getting the horse to work with me, that is what I like best."

"Tell me more," I said.

"Well, at first the horse doesn't trust you and pulls away. Then, after a while, it starts to work with you, and if you stick with it, in the end it is like the horse ends up dancing with you." She was smiling—beaming, actually. I was, too.

"So what is your strength?" I asked.

"I think it is teaching," she said, "but I only want to teach something I can be a part of in the end."

That is a strengths epiphany she can take with her and use for the rest of her life.

Stories like this one reveal why it is so important for children to begin chasing strengths at a young age. This is when their mind and intuition work together, allowing them to utter profound truths without even thinking too hard about it. Children have fewer filters. They start out knowing many things about themselves that adults work very hard at getting them to forget.

Here is an example from my own experience. Initially, I felt writing was a strength of mine. I began to observe how I felt every time I was writing. Most of the time I can produce a decent piece of writing, but what I observed was that I do not get a feeling of strength every time I am engaged in the act. I began to look for specific times when I felt strong during the writing process and when I felt depleted. I noticed that I could write forever when I was telling a story or trying to teach someone something. That simple distinction was a strengths epiphany for me.

Although I write an interesting newsletter four times a year, I don't look forward to writing it. That was an observation of depletion. I always volunteer to take on extra stories when the assignments are divvied up because I think I can write a good article. Before my strengths epiphany, I didn't recognize that while the articles I write may turn out well, I usually put off writing them, sometimes for days, delaying the whole publication and upsetting everyone in the process. That was another depletion observation. I am now more careful about volunteering to take on extra articles.

These small strengths epiphanies and depletion observations led me to examine myself while I am writing the articles. I decided that if I wrote all my articles more like stories instead of in the conventional way that I presumed someone should write articles in the school newsletter, then I would increase the enjoyment I experienced while writing them. I could cancel a feeling of depletion with the application of an activity that causes me to feel strong. *Aha*—another strengths epiphany. My stories improved tenfold, but I didn't stop there. Next, I noticed that while I hated to proofread, I enjoyed editing. I thought about that for a long time until it occurred to me that I got the same feeling from editing as I did when I rearranged my closet. My interest in editing is not due to my overall enjoyment of the writing process; instead, I like editing because I like arranging. Once into the swing of this mental activity, you begin to see that within each new understanding there's another gem waiting to be discovered. You become a strengths chaser! Here is the result of this particular series of strengths epiphanies: I feel strong when I am writing something persuasive or creative. I feel depleted when I have to write anything informational. I feel strong when I edit my own writing because I feel strong arranging my own spaces. I have no interest in arranging things for others and, likewise, no interest in editing someone else's writing. All this understanding has saved me from hours of feeling depleted and has allowed me to produce some of my best work.

I am devoted to identifying strengths because their identification is generative. They create an aha moment that is not static or final but instructive, pointing you in a new direction for your action. Because I have trained myself to think this way, I am therefore much more engaged in even the simplest activities of my daily life, always on the lookout for the next strengths epiphany. It is habit forming. The next time you talk with your child about the activities that seem to engage him, consider ways to unpack the details of his feelings. What questions might you ask to guide the conversation toward a deeper appreciation of the specific area that evokes that feeling of energy and strength? What follows are more examples of this process in action.

I was recently talking to my eleven-year-old nephew, Matthew. Matt loves to read so much that anyone would be inclined to say that reading is his strength, and at one level it is. However, I don't think Matt would read as much as he does if he had to read romance novels. Matt likes a specific kind of reading. He likes to read science fiction and fantasy books. That understanding in and of itself is a strengths epiphany because it produces the aha moment. As I explained earlier, strengths chasing is the act of peeling back the layers of preferences until you arrive at an understanding. The deeper you go, the greater the understanding will be. Sometimes, though, it is not a matter of going deeper but a matter of jumping over to a different activity to find true understanding by making a connection between one activity and another. In the last example, Adrienne had to jump into history and literature before she could have her most profound epiphany.

Matt told me something interesting about himself at a recent family wedding. There was an author at the wedding, and Matt was as excited to meet him as another child might be to meet his favorite basketball star. He told me that he had read all his books. I asked Matt if he wanted to be a writer, and he stopped and thought about that for a little while. He was not himself nearly as enthusiastic about writing as he was about meeting the person who wrote the books he loved to read. I could not explain what that distinction means; I could only take note of it and ask Matt more questions. I didn't ask them all at once. (I didn't want to be seen as the freaky questioning aunt.) Instead, I waited until the next time I saw him. We were at my father's house, and Matt and my stepmother pulled some brownies out of the oven. Matt became very excited. "You know why they call them brownies?" he asked me. I shook my head, knowing that no matter what my response, he was gearing up to explain it to me. His face became very animated, much the same way Adrienne's did when she was telling me about her love for epics. He began speaking quickly, as if his words could not quite keep up with the excited feeling that was pushing his ideas forth. That animated excitement is a sign of the opportunity for a strengths epiphany. Matt told me all about how brownies are mythical creatures, and then he proceeded to describe in vivid detail the land they lived in and the interactions they had and their social order with other fantasy beings.

"How do you know all this?" I asked him.

"I read about it. I've read all the Harry Potter books about five times."

"And this is all in Harry Potter?" I asked.

"Well, not all of it. I had to find out more about it on my own."

Matt may have a strength in visualizing imaginary places, and the reason he loves reading is that it inspires his ability to visualize these fantastical lands. He may have strength in researching the special characters in the books he reads, which pushes him to seek out more and more information. He may be interested in fantasy because he has a strength in understanding the imagination, which is a different strength than the ability to imagine. Only Matt will be able to pull these things together in order to understand himself and what his unique strengths are, but along the way his parents can ask a lot of questions and observe what he is drawn to, what he likes to talk about, and where his interests intersect. Of course, helping Matt form a habit of mind that chases his own strengths will involve a great deal of listening. Parents are encouraged to listen for the subtleties in their children's descriptions of their activities. Had I not been paying attention when we pulled the brownies out of the oven, I would have completely missed that Matt really wanted to talk about what he was reading.

In many respects, it is dangerous to simply label your strengths and call it a day. Labels are static. They don't change you, they describe you. For strengths to really work in ways that change lives, they need to become a thinking habit. They begin as the ahas that come from chasing them down. Once you catch an understanding of a strength, you cannot put it in a box and stash it under your bed with last year's tennis shoes. Instead, you are looking for the ahas that you can saddle up and ride off into the future. To find these, you need to develop a habit of looking for them. You start the habit with your children by asking them question after question about how they feel while doing certain activities. Likewise, you can make sure they engage in a very wide variety of activities, and the questions you ask can link the activities together. You may not always get succinct answers to the questions you ask. You may not get any answers at all, but don't stop asking the questions. If your children don't know the answers, simply ask them to repeat the question to you, repeat it in their own words. This will jump-start the habit and begin a journey of self-exploration that will eventually enrich all areas of your child's life.

Chapter 8

STRENGTHS ARE FOR YOUNGER KIDS, TOO

THE STRENGTHS CODE

Elise sits across from me at the dinner table. She giggles and smiles and flirts with me as if she is a twenty-year-old woman although she is barely fourteen months.

"Where did she learn that?" I ask her mother, Yanni.

"I don't know. She does things all the time that startle me, things she has never seen us do."

Children come into the world with millions of years of patterns encoded into their DNA. We are not random beings. We don't simply arrive in life bearing no resemblance to what came before us, and, similarly, we don't arrive arbitrarily into adulthood. Each of us represents an intricate design, a meshing of our natural tendencies—the things that came with us into the world—and our self-concept, which is developed through our perceptions, education, and expectations. When children are ready to name, identify, or discover their strengths, they access something that formed early in their lives—a combination of "nature" and "nurture." We don't improvise our strengths; they are part of a code that makes up our personalities. Adults can influence children's access to the code but not the code itself. People access the strengths code through a combination of positive memories and creative imagination. *Memory is the key to the past, and imagination is the key to the future.*

In the early years, parents can do four things to set the stage for a child's self-discovery:

- Record observations of preferences, quirks, and choices
- Stimulate imagination through creative play
- Create rich memories with tradition and ritual
- Model positive attitudes and positive approaches to life

It's never too early for you to begin molding your child's memories and his imaginations. A positive environment will give your child a sense of security and confidence, and your child will appreciate your observations—even if he disagrees with them.

Remember, strengths are not talents or skills, or what your children are good at. All those things are open to evaluation and criticism. Strengths are far more personal—they are the activities that make someone feel strong. Your child may be good at doing math problems, but unless she feels energized by that activity, a course of study or a career choice that has a heavy focus on solving mathematical problems will probably not yield a passion for the work or a happy life. Children begin life with a strong desire to please, but they don't go through adolescence that way. Beware: a child may abandon the pursuit of a true strength if he believes you chose it for him or it is something you are attempting to impose. When I was in fifth grade, my mother dragged me to an acting class, insisting I would love acting. At that time in my life, I was reluctant to do or try anything she suggested. The more she insisted acting was my true calling in life, the more I resisted. Years later, after I interviewed for my first teaching job, the principal called, offering me the position of high school drama teacher. I told him he must have made a mistake, I had interviewed for the English teaching job. He said he thought I would make a great drama teacher and asked if I would give it a try, which I did. I loved teaching acting, which led to my own acting with a community theater. Later on in this chapter I will give you suggestions about how to encourage without pushing so you don't accidentally steer a child away from a strength.

Your role in the development of your young child's strengths should be more like a personal assistant than a boss. You can think of this relationship in the same way Michelangelo thought of his sculptures. He saw a slab of stone and knew that a masterpiece was inside it, begging to come out. His job was to see it and release it. The strengths are already in your child. Your job is to help your child see and release them.

KEEPING A RECORD OF YOUR CHILD'S PREFERENCES, QUIRKS, AND CHOICES

One of the first things you can do to help a child discover strengths is to keep a journal in which you record the unique things you notice about her. This can begin as early as you want. The purpose of this is to keep a record of your observations so that later on, when the child is old enough to self-reflect and engage in some of the other activities already described (such as the questioning process that is involved in strengths chasing), she can review your early observations in search of clues or reminders of things that interest her.

I suggest that you keep either a written journal or a photo journal, or both. You can get a blank book and label it with your child's name: Kellie's Strengths Observations. You can divide it into the following sections:

- Preferences (Kellie likes wearing dresses more than pants.)
- Activities She Enjoys (She always plays in the sandbox.)
- Tendencies (Kellie tends to point to the photos as I read to her.)
- Quirks (She keeps her favorite toys in her laundry basket and gets very upset when they are moved.)
- Personality Traits (Kellie made a joke a yesterday; she seems to understand humor.)

Write down the specifics of your observations but try not to interpret them. For example, she may put her favorite toys in the laundry basket, but unless she tells you why, resist assigning a motivation for her.

Imagine how wonderful it would be to have a book from your earliest years that described the things you did and the traits you began to reveal when you were very young. You can do this for your child and take it a step farther by taking photographs of your child involved in the activities related to each category. Place them in your journal as evidence and as memory joggers for your child later on. For example, my friend Leslie tells me about her one-year-old, who after washing her hands and face always folds the washcloth and puts it back on the rack in a certain way. Leslie can take a photograph of her daughter doing this or of the folded washcloth, and next to the photo in the observation book she can write something like, "From a very young age, you were meticulous about cleaning up after yourself; you even folded your washcloth."

When your child is old enough, he can use this journal to discuss who he has grown up to be and what tendencies and traits were in him all along. This book becomes a powerful tool in helping to name and discover strengths later on.

As I was hatching this idea, I talked to my sister, Martha, who was pregnant at the time. Her first response was that she wished she had a book like that to look at—who wouldn't want a window into a past we cannot consciously remember? But she voiced concern about the time this may take with so many other responsibilities to juggle. We agreed that the time it would take was a form of front-loading. As she put it, "I am going to take photographs anyway, so why not have another purpose for them?" We both agreed on her next point: "I guess if I start this from the outset and make time for it, I may save money and time later. I know so many people whose kids are depressed, and they spend years and thousands of dollars trying to figure out how to fix that problem."

This is not to suggest that keeping a strengths observation journal will prevent depression or behavioral issues in every child. But I do believe that when you engage in a variety of these activities and follow this advice, you will have happier, more confident, and more creative children who are more resilient to depression than children who grow up in homes that do not consider strengths.

Little quirks can be clues to strengths. Take notice of your child's tendency to demand that you use a certain purse over another when you go out with him. It may signal a strength in something as seemingly unrelated as design. What initially may look like showing off could be an early sign of a child who has a particular strength for entertaining. Take note of the things your child does—anything that strikes you about his behavior. Here are a few of the kinds of questions that will guide you in making observations to add to the strengths observation journal:

- What causes your child to express joy and happiness?
- What are the things that keep her attention the longest?
- Are there sounds or words she reacts to more than others?
- Is she generous? How does she show this?
- Does she show sympathy? Is she caring or funny? Give examples.
- What are the differences between two children? Take note of all of them.

- What is the first thing he says in the morning and the last thing he says at night?
- How does he act in new situations or environments? What are the first things he notices or does?
- What books or movies does he prefer, and why?
- What frustrates him, and how does he address this?

Think of this strengths observation journal as a precious gift you will give your child when he is ready.

THE ROLE OF PLAY AND IMAGINATION IN CULTIVATING AND IGNITING STRENGTHS

> *You can discover more about a person in an hour of play than in a year of conversation.*
>
> —PLATO

Play is a primary activity for developing strengths. There was nothing wrong with Christopher Robin's desire to play in the Hundred Acre Wood without any adult supervision for long periods of time. Play is the activity during which people have free reign to explore, invent, express, and act on impulse. Creative opportunities have few rules, and the fewer the rules, the more freedom people have to volunteer strengths. Once you start to impose rules on and set procedures for activities, you begin to divide people into groups: those who are good at the task and those who are not. In creative play all are free to bring to bear any and all strengths they choose. The imagination knows no bounds. Imagination in play is the first step in the creative process. When children play, they experiment, test, and unleash their impulses. This is where strengths initially emerge.

Many studies indicate that play not only reflects but contributes to general cognitive and social development. Preschoolers who spend more time playing make-believe are advanced in general intellectual development and are seen as more socially competent by their teachers. Evidence indicates that fantasy play also strengthens children's memory. If you watch children play, you will notice that when undirected, they quickly flow into games involving elaborate fantasies, in which they take on imaginary roles. A metal jungle gym transforms into a giant sailing ship, and all the boys and girls climbing on it become pirates. Michael appoints himself Captain Hook and is quick to align with a heroine. Battles are fought, treasures lost and found, mutiny ensues—all in the span of a mother's or a teacher's relaxed half hour of sitting outside on a bench discussing the weather or last night's reality show.

During imaginative play, children are free to unleash and exercise their strengths. Watch children at play, and you will learn a great deal about what they prefer, how they socialize, and how they see themselves. Play encourages cognitive enrichment and emotional growth and influences personality development. Wonder, spontaneity, imagination, and trust are best developed in early childhood play. Adults know from experience that it is very difficult to relearn these skills later in life. The more we allow time for these early skills to become firmly established, the better we prepare children for the future, when they will need to build on these skills. The linguistic skills required to exchange different points of view, resolve disputes, and persuade others to collaborate so play can continue are numerous. These skills later become a child's Relationship Strengths or the interpersonal attributes they bring to teamwork.

Play can even help children get ahead in school. The stories children make up during imaginative play enrich their ability to use language and recognize narration, which is an integral part of learning to read. Likewise, play strengthens vocabulary. When new expressions appear in the course of an imaginative scene or game, children can guess their meaning easily from concrete cues in the situation. This is especially true for children who learn things kinesthetically, or hands-on.

Play is a very positive thing. It promotes a sense of enjoyment and opens people's minds to new thoughts and behaviors. And it allows for the regeneration of thoughts, which lead to new behaviors and ultimately enrich our ability to recognize our strengths. Play can be inspirational for adults as well as for children, and one of the current trends in business is to figure out how to inject play into the corporate environment as a means to stimulate innovation. Companies such as Best Buy and Yahoo!, which focus on developing their employee's strengths, also expend a good deal of time and energy on how to make their work environments more fun and, as a result, more creative and open to everyone's strengths.

Parents today spend a lot of time trying to control their children's play.

Recent books such as *The Hurried Child* by David Elkind point out the perils of overscheduling children. The biggest problem with scheduling every aspect of a child's day, including all his hobbies and all her encounters with others, is that is squelches the freedom children feel while playing. When children's freedom and imaginations are squelched, it not only takes the fun out of play, but it makes finding their strengths infinitely more difficult.

There are things you can do to inspire your child's imagination through play—no matter what his age. Here are some things to remember when considering your child's playtime and leisure time:

- Play should not always be competitive. Do not think sports teams constitute all the needs for play in a young person's life. "Play" is different from "game." The rules and the win-lose aspect do not inspire divergent thinking.
- Let children figure out how to do things for themselves. Constantly telling them how to do things can leave children feeling as if their originality is not valuable.
- Allow children to engage in activities without having to be the best. Try to avoid stating constant expectations. Unreasonably high expectations often pressure children to perform and conform within strictly prescribed guidelines, and they deter experimentation, exploration, and innovation.
- Telling children which activities they should engage in instead of letting them follow their curiosity and passions will result in performing to please rather than releasing passion. Too often parents want their children to engage in the activities they loved when they were young, rather than letting their children discover their own passions. I once knew a family that ran a tennis camp, and one of the boys didn't care for the game. His self-esteem suffered from the unspoken disapproval for his lack of interest in tennis.
- Resist the urge to evaluate everything. Overevaluation, whether negative or positive, constantly makes kids worry about how well they are doing, and this stifles their ability to take risks.
- Leave them alone to play and work sometimes. Hovering over kids, making them feel that they're constantly being watched while they are working or playing, is a sure way to halt their creative development.

There should be a balance between allowing children time for creative exploration, experimentation, and innovation and restricting choices and requiring children to obey rules and conform to social norms. Unfortunately, what happens is that life is often an all-or-nothing proposition. Thus, many children learn mostly about competition, rules, control, and conformity and little about the joys of exploration, innovation, and discovery as these elements pertain to their strengths.

Play Can Lead to Interests

Rhonda, Paula, and I sat on the sidelines of the playground at the Rumplestiltskin School in Eagle-Vail, Colorado. Recently graduated from college, my year of ski bumming ended when I crashed into a ski patrolman and ended up blowing out my knee. I turned from the slopes to my real calling, the schoolyard. Teaching preschool was one of the most fascinating jobs I ever had, and the most rewarding. I felt like an anthropologist, and the Rumplestiltskin School playground was my Bororo tribe. Outdoor play was my favorite time. I would sit beside the other two teachers and watch with utter fascination at the things children did and the ways they negotiated their relationships. There was a group of girls who played clapping and singing games every day. They started out nice enough and then slowly whittled the group from six to five to four. If you made one small mistake during the clapping part, you were kicked out. These games built great hand-eye coordination, and anyone without that suffered mightily at the hands of those who did.

Another group of kids played a game I referred to as "crash scene." Every day two trains of kids would run around the playground in circles until they crashed into each other. The minute this happened, they would all fall to the ground and then slowly rise up and take on roles. One child became the police who would quickly arrive at the scene shrieking a siren noise, another was a doctor, and one was a victim with a broken leg, and so on. Usually children tried taking on different roles. Sometimes new kids would play a few times and then drop off to work less boisterously in the sandbox. One boy, Jeremy, always played "crash scene," and in each instance he was the doctor. There were two times I remember telling him, no, he could not give Melanie mouth-to-mouth, and he looked at me as if to say, "What are you crazy, lady? Can't you see she is about to die?"

On rainy or snowy days, the kids played inside, and "crash scene" was not allowed due to limited space. On those few days I recall Jeremy playing hospital with some girls and their dolls. They lined the dolls up on the floor, and Jeremy would walk up to each one and ask what was wrong. The little girl would pretend she was the mother and tell Jeremy what the problem was. Jeremy pretended to take notes on each patient. He listened to their little plastic chests with an empty thread spool he used as a stethoscope, and once he ran over to me and said, "Miss Jenny, Mrs. Hunt's little girl is having a seizure. Would it be okay for me to save her life and do mouth-to-mouth on her?"

"On Mrs. Hunt?" I asked.

"No, on her daughter," he said, reassuring me and pointing across the room. Amy Hunt had a frantic look on her face and held up her doll for me to see.

"Yes, right away, hurry up," I instructed.

When it was time for show-and-tell, Jeremy brought in books about people being rescued.

"He's going to be a doctor," Rhonda whispered one day when he asked if we were going to see the fire engines and ambulances again.

"I actually think he will be some kind of paramedic or EMT. He seems to like the rescue aspect of all this," I said.

One day when Jeremy's father came to pick him up, he asked if he could talk with me privately in the office. He reached in his bag and pulled out a rag doll that was part of the school's toy collection "Does this belong to the school?" he asked, offering it to me.

"Yes," I said, taking it from him.

"I'm a pretty liberal guy, and I'm not one to jump to too many conclusions, but should I be worried that Jeremy is playing with dolls?" he asked.

"What did he tell you about the doll?" I asked him.

"Nothing. I didn't ask. I just found it in his backpack this morning and I was, well, frankly, I was worried."

"Well, if you ask him, he'll put your worries to rest," I assured him.

"What do you mean?"

"What are Jeremy's main interests?" I asked him.

"Well, he is a great skier, and in the summer he goes to day camp," he answered me.

"Yes, but what are his interests?" I asked again, truly surprised that he didn't know what was so blatantly apparent to us at Rumplestiltskin.

"Dolls?" He asked sheepishly.

"No. Actually he is very interested in emergency medicine," I answered in all earnestness. "You see, he took that doll home to see if he could stitch it up in the back, where there is a little tear."

"He likes dolls *and* sewing?" he asked.

"Sewing is what surgeons do," I reminded him, "but that is not the point. The point is that he has a real interest in taking care of people—or, in his case, dolls—that are hurt. He plays this game all the time. It isn't about the doll at all; it is about him developing an interest through his imagination."

"Well, maybe we should buy him a whole set then," he said.

"If you do, he will never sew up another thing again, and you can be sure of that!" I warned him.

Helping children pursue interests is not about pushing them to be the best at something or jumping into something you think they are a natural fit for. It is about observing the things they are drawn to and letting them explore them without your interference. When there is no test to pass, no expert to please, innate strengths can flourish through interests. Just don't confuse interests with strengths. Strengths are forever; interests change and grow throughout life, attaching to strengths like a mollusk to a coral reef. It is in a child's interest that his strengths are observed. Ask, listen, watch, and wonder. Children are full of surprises.

SHAPING MEMORIES TO RECALL STRENGTHS

> *Memory believes before knowing remembers.*
>
> —WILLIAM FAULKNER

Picture two houses separated by a tall grassy field. All summer long the children of the families living across the field from one another run back and forth between the two houses. In June, when the children get out of school, the grass is high, and they must push through it to get to the other side. For the first several weeks this is chaotic until they have established a common pattern that creates a trail. By July there are several well-worn footpaths between the houses, and the children don't think twice about how to cross the field. Our minds work something like the field. Our thoughts are chaotic and random without establishing pathways or patterns in them. These pathways form through repetition. The more times we repeat an activity, the more defined its pathway in the brain. When we repeatedly see, hear, or think something, we remember it, and it becomes relevant and meaningful to us. In short, for there to be meaning, a pattern must first be established.

Parents can help lay the foundation for discovering strengths by providing children with positive memories. The more these positive memories are organized and established into patterns at an early age, the easier it will be later on for your child to travel back and retrieve them from their storehouse of memories. Adults help organize memories for easy access with the use of traditions, rituals, and family tasks. As a parent, you cannot guarantee what your child remembers, but you can ensure the memories they access in the future are meaningful and positive as well as rich, vivid, and easy to pick out. Memories serve as transmitters of meaning. The following sections show how memories of family and school traditions and rituals inform the discovery of Relationship Strengths, and memories of family and school tasks inform Activity and Learning Strengths. When you guide young people to discover their strengths, you are essentially asking them to remember something that has always been true about themselves. Here are some ways you can shape those memories from a very early age, so children can use them later to recognize their strengths.

TRADITIONS AND RITUALS

Memories of traditions and rituals will help children discover Relationship Strengths because they focus on positive interactions with others. When you ask children to reflect on the things they do that make them feel proud and strong, they need to have a bank of positive memories to look back on. For some reason the negative times are easier for kids to spot. When families develop traditions and rituals, they are making conscious choices to develop positive memories.

Traditions are the repeated activities a family or group of people do together to create shared meaning about their social interactions. The most obvious traditions families practice have to do with celebrating holidays and milestones such as birthdays and graduations. Families can invent their own traditions, and these traditions can take place anytime. Rituals are pretty much the same things as traditions, but they involve using ordinary objects or repeated actions to consciously enhance and create deeper shared meaning. Most notably, rituals are used in religious celebration: taking Communion, lighting the menorah, praying at sunset. Like traditions, rituals can be created to enhance positive meaning in their family lives. These do not have to be religious. The more times a family repeats actions that convey deep positive meaning, the stronger the memories will be, and those are the memories that will stand out in a child's mind when he is asked to reflect on his past.

Good schools do this all the time by building rituals and traditions into the culture to form lasting and significant memories for children. For example, as a tradition, every year a school may hold an end-of-the-year field day where instead of classes, students and teachers have fun competitions. The purpose of this tradition is to convey the idea that hard work can be rewarded with fun. One of the rituals on field day is an opening ceremony, during which time all the children get T-shirts designed by their teachers that have a slogans on them about how great the year was. Later in life, children will remember this day. It may spring to mind ahead of the days when they felt anxious or unrecognized because the meaning of this day was deepened by the tradition and its rituals. Later on, when a child is asked to "think back on a time in your life when someone else did something for you that felt good," memories like this can spring to mind. The more memories like this a person has, the better.

Here is an example of how this can happen in the family. A family may have an annual Fourth of July tradition at their grandmother's house. A barbecue, fireworks, and a softball game may all be parts of the tradition, which conveys the values of family closeness, fun, and enjoyment in one another's company. A ritual may be added to this tradition to further enhance its meaning. An example of this may be that every year at the Fourth of July barbecue, just before the family leaves, each person places a rock with their name on it in a garden beside the house. Looking back, the rocks come to represent the solidity of the family or an attempt to make permanent an otherwise fleeting moment. These are the kinds of positive things that will stand out in children's memories for the rest of their lives. Children will draw upon these recollections when thinking about what their Relationship Strengths are.

A Summer Tradition

Every summer the Wooden family packs up the minivan and drives eight hours north from their home in the Wisconsin suburbs to a summer cabin in the lake country. Every time they make the journey, they stop at the same Chevron station about halfway into the trip. This particular station has a giant teepee in front of it, and the children start talking about it as soon as they leave the driveway. "Are we almost at the teepee?" they ask every fifteen minutes from the backseat of the minivan. On the drive up, they play Spot the Cow, listen to the same CD, and argue over who will get to sleep in the top bunk. Later in life, each of the Wooden children will recall these memories in different ways. Susan may remember the drive up and the stop at the teepee; Lucas might recall the games they played at night; and Fran may remember how it felt to swim in the lake.

The Woodens have a ritual they do every year when they arrive at the cabin. Together, they go to each room, gather up all the clocks, and put them, along with their watches, into a drawer in the kitchen that they agree not to open until the morning they leave.

For each member of the Wooden family, this becomes a rich memory that they can access when they are ready to create the self-told stories of their lives. These stories serve as access points into discovering strengths. When children have rich and memorable family traditions, they are able to connect to good feelings about being with other people. They can reflect on their contributions to those times or identify specific details that serve as clues to what makes them feel good interacting with other people.

Parents and teachers can begin traditions and rituals at an early age. It is important to document these traditions with photographs for children to refer back to later in life.

FAMILY TASKS

One of the best ways to prepare young children for using their intuitive ability to discover Activity Strengths is by assigning family chores. Giving children a variety of chores to perform, with choices about what they will to do and how they will do it, will prove to be rich preparation for accessing strengths when children are ready.

I think back on my childhood and remember the many chores we had to do around the house—everything from doing the dishes to cleaning our rooms—but there is one memory that stands out.

One day my father bought my brothers and me new sleeping bags for an upcoming family camping trip. They were these big, heavy brown canvas things with flannel on the inside. The flannel interior had pictures of ducks on it. My brothers and I each had to practice rolling up our sleeping bags and putting them in the small stuff sacks they came in. I think the purpose of the exercise had something to with taking responsibility for our things on the trip.

So there we were in our living room, the three of us kneeling at one end of the spread-out sleeping bag, ready to roll to my father's instructions.

"Roll it once as tightly as you can, then put your knee on top of the rolled part to hold it in place while you use your hands to smooth out the bag in front where you are going to make the next roll," he directed us.

I rolled it very tightly and smoothed it out. We kept doing this until it was in a tight, neatly rolled oblong that looked like a hotdog. This hotdog shape was only successful if it fit in the sack. It took us several tries to get it just right. I remember that I loved doing this. I was certain I could roll it in the smallest possible ball, so small that there would be extra room in the bag.

"Look, the bag is too big," I proudly announced.

"Great work!" my father praised.

To me, this activity was somehow different from, say, cleaning my room or doing the dishes. I think back on all the chores he asked us to do, and I have a fond and energizing memory of another one.

We lived in an old English Tudor house with a room referred to as the sunroom, because it had three walls of windows. One day my father brought home three squeegees, three bottles of blue Windex, and several rolls of paper towels. He said that we were going to learn how to wash the windows. I was again very excited about this job, which is why I remember it over all the thousands of other interactions I have forgotten. My father was once again very precise in his instructions. We were to spray the entire window with Windex and then apply the squeegee. After each swipe of the squeegee on the window, we were to wipe the squeegee with a paper towel—wiping off all the excess fluid—and then place the squeegee back on the window directly where it stopped being perfectly clear and repeat the activity. My father explained the importance of this method: it was so there would be no streaks on the glass. We did this all afternoon like a scene from *The Karate Kid*.

I still clean windows that way, and I still roll my sleeping bag as tightly as possible, taking great delight in getting it smaller than the stuff sack. The memories that stick in young children's minds are windows into their strengths. Today I have a strength for tasks that require tight, precise, sequential ordering. The seed of the strength for this activity was always in me, which is why I remember these activities more than the countless number of dishes I washed and the endless times I had to clean my room.

Today my job requires a lot of me, and none of it has to do with washing windows or rolling up sleeping bags. In fact, I function in a cerebral role. However, the times I am asked to pitch in and lend a hand in a physical activity, I always gravitate toward the jobs that require sequence, precision, and placement. For example, if we have to set up an event and I am needed to lend a hand, I know that I want to fold the letters and stuff them into the envelopes more than I want to carry all the chairs into the room. Folding the invitations is precise, and the process is sequential and tight. This activity, oddly enough, fits with my desires.

As parents, you can give young children a variety of tasks, and later in life they will recall the ones that naturally appealed to them and those that didn't. At age four, five, or six they will not be able to articulate what they feel strong doing and what depletes them, but later, when asked to recall tasks, they will remember those odd details and be able to transfer those memories to their current tasks and thus identify strengths.

When you assign tasks to your children, it is critical to observe and ask whether they enjoyed them or not. They may not always be able to tell you why they did or didn't, but you may be able to see for yourself. If you avoid judging them or considering them lazy for not enjoying the task, you can actually get the best out of them by reinforcing and finding ways to put them to work on the activities that strengthen them. Let's be clear. Just because children have the responsibility to do a chore doesn't mean they will eventually love doing it. Nor is this to suggest that children should not be required to do chores they don't like or study subjects that they do not enjoy. Discovering strengths is not an excuse for avoiding tasks you do not love.

Family chores teach kids responsibility and the skills to start, work at, and complete a job. They also help kids identify the things they like to do and what they don't like to do. Sometimes parents use family chores as consequences for misbehavior. This can send the message that working or cooperation is a punishment. A better way to help children discover strengths is by making family chores a tradition, something you do together. This way you can build both Activity Strengths and Relationship Strengths at the same time. Here is story about how a family tradition evolved around a weekly family task. Because of the strong impression it left on the child, his teacher was able to help him connect to a Learning Strength.

Hawk's Story

Hawk was too cool for school. I can still see him sitting there in the first row, third seat from the front—a miniature Fonzie in his leather jacket, with an attitude to match. He was the first student I ever really taught.

Hawk was twelve years old and didn't trust anyone. Kids aren't born not trusting; they get that way for one reason or another. I think with Hawk it was an odd combination of his feeling insecure about his penmanship—which was practically illegible—and being very different from his parents, and they were not entirely comfortable with that. I had met Hawk's parents; they were a delightful, well-educated, and politically passionate couple. Hawk's father had a longish gray beard and piercing green eyes. He wore a faded jean jacket with a peace sign patch on the sleeve. A little button on his lapel said, "No Nukes." His wife had a long black braid and looked like an Eskimo Buddha. They told me they worried that Hawk's tendencies were so different from theirs. I remember thinking, "Just keep celebrating who he is. Let him be completely Hawk."

My goal was to get Hawk to trust me. If he trusted me, he might eventually trust himself—which is what people need in order to discover strengths.

Hawk loved to talk. He was always late for his afternoon classes because he couldn't end the conversations he began over lunch. Hawk also feared writing. Every time I gave the class an assignment that included writing, he would slump down in his chair and snarl, "This is so stupid."

One day, as a companion assignment to *Treasure Island,* I asked the class to recall and write a one-page story describing a family tradition. Aware that Hawk hated to write, I told him he could tell me his story. His face lit up when I said that, and just as quickly he looked around the room at the other stunned children looking wide-eyed in his direction. He made a sour face, as if he had just smelled a rotten fish, and looked off in another direction.

"It's okay," I told him later when no one else was listening. "I can come in early tomorrow, and you can tell me your story before school."

"Come in early?" he protested, thinking he was somehow in trouble with me.

"Yeah, to tell me the story, so the other kids don't know. I hate getting up early, but I will come in so you can get this assignment done."

He considered this a moment and then said he would think about it. I told him that whatever he decided, I would be there at 7:30 a.m.

The next morning I woke up ten minutes later than usual, and in my haste, I almost forgot about my meeting with Hawk. When I finally arrived, Hawk was sitting staring at his reflection in the newly polished hallway floor. He didn't look up.

"Thought you weren't coming," he said.

"I overslept," I confessed.

"We can just forget it," he said.

"Forget it? I just ran five blocks without any coffee. I can't forget it. Let's get down to business."

Hawk went right to his seat in the first row and sat down, not bothering to remove his jacket.

"Okay," I said, taking my seat at the teacher's desk. "You are going to tell me about a family tradition."

He didn't hesitate. He jumped right in and began talking in an animated way that I had not seen before.

"My dad," he began. "My dad is this nature freak. You've seen him, right? He's all save the whales, and boycott grapes. He gets all our food at the Willy Street Co-op—you know, that big one down on Williamson Street?"

I nodded affirmatively.

"Well, every Saturday morning since I was a little kid, he forces us to get up really early, like 7:00 a.m., to go to the co-op with him and get our weekly food. It is such a drag. We have to get all the plastic bags together first, because you have to bring your own bags. Recycling." He rolled his eyes. I smiled. He was very amusing.

"So we get in the store and my two sisters and I each have a job. Me? I have to get the spices. So I go to the spice aisle, and, you know, all the spices are in these big glass jars. I guess they aren't so big now, but when I was little, they seemed gigantic; I could barely turn the lids. And my job was always to fill the little jars we brought from home—you gotta bring those from home, too—which is, like, such a rip-off."

Then he stopped. I waited until it was clear he was not going to continue.

"So that is your family tradition?" I asked.

"Yeah, that's the story. It's what you asked for, isn't it?"

"Yes . . . I suppose it is what I asked."

"So can I go now?"

"No. I want to know more about that. Tell me some more details."

He thought for a moment. "Well, my sisters always have to use lists to remember what they are getting because they always get sidetracked in the aisle that sells soap and candles and all that girl crap. Me? I don't use a list, and I am always finished first," he pointed out, beaming.

"So are you proud of finishing first?"

"I always finish first."

"How long have you been doing this?"

"I told you, since forever."

"Do you like it?" I asked.

"What's not to like?" he answered.

"What is it you like about it?"

"Don't you get it—I'm not a hippie. I don't look like anyone in the store, but even when I was little, I could still find the spices and fill the jars. That is what I like."

"Is it something you will keep doing?"

"Hell, no. I am going to shop in a real store and eat real food when I can shop, somewhere where you at least get bags and the food is already in jars."

"Okay. That's good. So tell me—what do you remember about that tradition that you like?"

"Don't you get it?" he asked with a pained expression.

"I am trying to," I said gently.

"I can do the hardest job and do it faster than my sisters, and I don't need a list. I just told you that."

"You feel energized by doing something difficult, and you like that you are fast and precise?"

"Well, duh!" he said.

"Then that is the kind of job I will give you in class when we do the next project."

We sat quietly a moment until Hawk shrugged.

"Okay. Can I go now?"

"Yes. Look, I am sorry I was late. Thanks for coming in early. And on Saturday I'll look for you in the co-op. I stop by there sometimes."

"Well, you can forget about seeing me there. We go really early. You're probably still asleep."

"Good point." We ended our meeting.

A week later we began a project on *Treasure Island*. I listed all the jobs on the blackboard, and next to them I wrote how long they would take and which were the most difficult. One of the jobs was gathering all the information about the characters and putting them into a chart. Someone needed to complete it quickly so the other group members could move on with their assignments. Next to that job description I wrote, "Rather difficult, needs to be done quickly and must be specific."

When I was finished writing, I turned to look at the class, but I already knew his hand was up, ready to volunteer.

Hawk, like most children, needs a network of people working on helping him see his strengths.

Chapter 9

BARRIERS AND BRIDGES: MAKING THE STRENGTHS LIFE POSSIBLE

People do not lack strength; they lack will.

—VICTOR HUGO

THERE ARE SO MANY ELEMENTS THAT GO INTO EDUCATING AND RAISing healthy, confident children who are prepared to take on life's challenges. Discovering and developing strengths will not ensure that life will always be easy or uncomplicated. Everyone will face barriers and experience failure. The suggestions, ideas, and insights outlined in this book provide bridges to the future by showing parents and teachers how to create positive, supportive environments that will provide children with direction and the kind of resilience people need to navigate a lifetime of choices and opportunities. Along the way, the models you provide will speak as loudly to children as any method or exercise from a book. How you conduct your own relationships, the philosophies you base your discipline on, how you make decisions, and whether your approach to life is positive will have a great effect on your children's ability to put the strengths they discover to work in the real world. Many people will worry whether this approach is too soft. They will wonder if there is virtue in confronting weaknesses. There will be many questions: How can children from broken homes develop strengths? What if parents are not able to do the things in this book—what happens to those children? What happens when children act out or do things wrong? How can you focus on their strengths and still teach them that what they are doing is wrong or inappropriate? These are all good questions, and there are no simple answers to them. In this chapter I will address the following issues:

- How a strengths environment involves a general positive outlook on life
- Importance of building self-esteem without perpetuating false confidence
- A discipline system that is strengths-based and holds kids accountable for bad behavior
- How developing strengths engenders the resilience needed to handle setbacks
- How we can help children from dysfunctional homes

A POSITIVE OUTLOOK ON LIFE BEGINS WITH YOU

To think negatively is like taking a weakening drug.

—REMEZ SASSON

The most fundamental way in which you can support children on their strengths path is by demonstrating a positive outlook on life and by committing to finding strengths in others. Should your child hear you speak disparagingly about others, always highlighting their faults and apparent weaknesses, you will undermine your effort to help him discover his own strengths. Your child's mind will not be open to discovering his own strengths if he doesn't believe his parents are open to discovering them in other people.

Several months ago I was invited to dinner at the home of Sarah, a woman I'd met while on vacation. When we arrived, Brooke, Sarah's twelve-year-old daughter, greeted us. I felt as if I'd already known this child, since Sarah talked about her quite often over the course of our five-day retreat.

"Hello, I'm Brooke," she said with a huge smile that bore a mouth full of plastic braces.

"Brooke, I have heard so much about you. I'm Jenifer, and this is my husband, Nick," I said as I extended my hand.

"What did you hear about me?" Brooke quickly asked.

"I heard that you enjoy swimming," I replied, "which interested me because I loved to swim when I was your age."

Brooke, an only child, sat next to me at dinner. Sarah sat at one end of the table and her husband, Stu, a stocky, dark-haired health-care provider, sat at the other end. Maggie and Jim, their friends from college, sat across from us. The conversation was lively as we tested the waters with current events—"Imus continues to get a lot of press and attention" and "How did Sanjaya get so far in the first place?"—before moving on to the topic of children. "No, we don't have any, but we run a girls' boarding school."

Brooke pushed the peas around her plate, perked up and contributed when the conversation turned to *American Idol,* then asked twice if she could be excused.

"Not yet, honey," her father said.

"A girls' boarding school? That must be something," remarked Maggie.

Maggie launched into a story about a neighbor of hers who sent her daughter away to boarding school for being bad. She asked me if the girls at my school were bad kids. I wanted to say I didn't believe in bad kids, but I held my tongue.

"I didn't really know her that well," Maggie continued. "I just heard that she was a lazy kid, which is a shame because her parents are both so wonderful and successful. She started out on the soccer team with my Lizzie and then just dropped out—gained a bunch of weight and, according to Lizzie, she started to lose her edge in school. I told Lizzie she couldn't hang around with kids like that.

"Her brother is really great. He was all-state lacrosse and ended up on a scholarship to Williams. A real winner of a kid."

Brooke shifted in her seat. "Mom, can I please be excused now?" she asked.

"Yes. Why don't you get going on your homework? You have a test in English tomorrow, right?"

"Yup," she said, standing up from the table and accidentally knocking over her glass. Water rushed across the table.

"Oh, oh, I'm sorry," she said, her face turning the same shade of pink as the tulips on the table. She started to cry, and Sarah jumped up.

"Brooke, it's okay. It's just water. Don't worry," she said, tossing her napkin on the spill. All eyes were on Brooke, who was visibly more disturbed than the situation called for.

"Brooke, are you okay?" her father gently asked.

"No. I mean, yes. I just—" The telephone rang, and as her father rose from his chair, she blurted out, "I quit the swim team, my coach is going to call, I quit the swim team today." She looked terrified. "Please don't hate me. I'm sorry. Don't think I am bad or lazy or a jerk like Lizzie's friend," she said, crying.

Though her parents never disparaged her, Brooke was nevertheless adversely affected by hearing others making negative comments about children. Negativism is something that spreads easily when it goes unchecked, as it did during the dinner conversation. In fact, negative thoughts and words spoken about one subject can spark a chain reaction, as happened with Brooke. But eliminating the negative is not enough. One false premise that many people live by is that if they don't hear that they are being talked about in a disapproving way, they don't know it is happening. People use this idea all the time to justify their negative discussions of others. The old adage "If you don't have something nice to say, don't say anything at all" is only a small start. Simply eliminating the disparaging words is not enough. Children feel disapproval and criticism even when they are not privy to the conversations. I see this happen all the time in boarding school. The teachers meet to discuss student behavior, and if there are negative or cynical anecdotes shared, the students intuitively sense this. One of the ongoing complaints students have is that teachers talk negatively behind their backs. When I ask them how they know this, they say that they can sense it. They are rarely wrong about their intuitions. People know when they are being disparaged by others. If you truly want your children to believe in and develop their strengths, you must be a model of positive thinking as well as positive conversation. This will involve accentuating the positive in everyone in your life. When you do this, everyone will win. It just doesn't feel good to hang around with fault finders. They don't make good spouses, friends, parents, or bosses. This is perhaps the most difficult habit to change, and it begins with your words.

Does this mean that to develop strengths we must all become Pollyannas? Absolutely not. Humor, intelligence, and creativity allow for complexity and depth in people's lives. A good laugh, a smart dialogue, and a great new idea don't need to come at the expense of another person—in fact, the funniest, smartest, and most creative people are usually the most positive ones.

BUILDING SELF-ESTEEM, NOT FALSE CONFIDENCE

People always ask me if it is possible to overdevelop strengths. They wonder if all the focus on a person's strengths will give them a false sense of pride or accomplishment. Self-esteem is an important component of building children's strengths. But building self-esteem has become confused with praise. Praise is something that comes from the outside; self-esteem is something that is built from the inside. Children shouldn't be told that they are good at something if they are not. Real self-esteem is built when a child accomplishes real work at a high level. Parents and teachers must keep raising the bar and coaxing children to achieve their best, supporting them and believing they are capable in the process. Improvement only happens when children are asked to stretch beyond their comfort zone. There is a certain amount of discomfort that accompanies any challenge. It is in this zone, the challenge zone, where people develop a sense of self-esteem. To tell a child her average work is outstanding is to sell her short. Besides, she knows it. She can ascertain the quality of the work around her done by others and compare her own. False praise says you don't believe she is capable of outstanding performance. The act itself accomplishes the opposite of what was intended. In short, intelligent and well-guided strength development in children and young adults results in improved performance and, ultimately, excellence. That is the source of genuine self-esteem.

DISCOVERING STRENGTHS: A COMPLEMENT TO ALL LEARNING

The nature of development—in any area—is such that there needs to be both discipline and self-reflection involved in the process and the outcome. This is true with respect to discovering and nurturing strengths. If a child feels strong when she is leading, then that feeling will only serve her well if she is a good leader. If this child is a bad leader, she may feel strong, but she will have few, if any, followers. The repeated feeling of strength will not, in and of itself, allow her to be an outstanding leader. She will also need guidance and coaching. Any child's improvement in skill-related performance depends on his or her commitment to the repeated practice of that skill. The feeling of strength is simply the underlying motivation behind the practice. Here is an example to illustrate this.

Remember our friend Martin, who has a strength in debate? Martin's *strength* in debate does not necessarily make him *skilled* at debate. Having the strength means that when engaged in that activity, he feels energized and alive. He loves to debate. Still, it will take repeated practice for him to become an expert debater. The chances are good that his strength in debate will keep him focused on developing that skill. If, on the other hand, Martin were *skilled* at debate but didn't feel a particular *strength* in that area, he might never devote himself to the practice it will take to become an expert. Does that mean that if a child does not have a strength or an affinity for an activity or a task, he is not supposed to practice it? No. If Martin needs to learn to debate, then regardless of his strength or lack thereof, he will still need to develop that skill so he can perform well. However, if he chooses a job or a course of study that involves debate just because he has a skill for it, it won't end up bringing him the kind of ultimate satisfaction and renewal he might discover using and developing a skill that also makes him feel strong.

You Probably Won't Find Your Life's Calling in an Area of Weakness

What does it mean when a child has neither skill nor strength in an area that he needs to learn in order to participate in school and work? Let's say, for example, that Martin has neither skill nor strength in anything mathematical. Now what is he supposed to do? He has to learn math, doesn't he? Yes and no. Yes, he has to learn to use math. He needs to have the skills that will bring success in the aspects of life that call for a knowledge of basic math. But he doesn't need to be an expert in it. We are burdened by a huge misconception that children have to be good at everything in order to be successful. In our rush to make them experts in areas in which they are not, we rob them of the time to develop expertise and consequent self-esteem in areas in which they excel. You'll recall I've said I was terrible at math in school, but I ended up with a life that is rewarding, meaningful, and happy. Math is not a significant source of self-esteem for me. Children can fail at things and still find significant success elsewhere. They can be average at things and still live happy lives. Most of us are like that.

PHILOSOPHY OF A STRENGTHS-BASED DISCIPLINE

When I tell someone that I am a high school principal, I am often asked, "What is it like to have everyone afraid of you?" This question makes me smile. The reality is that no one is afraid of me. In fact, I love to discipline children. It is the one transaction that will cause them to remember you for the rest of their lives; it is one in which you can really teach them something and can build the most powerful relationship. When considering how to influence a child's behavior, most people think only of the negative side of the discipline system: punishment. However, a strengths-based approach focuses on two components, both of which can be considered positive. A discipline system is not only about correcting wrong actions; it is also about ensuring right actions. It is both proactive and reactive. A philosophy of a strengths-based discipline can be applied at home and in school.

It Is Better to Be Proactive

The first component of a strengths-based approach to discipline is proactive. It involves establishing guidelines and expectations about behavior. It allows children choices in their actions and is clear about the consequences of those choices.

A strengths-based discipline is based on the premise that children are in relationships of personal growth with adults. This means that adults have a responsibility in the relationship to act as role models and to continue to grow and develop. Discipline is an interactive system. It isn't something adults do to children but something they are involved in *with* children. Here are some basic guidelines for the proactive aspect of a strengths-based discipline:

- Seek your child's input, and offer him reasonable choices.
- Don't demand obedience without allowing for questions.
- Work to discover ways to inspire your child to a greater good.
- Recognize your child's uniqueness, even if the unique qualities seem bothersome.
- Do not back children into corners.

The Latham family has several expectations for behavior that are clear. They are expected to share, they are expected to call if they are going to be late, and they are expected to act respectfully in public places. When the Latham children share or act with considerable respect, or come home on time, their parents thank them for cooperating. In the Latham family good behavior that follows clear guidelines is rewarded with gratitude and appreciation. This is better than praise. Telling your child you appreciate that he follows the family guidelines is far more rewarding than telling him he is a good boy. Children develop positive self-concepts more easily when you focus on how their actions affect the expectations of the relationship rather than on some value judgment of the kind of person they are. Remember, a positive self-concept is critical for the discovery of strengths.

If Mrs. Latham and her son Ricky are in the grocery store and Ricky starts yelling and running up and down the store aisles, Mrs. Latham can give Ricky a choice: "Either you stop running or you'll have to sit in the cart" or "Either you stop running or we will leave right now, and you won't be able to come with me next time." Ignoring the behavior, trying to quell it with anger, giving in to it, or placating it will only reinforce it. Proactive discipline sets expectations, offers reasonable choices, and follows through on preestablished consequences.

A LITTLE EMPATHY GOES A LONG WAY

Children need empathy and assurance to guide them through adolescence, but more often than not, they receive criticism and corrections. Adults, unable to recognize the mood swings, tears, and confusion as an awakening, fail to hear that young people are calling out to be believed in, validated, and supported unconditionally as they emerge from childhood. My words may sound peculiar, since for so long we have been conditioned to see this remarkable time as a necessary burden and a troublesome condition, but it is precisely our long-standing failure to understand and listen closely to kids that causes them to act in desperate and risky ways. Truly, this time is cause for celebration and our most careful attention. Yet this approach is underutilized by most schools and parents; nowadays, we are more inclined to medicate our children during their time of awakening, simply because we become frustrated trying to understand and cope with what is really happening to them.

Justin played on the junior varsity basketball team. Although he was not naturally talented in basketball, he loved being on the team. He was usually the first one dressed for play on game day, even though he never actually played. He seemed happy to sit on the bench, where he clapped and cheered his teammates on. At every game I made a mental note to ask the coach if he would let Justin play once in a while. One day the players were supposed to leave school early for an away game, and Justin's biology teacher asked him to skip the game and stay in class to get extra help for an upcoming test. He ended up in my office after he refused to stay and called the teacher a jackass. I returned from a late-afternoon meeting to find him slumped in a chair in the reception area outside my office.

"Justin, I understand you had a bit of a run-in with Mr. Walker. Just let me put these things away and check my messages, and I'll be right with you."

I entered my office and watched him through the window as I straightened up my desk. He tapped his foot nervously, and his jaw was clenched. I asked him to come in, and he sat in a chair in front of my desk. I stayed on the other side, in my chair, something I usually don't do when I have visitors, but he was tense, and I think he appreciated the distance.

"So you want to tell me about it?" I asked.

"You already know, so why don't you just suspend me and get it over with?"

"I might do that. But what I want to know is why it means so much to you to go to the game. You have never been in any kind of trouble before, so what is different about this?"

"Walker has no idea," he said.

"No idea about what?" I asked.

"No idea about basketball. He doesn't get it."

"*Hmm.* So you don't think Mr. Walker understands how important basketball is to you?"

"If he does, that is even worse."

"You sound pretty angry with him."

"Well, he told me that I had to stay and study for the biology test because last time, when I got a C minus, my mom got mad at him and said he didn't help me enough. So I told him that Coach Chapman would be pissed that I wasn't at the game."

"Yes, and then what?" I asked.

"Well, then he said that it didn't matter because I didn't play anyway. And, well, what the hell does he know anyway?"

"So he hurt your feelings when he suggested that it doesn't matter?"

"Yeah, so I got pretty mad and it was stupid, but I called him a jackass."

I sat quietly and looked at him. I was caught in a dicey place that all school administrators know well. I had to support the teacher, but I also wanted to support Justin.

"Justin, what you said was wrong, and you'll need to have some consequence for that, but I hear you saying that the team matters very much to you."

"I guess it was his thinking the team didn't matter to me just because I don't play much. But the team counts on me to cheer them on from the sidelines."

"Like the coach?"

"Sort of like that."

"I see. So that's why you like basketball so much? Well, that is very important then. It is something you should take seriously, and so should we. Thank you for telling me that. Justin, you were wrong to call the teacher a name and walk out, but it was right for you to go to that game. I'll make sure this doesn't happen again if you make sure how you handled yourself doesn't happen again. I'd like you to apologize to Mr. Walker, and I'll have a talk with him, too. Can you do that?"

"Yeah, I suppose," he said, and smiled.

WHEN YOU MUST REACT

People become motivated by relationships, not fear of punishment. That said, it is important to remember that treating children with the same respect you would afford an adult does not mean giving them a pass to act in any disrespectful, uncontrollable way they want. It does not mean you act as their friend. Children do not want adults to be their friends. They want them to be role models, to set guidelines, and to hold them accountable. Children want adults to notice them and respect them, to make the boundaries clear, and provide consequences for when they cross the boundaries. When children are defiant, it often signals that particular emotional needs aren't being met, so they act out in ways that attempt to meet those needs. For example, if a child feels unnoticed, she may purposely go against an expectation just to get your attention. Remember the example in part 1 about when I stole my stepmother's bracelet? I stole it not because I was fundamentally a bad person; I did it to get attention. When this kind of acting out happens, adults must react. How you react will determine whether you are continuing to build on the strengths philosophy. In general, adults are encouraged to take the necessary time to react to mistakes in the following way:

- Discover what went wrong.
- Get the child to accept responsibility.
- Plan for the future.
- Assign a consequence.

Discover What Went Wrong

In any serious situation involving your child's behavior, don't assume you know all the facts and motivations before you sit down to talk. Give your child the opportunity to tell you what happened. You should also be prepared for your child to lie to you. When faced with the prospect of punishment, most children are afraid, and they often lie to avoid consequences. The children who do this most often are the ones whose parents have told them that the absolute worst thing a child can ever do is lie to them. I value truth telling maybe more than any other virtue. That is why we must be able to call a child on lying and not have the world fall apart. Saying "Stop lying, we need to get to the truth" is a much safer approach than saying "You'd better not be lying because I can forgive you for anything except lying to me." I hear parents say that to kids all the time. It doesn't work.

Children who convince their parents that they were not to blame or did not play a significant role end up making repeated mistakes. They learn they can "snow" their parents. Parents want very much to believe in their child's innocence in all matters. My rule of thumb is "If it walks like a duck and quacks like a duck it probably is a duck." Bad behavior stops when kids are encouraged over and again to accept responsibility. This means getting to the truth and not letting them off the hook with regard to consequences.

Accept Responsibility

One time a group of girls from school got caught stealing from a store at the mall. I had to drive down and pick them up from store security. Of the four girls, two of them were dismissed from the school and two stayed and became successful students. In the beginning, all the girls lied about what happened. The two girls who ended up being asked to leave were the ones who persisted in their lying even after we told them we knew they were lying but they would have a chance to stay at the school if they told the truth. One girl's mother lied for her, insisting that the policeman planted the stolen earrings in her handbag. The two girls who remained at the school have grown into lovely young women whom I trust. They were able to accept responsibility for their actions and not blame anyone else. At first they lied, but when they figured out that we were more interested in their personal growth than in punishing them, they were able to admit the action and then explain why they did it. The payoff for getting kids to move from defensiveness to taking responsibility for their actions is huge. It is important in this phase of the discipline process to resist giving advice. Children need to participate actively in the process, and they often shut down once giving advice begins. For example, a young girl admitted to using her roommate's cell phone for long-distance calls, and before she could explain why (an important step in the responsibility acceptance phase), the teacher interrupted and began telling the girl about her choices and why what she did was wrong. The student stopped explaining and became a passive listener, not engaging in examining what she did or why. The process of accepting responsibility may take a long time. Five hours passed between the time I picked up the girls at the mall and when they finally admitted the mistake and accepted full responsibility. This time involved the students' thinking about the issue, writing down the facts, discussing it with teachers, and reflecting on it. It was not easy to step back, yet it was the only way to get the girls to change their behavior and move toward the next step.

Plan for the Future

Once your child has accepted responsibility, you can discuss his strengths and how he will use them to make better decisions in the future. He may have used his strengths to make the poor decisions, and in that case you should also discuss that misuse and how he can properly refocus his strengths. This step is where you move from reaction back to being proactive, setting new expectations and discussing the choices that are available. It is important to let children know that their future appropriate behavior is always much more important than the missteps of their past.

Assign a Consequence

Consequences should always be part of any reactive event. Children should know that for each mistake there will be a consequence. These consequences should be actions that you are prepared to follow through on and that are not so excessive as to derail the work you did in the previous steps.

As I indicated earlier, this is not a comprehensive book on parenting; rather, it is about how to develop strengths in children. Strengths are not excuses. Children need gentle discipline, a ready ear, and understanding. Most of all, children need a sense of purpose in life. In trying to ascertain what that purpose is, they may act out. There will be times when they make big mistakes, and so will you. Finding strengths is not about being perfect.

Sometimes, depending on the severity of the situation, when children act out, the best thing to do is apply humor to the situation. Take the following story as an example of how humor can turn an "out-of-control" time into an opportunity for strengths acknowledgment.

DEVELOPING STRENGTHS ENGENDERS RESILIENCE

> *In order to succeed, people need a sense of self-efficacy, to struggle together with resilience to meet the inevitable obstacles and inequities of life.*
>
> —ALBERT BANDURA

Late one Saturday morning, I was sitting on the lawn of the parkway next to the Charles River in Cambridge, Massachusetts, cooling down after a run. A few yards away from me, a family of four—mother, father, teenaged daughter, and younger son—were having a picnic. The father and son were feeding bits of bread to an aggressive pair of ducks that were pecking the food right from their hands. The girl was visibly uncomfortable with this.

"Those ducks are gross. Get them out of here," she whined.

Her brother and father paid her no attention and went right on feeding the ducks. She continued to protest, her voice growing increasingly louder, and her family members continued to ignore her. This went on for several minutes until one of the ducks stepped over to her and tried to peck at her sandwich. This was the last straw.

She jumped up and began shouting hysterically, "Get out of here! I cannot believe it! This is SO GROSS. What kind of disgusting freaks are you? You are supposed to be my family? Those ducks are diseased!"

She stomped around, gesturing wildly with her arms. "You all totally suck!"

Her mother, brother, and father sat staring at her with expressions of awe and disbelief.

She continued, "Maybe I don't even belong in this family. Maybe I was adopted, maybe an alien spaceship dropped me off by accident into your living room. Well, guess what? I am ready to leave now!" She was panting by the time she finished. She was acting . . . well, quite fresh, I thought.

When she finally finished her scene, very much out of control, no one in her family moved or said anything. They just sat there speechless—stunned, I suppose. Then a curious thing happened. Her mother started to clap, and the father and brother joined in, clapping and shouting "Bravo!" until she stopped, began to laugh, and finally sat back down to resume her lunch. I delighted in witnessing this little drama, and I retell this story often. You might look at such a scene and think she was acting disrespectful, inconsiderate, and rude; or you could see a girl who just might have a flair for the dramatic, strength in acting and speaking her mind. Rather than correcting or punishing this behavior, the girl's family applied humor to the situation, validating the strength in it without allowing the out-of-control aspect to become a conflict.

Humor is one component of resilience—the ability to overcome personal setbacks. The family in the duck story is demonstrating the ability to look at life's troubles and see them as absurd. There are many things families can do to raise resilient, emotionally hardy children—the ones who get up each time they fall, who do not become depressed, hardened, or neurotic from life's challenges. Resiliency research shows that children who are singled out by their parents as being important or special in some way are more resilient. Research also demonstrates that children whose parents encourage their gifts and talents are more resilient. Furthermore, parents who assign their children family responsibilities create opportunities for them to become more resilient because they develop a keen sense of purpose and direction. Parents who model positive outlooks and involve their children in discovering strengths will be the ones to raise the most confident and resilient children, ready to handle life's inevitable challenges.

ARE STRENGTHS THE CONCERN OF POOR, MARGINALIZED, OR DYSFUNCTIONAL FAMILIES?

Nothing has more strength than dire necessity.

—EURIPIDES

My experience as a high school principal began as an intern in a poor Boston public school where armed guards patrolled inside the building. Classrooms were stark. The only things to be found in most of them were desks with the chairs attached. There were no bulletin boards, no artwork, no books. The place felt more like a disorganized prison than a school. Many of my classmates wondered whether I was frightened at the school. It was a fair question, but I was not afraid. In fact, I asked to be in that school. I wanted to see what the students were like, and I was not surprised by what I found. I observed classes at this school for two months. What I saw was that, like any kids, these kids wanted to be noticed, appreciated, and listened to. They wanted someone to take them seriously, no matter how angry or out of control they appeared. Most of the kids, no matter how hardened they seemed on the outside, were nice when I got them alone and showed them I was not afraid of them.

I ended up going to a second school, a suburban upper-middle-class school that bused in some of the kids from the neighborhood of my first internship. My project while there involved discovering why the bused kids had such a difficult time fitting in with the suburban kids. Why did they sit alone in the lunchroom? Why didn't they stay after school and join any clubs? I decided I would do an ethnographic study of them. I met with them regularly about the project. Initially they wouldn't talk to me. When I asked them questions, they made fun of me and tried to scare me away by swearing and talking about street life. I returned to the same table every day for two weeks before asking if I could take their photographs. They loved this idea. I made their photos into posters and hung them around the school. They started to talk to me regularly then and said that other kids started talking to them, too. I spent the next few weeks finding out as much as I could about them and took more photos to reflect what I discovered. If they babysat their brother at home, for example, I went to their house and took a photo of that.

Along the way I discovered that they hadn't integrated because no one ever really talked to them. The teachers didn't call on them in class, they were not invited to join clubs, and, in general, no one paid much attention to them. This came as a surprise to the teachers, who thought they did pay a lot of attention to them. They may have been paying attention, but they didn't interact with them. When I asked the same teachers if they knew what the students did after school or on the weekends, they had to admit they knew nothing about them outside of school. When I visited these students' homes, I found some of the most invested parents I had ever met. They spent a lot of time talking to me about their children and telling me about their dreams and hopes for their future. There were many people connected to these kids. From that experience I came to know that income and race are not indicators of whether strengths will be developed. In fact, I predict that many poorer families, once they hear more about the strengths movement, will invest more heavily in trying to help their children develop their strengths—they have to in order for them to get ahead. During that internship, I discovered that people who live in poverty have developed more intense social networks than many of my middle-class friends. My observations about the Strengths Movement is that poor people and otherwise marginalized groups will embrace these philosophies and methods wholeheartedly, much the same way I have seen marginalized students embrace them. If you give the disenfranchised a breath of life, a genuine moment to shine in their own light, they will rise up.

The children who will need help with this are the ones who come from dysfunctional families or families that are too busy to enact these methods with their children. This is when a variety of different institutions can come into play. In addition to the school, there are after-school programs, social services, youth groups, church groups, and health-care professionals playing a role in caring for children. The vast network of institutions that care for children when their homes are not up to the task have a stake in the Strengths Movement. This book is especially important for those whose duty it is to care for children from dysfunctional homes. These children, perhaps more than others, need their strengths developed. And it will be important for these outside institutions to see how focusing on strengths is so crucial for the children they serve. The exercises in part 3 can be accomplished with a wide variety of people in a multitude of settings. Children from dysfunctional homes will need other people in their lives to pick up on these ideas. Since all children have to go to school, the school naturally plays one of the most significant roles in developing strengths. As a nation, it will be up to all of us to support the spread of the Strengths Movement in our schools.

Chapter 10

THIS APPROACH IS FOR LIFE

With the new day comes new strength and new thoughts.

—ELEANOR ROOSEVELT

MEANINGFUL LIVES ARE THOSE THAT ARE FILLED WITH MEANingful work, regardless of whether you actually are paid for that work. Most people end up spending over half their waking lives at their jobs, yet statistics show that fewer than two out of every ten people report actually playing to their strengths at work. Work not only occupies the time when we are there, but it is often what we think and talk about outside of the workplace.

Without an inherent sense of meaning, one's daily activities are simply empty tasks. If children are to end up happy, whether in school or in life in general, they need to have the opportunity to engage in the practice of developing meaningful relationships and finding the strengths and talents that will sustain their work. There is no better time to begin this process and engage in this practice than in childhood.

The people I worry most about with regard to strengths development are the children who have intellectual ability. Rarely do the parents and teachers of children with strong intellectual ability believe in their need to develop strengths. After all, they already have what it takes to be successful, don't they? Intellectual ability is only one kind of ability, and, frankly, it is becoming increasingly uncommon. Alone, it is not enough to guarantee meaningful work or fulfilling relationships.

The world contained inside our schools and the world beyond their walls seem curiously at odds in the opening of the twenty-first century. As creativity theorist Ken Robinson points out in his book *Out of Our Minds: Learning to Be Creative,* "The relationships between education and the world we actually live in are being stretched to breaking point [*sic*]. . . . The pre-occupation with academic ability is an example of functional fallacy: the tendency to confuse particular purpose with a general one. . . . To educate people for the future, we must see through the academic illusion to real abilities, and how these different elements of human capacity enhance rather than detract from each other."

While the twenty-first century is a grand time to be alive, because there are more innovations and exciting opportunities than ever before, we are faced with a rethinking of ideals we have always held to be true. Some principles and truths remain universal and timeless. Others will no longer serve a purpose in the future. Some we simply got wrong and need to change. Now is a good time to ask, "What is the purpose of our schools?" To answer that, we must be willing to step outside of the notion that education is a finite process leading students to a destination. The ultimate reality in both school and life in general is that the function of neither is static. Learning—in every sphere—is a process of continual human development.

There is a strong and necessary connection between the home, the school, and the workplace, and I am increasingly perplexed by the way we compartmentalize these arenas as if they didn't influence one another or greatly affect one another. If I have learned anything while writing this book, it is that the strengths story is a story about convergence, about how good ideas know no boundaries, and about how, if we truly wish to change the future for our children, we need to see past our traditional categories and hierarchies of thought.

In the final days of writing this book, I found myself on a highly unlikely journey. I was traveling by car, then bus, then plane across the country with business expert Marcus Buckingham, calling the nation to action around the concept of the Strengths Movement. As Marcus toured around the country spreading the word about strengths to businesses, I joined in spreading it about strengths in schools. To call it unusual that a school head from a small girls' boarding school in northern New Jersey was on a book tour with a business author would be a massive understatement. It is not "the road less traveled" as much as the road never before traveled, at least to my knowledge. In my professional circle, this is not how we spend our time. Yet, somewhere along our paths, Marcus's business world converged with my academic world. And that is what motivated me to write this book. My premise is that everything is converging; that is, the knowledge we have about one area will soon cross over and be recognized as useful in another seemingly disparate area, and the future will depend on people who can recognize where this synthesis will be most useful. For me, this idea really hit home one evening while I was finalizing this book in a small room in the Milwaukee Athletic Club, close to home but not quite there.

On a gray and windy afternoon, I had flown from the book tour's stop in Minneapolis to my home city of Milwaukee, Wisconsin. I had been in seven cities on the East Coast and in the Midwest, and what was clear to me was that people wanted to know how both their businesses *and* their children could benefit from strengths building. On the day I arrived in Milwaukee, I had a very short time to get the proposal for this book ready before we headed back out to twelve more cities. Instead of going home to my family, I called my father and asked him if I could check into his club to finish my work in solitude. I told him snippets of what I was doing: traveling on a book tour to twenty-two cities, meeting with Best Buy and Yahoo! executives, writing a book, appearing on a national PBS pledge show, meeting with the president of the National Association of Independent Schools to call the school heads along the book tour to hear the message about strengths. I could not explain the whole trajectory that had led me so suddenly from running a little boarding school to participating in all these seemingly disparate events, but he trusted that what I was doing was in some way meaningful and important.

I took a small, musty room on the eleventh floor of the Milwaukee Athletic Club, and after a long day of revising, I decided to venture down to the restaurant to grab a bite to eat. The Milwaukee Athletic Club is a professional place where businesspeople meet to connect professionally and socially. When I entered the first-floor pub at six o'clock on a Thursday evening, I encountered a room full of baby-boomer businessmen in dress suits. I was one of three women in the room. There were seven flat-screen televisions, all playing one of the first games of the NCAA men's basketball tournament, March Madness: Xavier versus Brigham Young University. Local favorite Marquette had just suffered defeat at the hands of Michigan State. After a full day of thinking and writing about children, I felt suddenly stunned and awkward sitting at the bar to catch a meal. Everyone in the room was talking business with colleagues, watching the basketball game, playing pool, or checking their BlackBerrys. I knew someone was going to ask me what I was doing there. It was a club; new faces are a curiosity. My mind raced. I didn't feel comfortable telling anyone I had checked in to work on a book because that would lead to too many questions about what the book was about. These people didn't look like a group who had assembled to focus on their kids. Not that they didn't care about their kids; it was just not the reason for their being in the room.

After about ten minutes, a man seated next to me asked the inevitable question: "What brings you here?"

I told him that I was working on developing a solution to the nation's economic future. He perked up.

"Yeah, and what is that?" he asked, a bit skeptical.

"Well," I told him, "don't you find that it is increasingly difficult to get good employees to advance your corporate mission?"

"You got that right."

"What I am working on is developing the next American workforce that will advance the United States' economic interests in the new global economy."

"*Hmm.* That sounds interesting. What are you doing?"

"I am doing several things: I am leading a school that develops strengths rather than focuses on weaknesses; I am speaking to companies about how to get their organizations to support what we are doing in our school; and I am writing a book to promote these ideas."

"So what are the business ideas?" he asked.

I started telling him about some of the ideas. I explained Marcus's books and the work of the Gallup Organization, and I told him about the Affinities Program. Like many businesspeople, he found this all very interesting.

"I think that may work very well in business," he said.

"Of course it will. The sector doesn't matter," I explained. "Universal principles work everywhere."

For too long, people have compartmentalized their lives. In doing so, we miss the point that development of strengths in children in schools and development of strengths in the work world serve the same ends—generating meaning and productivity.

I tell this story because it is ultimately about the future of families, schools, and the American economy. The Strengths Movement is the common denominator. As we advance in the world, your children will need to be prepared to enter a workforce that is entirely different from the one we are in today. The world is in transition, and what we will all discover is that the secret to success and meaning in the future lies in understanding the interconnectedness of everything. Discovering and developing strengths in children will create a society that will allow everyone to benefit and flourish.

In December 2006, the New Commission on the Skills of the American Workforce published a report called *Tough Choices or Tough Times*. This document describes what needs to happen in American education to prepare workers to compete in the global economy of the future. Every recommendation in the report relies on building the strengths of the next generation, both students and teachers. If that is the case, then the Affinities Program and similar strengths-building programs will be more than just another innovation in schools; they will be one of the answers to the problems of the future of education. The "real world"–"school world" dichotomy must be broken down. Schools need to become more relevant. Businesses also have a great deal to learn from schools. We need a genuine partnership between those two worlds to advance our mutual interests. Business and education are intricately bound together. Without a great educational system, there is no great future workforce. Without great programs in schools, businesses are left to spend millions of dollars educating and reeducating their employees. Beyond making schools happy and vibrant places, developing strengths in children will help businesses be successful in the future. This is a win-win proposition.

Meanwhile, ensconced in my chair at the Milwaukee Athletic Club, surrounded by businessmen and fathers, my thoughts traveled to the more recent past and our tour of the country. Our audiences were mostly businesspeople. Like the men surrounding me, most of them were also parents. In every city we visited, people approached me after the program and asked if they could get a copy of the curriculum. In Washington, D.C., a woman said, "We need this at the university level, but in order for that to happen it practically needs to be legislation." Marcus Buckingham turned to me and said, "This should be a law." Earlier, when we were at a question-and-answer period following filming the PBS show that features Marcus and the Purnell School, a man approached the microphone and said: "This is all well and good, but until the lawmakers hear this it won't do what you want it to do. Do you have any plans to go to Congress with this?" In each city there were parents who came up to us, men and women alike—some in tears—saying, "Please make this happen. Make them change the focus from human weakness to potential." "Them" needs to become "us."

There are vast reserves of untapped potential residing in our children. Their strengths are as various as the children themselves. When we acknowledge that and truly know our children, everyone wins, and everyone is worthy of a highlight, each in his and her own right. Moreover, we will ensure our competitive edge as a nation. A national strengths awakening will take a revolution. In the long run, it is what will save us all. It is a big job, and it requires everyone's strength.

PART 3

CREATE YOUR FUTURE, PLAY TO YOUR STRENGTHS
WORKBOOK

THE IMPORTANCE OF DEVELOPING YOUR CHILD'S STRENGTHS

In this complex world, it takes more than a good school to educate children. And it takes more than a good home. It takes these two major educational institutions working together.

How we develop children's strengths and affinities is a variable too frequently left to chance. Most schools and parents provide children with myriad experiences and then hope that one of them will spark an interest that will somehow flame into a passion. This is the goal, but history demonstrates that too few children actually leave school with a real interest in learning, let alone a passion for anything.

High-earning individuals are now working more than sixty hours a week. According to a May 2007 report in the *Christian Science Monitor*, most workers say that they are putting in an average of 16.5 hours per week more on the job now than they did five years ago. I can't imagine spending that much time doing something I didn't love any more than I can imagine sleeping eight hours a night on a mattress that was terribly uncomfortable. Most adults I know don't even think about work in terms of feeling committed, passionate, and excited, yet they hope that children will find careers that they love rather than jobs that merely serve the purpose of bringing home the bacon.

The journey to fulfillment begins with introspection, risk taking, and, most of all, knowledge of and then faith in one's own unique combination of strengths.

Security is what most people crave. We believe that if we go to school and get a good job, we will be financially secure and that this security will allow us to have free time to make friends and engage in leisure activities. But security can be an illusion. Things seldom turn out as planned. We cannot simply prepare our children for lives of security; we must also instill in them a sense of hope and the ability to be resilient in the face of uncertainty. If we have learned anything, it is that the twenty-first century is an uncertain time. One needs to know where children would like to go but must also realize that they are likely to end up somewhere different. The discovery and development of inner strengths will help shape children's understanding of what moves them forward with purpose, as well as teach them how to cope with uncertain times.

FROM THEORY TO PRACTICE

This part of the book offers concrete suggestions for activities that parents and teachers can use with children of every age to stimulate the recognition and development of personal strengths. Many activities in the workbook are adapted from the Affinities Program, the school curriculum outlined in the appendixes. The Affinities Program is a four-year curriculum designed to help high school students develop their natural strengths and plan their future accordingly. The Affinities Program also outlines a model for developing a whole organization devoted to building on everyone's strengths. I have modified many of the activities from that program and organized them in the workbook by age group so that you can begin to put theory into practice with children of any age.

WHO CAN USE THIS WORKBOOK?

Everyone can use this workbook. The workbook functions best when the person using it has a partner, since many activities invite you to discuss and reflect on your ideas with someone else. This is much easier when the partner is also doing the exercises, but that doesn't have to be the case. The workbook can be used in a variety of ways by

- parents with children at home;
- teachers and students in the classroom;
- older children, either on their own or with partners;
- work groups;
- grandparents with grandchildren;
- child care groups and social service groups; and
- youth groups, such as Scouts, Junior Achievement, and church groups.

You can use this workbook repeatedly throughout your life. Your answers may change as you grow, develop, and encounter new experiences. It is up to you to decide how much effort you will put into this discovery. The effort is not for anyone but *you.* You deserve this workbook and the future it promises.

WHY IT WORKS

At first glance, the activities and exercises may appear involved, time consuming, or even bizarre. Their purpose is to get you and your child to think differently about yourselves and the world around you. If these exercises were familiar, you would not learn anything new from them. If they were simple and easy to do, you would have figured all this out a long time ago. Changing perceptions takes work and a bit of commitment, but the process is a positive one and the payoff is as important as anything you will ever do for yourself and your child.

As in any life-changing program, there are practices to adapt that lead to habits. The habits create the change. You can compare this program to a diet. When you follow a diet, you change your body; a diet is based on omitting certain foods and usually involves a form of sacrifice in order to reach the ultimate goal. This program is like a diet for the mind. You are going to feed it with all kinds of interesting new foods, and in the end, your mind will be changed, but the sense of sacrifice will not feel bad. You will never feel deprived doing these activities.

Some of these activities are more easily adapted in the classroom. If you come across one and think, "Who would ever go to the trouble to do that?" or "My kid would never go along with that," you can assume it works more effectively in a school setting. But keep this in mind: you cannot do one exercise and expect change. Anyone who is committed to this process should attempt to complete all of part 3. If one activity feels cumbersome and your child doesn't want to do it, go on to the next, but don't give up. I promise your thinking will change, and soon you will notice that the process feels positive and stimulating. There is nothing to lose and everything to gain.

DEFINING STRENGTHS

In seeking out children's strengths, we need to be clear about what we are looking for. As we've seen earlier in this book, strengths are not necessarily talents, nor are they skills. Simply put, strengths are activities that make a person feel energized, empowered, and strong. Strengths do not necessarily turn into talents through practice. They exist well beyond what you like to do or what you have a preference for. Strengths are innate. They are dynamic and precise. The more precise and accurate people can be in defining their strengths, the more likely they will be to develop them in the service of their success.

When strengths are tied to interests or affinities, children can develop skills because they are inclined to practice longer. Once children develop skills that are a result of their strengths, they are able to find activities that will allow them to experience what author and psychologist Mihaly Csikszentmihalyi calls *flow*—the act of being so absorbed in an activity that you lose your sense of time and place. Talent and skill have the opportunity to develop to their greatest potential when a person is in a state of flow. In order to bring flow into your life, you will need to understand what your strengths are and develop them.

The Strengths Inventory included in the appendix of this book is a starting point. It can be used in combination with the Strengths Profile, also found in the appendixes, as a tool to summarize all the work you do in part 3. When used together, the Inventory and the Profile create a vivid snapshot of a strong person. This information will change and grow as you develop your thinking about strengths.

Inside you and your child are the keys to your success. They are your strengths. This workbook will help you reveal those strengths and enable you to bring them into play in your everyday life. This is the key to success.

CREATE YOUR FUTURE, PLAY TO YOUR STRENGTHS

CONTENTS

HOW IT WORKS

THIS WORKBOOK WILL HELP YOU DISCOVER, DEVELOP, AND USE your strengths to determine your future. When you are finished, you will have developed a new way of thinking. You will be on the road to having many "strengths epiphanies." This workbook will not label your strengths for you; it does not show you how to overcome your weaknesses. Instead, it will begin to change how you think about yourself and other people. The thinking you develop will focus on the positive. Once your mind has changed, your actions will follow and your life will develop to its full potential.

The workbook is divided into four sections:

- Activity Strengths
- Relationship Strengths
- Learning Strengths
- Looking to the Future

Each section is divided into two parts:

- Discover (the strength)
- Develop (the strength)

There is a practical sequence to this book. It is most effective when done in the order it is laid out. That said, you do not have to complete every exercise; just don't skip around, back and forth. Activity Strengths come first because it is necessary for a person to understand himself before moving on to understand his Relationship Strengths and who he is in relation to others. Learning Strengths are featured last because learning is ultimately a relationship between the student, other students, and the teacher. Learning is facilitated when people understand themselves and their Relationship Strengths. Of course, the application of these strengths is a simultaneous process. We can pull it apart neatly here, but in real life, all three work in concert to make us who we are.

STRENGTHS: A DEFINITION

Strengths are

- verbs;
- innate, i.e., no one can give them to you or take them away;
- things that can be transferred to a variety of activities;
- used to engage talents; and
- specific and precise.

They

- combine with other strengths, and
- make you feel good and strong when you are using them.

Contrary to popular belief, the opposite of strength is not weakness. The opposite of strength is depletion. If an activity is not engaging an individual's strengths, thereby energizing the person, the activity is depleting.

Knowing your strengths and putting them to use is empowering and fulfilling. They can give people agency, freedom, and independence. Parents and teachers are often good at seeing the potential in children. They are inclined to point out talent and hope students develop those talents. However, in order for their true strengths to emerge and grow, children need to self-identify them, for ultimately they are the ones who know best what makes them feel strong. Adults can help in this endeavor.

DISCOVER, DEVELOP: AN EXPLANATION

- Discover

To discover Activity Strengths, Relationship Strengths, and Learning Strengths, you will need to

- funnel and name, and
- reflect.

Funnel and Name

The starting point in discovering strengths is paying close attention to everyday activities and being able to describe them. What are their various parts? How do some activities compare to others? Many of the suggestions in this workbook will ask you or your child to describe simple, everyday activities as a way to begin forming awareness about the things you do during the day both inside and outside the classroom. By isolating and breaking down some very simple or routine activities, you begin to see how *all* activities and routines consist of various parts or steps. This understanding is an important step in discovering strengths, because it allows you to pick out, or funnel, the parts of an activity or behavior that make you feel energized and the ones that don't. **The ability to do this is the foundation of discovering strengths and applying them in all areas of life.**

The act of funneling and naming strengths is recursive. This means that you will be able to repeatedly look at what you believe is a strength and break it down until it becomes perfectly clear that you have named it in the most specific way possible for you. As we saw in part 2, there is a major difference in saying "I have a strength in writing" and "I have a strength in creative writing." Funneling is the action that allows you to hit your target and name the strength with precision. The more precise you are, the better you will be able to match your activities to your strength. We find the real strengths by funneling things down to their core.

If your child is not old enough to do this, you can do it with him and work to develop this funneling skill as a precursor for naming strengths later in life. Once your child is able to name her strengths, she will find that they can be transferred to a variety of activities.

Reflect

Reflection is an essential part of strengths discovery and development, and it is best done with a partner or a small group. This step involves talking with someone else about the activities you are doing. Most of our lives, we are conditioned that it is inappropriate to talk about ourselves, especially the things we are good at. In this step, which you will find after some of the activities, people are encouraged to talk about themselves, how they feel, and what they are thinking. As pointed out in part 2, developing strengths involves cultivating a new way of thinking about yourself. For younger children (aged four to eight), the best reflective partner is probably a parent, guardian, grandparent, or substantially older sibling. Older children can collaborate with siblings, cousins, or friends or with parents, guardians, or grandparents. My experience has shown me that children in grades five through nine are eager to share their thoughts with a willing listener, but this usually requires an adult to help guide the conversation. Because this practice may be embarrassing for teenagers, who are in their most self-conscious stage, older children may work better with peers rather than parents. This will be less true of girls than boys, who may feel more comfortable if they can discuss with just their fathers. Some boys will discuss personal matters with ease with female friends. If I had a teenaged son with a girlfriend, I would encourage them to use this workbook together. I often hear my friends complain that their child is spending too much time with their boyfriend or girlfriend. You can use this to your advantage by suggesting that you will allow them to spend time together if they are collaborating on discovering their strengths.

Self-reflection and the Young Child

When your children are between the approximate ages of four and eight, you will mostly be preparing them for the act of self-reflection, which is necessary in order to discover strengths. I cannot stress enough the importantance of self-discovery. You simply cannot define your child's strengths for him. If your child is too young to be able to self-reflect (a skill that usually develops around preadolescence in roughly the fourth, fifth, or sixth grade), you can still find many activities in this workbook that will help prepare your child for self-reflection when he is older. These activities focus on

- asking a series of questions;
- asking children to make choices between objects or select things from a group;
- engaging them in drawing;
- guiding them in storytelling;
- developing the ability to put things in sequences; and
- recording their feelings and thoughts to later serve as memory triggers.

DEVELOP

To develop Activity Strengths, Relationship Strengths, and Learning Strengths you will need to participate in exercises that allow you to practice using your strengths. This workbook introduces a few exercises for each strength to get you or your child started. They are only the beginning of a lifetime of developing strengths. You may find some of these exercises too complicated to do at home. That is okay. Some of the things listed here are more easily accomplished at school. It is up to you to make that call. Some exercises will take longer than others, and some may be repeated. There is no rule, except that you are encouraged not to attempt to cover too many concepts at once.

ARE THERE ACTIVITIES FOR CHILDREN OF EVERY AGE?

Adults of any age and children aged four to eighteen can do the exercises in this workbook. Unless noted otherwise, the activities are for children aged four to eighteen.

Ages 4–8

Most of the activities are not developmentally appropriate for children aged four to eight, but there are still plenty of things suggested here for you to do with your young child. Throughout the workbook there are sections entitled "For Young Children," for children under eight years old. These sections give suggestions for modification if your child is unable to comprehend the described exercise. Parents who have the time to invest can modify any of the exercises as they see fit. With younger children, you will mostly be observing and recording behaviors as explained in part 2 and in the section on self-reflection.

Ages 9–13

The ideal age for your child to begin this workbook on her own is about ten or eleven. Most children at this age (both male and female) will be eager to work through the exercises with you or on their own. By middle school, students often feign disinterest. But the more they see you doing the activities and showing interest, the more they will want to join in the process.

Ages 14–18

In general, a school setting is a good place for teens to engage in many of these activities. Teens will be reluctant to do any kind of activity that seems like homework on their "free time," so you will have to be creative about how you get your teen to do this at home. I have helped you out a little with this hurdle.

In some sections, entitled "As Added Incentive," I list suggestions "for reluctant teens." Some teens are just way too cool for family activities of any kind, including sitting with you to answer these questions. That is normal and doesn't mean they aren't interested in discovering their strengths. There are ways you can encourage them to participate without making it a "program you want them to do." Sometimes, these things are better left to no spontaneity. You can simply sit down with one of the exercises and say, "Hey, can we do this now?" Whereas some might feel averse to the book, there are probably a lot of teens who will want to read it with you. (I think they will enjoy the observations about school in part 1, actually.) My experience with teens tells me that when you treat them as equals, as the adults they have not yet become, they rise to the occasion. So don't assume they will not want to do the activities in this book, for you might find otherwise.

Older kids can take this book and do the activities for themselves. High school girls will be more willing to do them as presented. High school boys may be more or less willing to engage in these as part of a program outside of school. Many will want to do this alone rather than do the exercises with you. For both teen boys and girls, I suggest that, when possible, fathers become deeply involved in this process and these exercises. At times, it will help the child if the father takes the lead in initiating the activities. When teens see their dads doing things, they are much more apt to become involved than when their mothers suggest they participate. However it is done, this work, while fun, should also have an air of consequence to it. This is not some touchy-feely activity. It is about developing strengths to pave the way for a fulfilling future, one that is determined by the kids themselves. When presented this way (and it is *all* in the presentation), you will sufficiently motivate most teens.

To make these activities more engaging for teens, especially those working on their strengths outside of the classroom, I have set up an island in *Teen Second Life* called *The Strengths Movement.*

Second Life for Teens

To interest teens, you need to meet them where their interests lie. *Teen Second Life* is a virtual reality where teens can go to meet other teens. Adults (over age eighteen) are not allowed in *Teen Second Life,* as it is intended to be a place created entirely by teenagers. However, educators who have passed extensive background checks have access to selected spaces to host educational events in *Teen Second Life,* and many creative educators are setting up dynamic real life projects in this online world. *Teen Second Life* is the perfect instrument to use as encouragement for your teen to complete the exercises in this book. After your child takes the Strengths Inventory, he can get to *Teen Second Life* by signing on to www.strengthsmovement.com and entering through the *Teen Second Life* portal. There will always be an adult present at the Strengths Movement events in *Second Life.* Events will include such things as international discussions about strengths, future hiring fairs, and online classes. Your teen can also find a reflection partner on this island, another teen who is working through the book.

As in real life, there are many wonderful and exciting educational things happening in *Second Life.* Likewise, there are also many frivolous things happening. My intention in establishing the Strengths Movement in *Second Life* is to open up a healthy place for teens to meet other teens from around the world to talk about their strengths and form a community of young adults who believe that using their strengths will ultimately be the secret to their success. There is also a Strengths Movement Island in the adult *Second Life.* Parents and children aged fourteen to eighteen can talk about their virtual strengths experiences over dinner. I guarantee you that if both you and your child have been to *Second Life* together, there will be plenty of fodder for your discussion about strengths.

SUPPLIES NEEDED AND TIME INVOLVED

Most activities will require making observations in a Strengths Journal. You can use any notebook, but you should keep the notes you make from session to session all in one place because you will refer back to them later. Some of the questions ask you to write the answers using colored pens. I suggest you use a red, a blue, and a green pen. You will also need two different kinds of stickers to indicate both positive and negative preferences. This color-coded approach will help you to quickly identify positive activities when you return to the journal later. If your child is too young to do the activities herself, you can fill the answers out for her and, as suggested in part 2, you can give the journal to her later, when she's old enough to do it alone.

Ideally, you will spend one hour a week on these activities. At this pace, it will take about six months to comlpete the workbook exercises. If you are in a classroom setting, you can set aside a regularly scheduled time to do these activities. If you are doing them at home, you can work around the family schedule.

ACTIVITY STRENGTHS

AN ACTIVITY STRENGTH IS SOMETHING THAT MAKES A PERSON feel good while he or she is doing it. Some activities are natural magnets for an individual's strengths, but other activities are not natural fits. One of the goals in developing Activity Strengths is to make you more mindful of the everyday tasks that make up your life and the different elements involved in those tasks. The exercises in this section are useful for funneling the common activities you do each day.

You may question how these simple exercises will lead you to understand your strengths. Simply put, they train your mind to recognize various aspects of the things you do and how you feel when you are doing them. If you are like most people, you go through your day doing hundreds of things on autopilot. The goal of these exercises is to train your mind to recognize subtle distinctions in these activities that can mean the difference between strengths and weaknesses. Ultimately, you are going to see all your activities differently when you come to understand that some aspects of them energize you and others deplete you. For now, you will begin with simple distinctions and learn to see some commonplace activities in a new light.

We begin the workbook with a look at some of the activities that families do together, because these are the ones you are most familiar with and may most often take for granted. The exercises that follow are only the beginning. You can add to them, use them to brainstorm other ideas, or do them repeatedly, as part of a routine. The most important thing to remember is that strengths do not develop in one-shot, *been-there-done-that* attempts. Fulfilling lives with minimized anxiety and maximized purpose must be earned. The place to begin is to recognize and reflect on everyday activities.

DISCOVER

By the end of this section, you should be able to

- idenfity Activity Strengths and
- describe Activity Strengths to others.

Examine Activities in the Home

Often we have strengths in one part of a sequenced activity but not in the whole. These simple exercises can provide clues as to which parts of a much larger activity (such as planning a project) a person will naturally have strength. This section serves to get you thinking in sequences and seeing how one job is made of smaller parts. There are four exercises in this section, followed by a reflection. Some of the questions ask you to make lists, and some ask you to make choices about the things on the list. Some of the questions will seem easy, and others may appear more difficult or even tedious. They may take longer. The purpose of this is not to arrive at a single answer about strength. As defined in part 2 of the book, strength development is a new way of thinking. These exercises will show you that new way. You are developing insights—epiphanies—not static definitions. When you begin thinking about specific things you enjoy doing, you begin to observe yourself in your activities. Remember, when you feel strong and energized doing something, you are more likely to continue repeating the activity, more likely to keep at it longer, and more likely to develop skill or talent in that area as a result. But remember, these household activities are not the only activities you may engage in or feel strong doing. **They are the simplest examples that will give you insight into ALL your activities.**

As Added Incentive:

- Tell children that when they finish this assignment, you will reassign their family chores and obligations so they better accommodate their strengths. There is a sample family chore chart in the appendix.
- Ask your older child to complete this exercise as a way to begin reflecting on a potential college-essay topic. Tell him that it will be a great topic to write about his strengths and how he can put them to use at the college level

For Young Children:

As you work with young children on various tasks—putting away toys, getting dressed in the morning, eating meals—point out each aspect of the task as you are doing it. (For example, when getting dressed, say, "Now we are picking our clothes. First we put on the shirt. Next we . . .") This simple verbalization of process will help children begin to recognize sequencing, a skill that will later facilitate discovering activity strengths.

FUNNELING QUESTIONS

Directions: To do this section, you will need a green pen, a red pen, and two kinds of stickers. Choose one sticker to represent the positive and the other to represent the negative. Break each activity listed below into at least three smaller parts. (For example, cleaning up can be broken into clearing the table, washing the dishes, and emptying the dishwasher.)

In the Kitchen

- Cleaning up
- Cooking
- Grocery shopping

In Your Room

- Making the bed
- Doing your laundry
- Straightening things up
- Decorating

For the Household

- Cleaning the windows
- Dusting
- Rearranging the furniture
- Paying the bills
- Cleaning the bathroom
- Fixing broken things
- Taking out the garbage and recycling

Family Interactions

- Shopping
- Wrapping gifts
- Entertaining guests
- Talking about problems

GREEN JOBS/RED JOBS

- Make a list of all the chores you have to do at home. If you don't do chores, then list all the activities you can think of that families do on a regular weekday at home.
- Of the jobs/activities you listed, using a green pen, underline the jobs you like doing the best. Using a red pen, underline the ones you like doing least. Make sure all the jobs are underlined either in green or red.
- Look at the jobs you underlined in green, and for each one explain in no more than two sentences exactly what it is about the job that you enjoy doing.
- Now, look at the jobs you underlined in red, and for each one explain in no more than two sentences exactly what it is about it you dislike.
- Now, look at your green list again. If you had to choose one job to do and you could stop doing all the rest, which is the job you would choose to keep doing? Put a positive sticker beside that job. Write one sentence about why you like doing that job more than the other green ones.
- Now look at your red list and choose the one job you dislike the most. Put a negative sticker beside that job. Write one sentence about why you dislike that job more than the others.

WANT TO DO/DON'T WANT TO DO

- Make two columns on a page. Label one column "Want to Do" and the other column "Don't Want to Do."

WANT TO DO	DON'T WANT TO DO

- Look over all the jobs and activities you have already written about in the green/red exercise and put them in either the "Want to Do" column" or the "Don't Want to Do" column.
- Place a positive sticker next to the top three jobs/activities you like the most and a negative sticker next to the three you like the least.

For Young Children:

Give your child a choice of three chores (for example: making the bed, picking up toys, doing dishes). In your child's strengths journal, make a note of what he chooses. Watch your child as he does the chosen task and make note of what he does with ease and what frustrates him.

MAKING CONNECTIONS

There are two parts to this exercise.

Part A: Fill in the first blanks below with one of the chores from either the Funneling Questions, Green Jobs/Red Jobs, or Want to Do/Don't Want to Do exercises. Choose either an activity that you said you enjoyed or one that you wrote in green. Fill in the blanks below it. Repeat this with a second chore.

- *I like this action:* ________.
- Now name all the various parts of the action, breaking it down into its smallest parts. (Come up with at least three parts.)
- *The part I like best is* ________. (Choose one of the three parts.)
- *If I could put what I enjoy doing about this activity into one word, the word would be* ________.

Example:
I like this action: grocery shopping. Break it down: making the list, choosing the food in the store, putting away the groceries. The part I like best is making the list. One word that describes what I like best about this is planning.

Part B: Look at the two words you came up with to fill in the last blank in part A of this exercise. You are going to use these words to help you think of a few more things you do that you have not yet listed. Fill in the first blank below using one of those words, and then make a list of as many other activities you can think of where you also use this word. (For example, I would use the word *planning* from my example in part A to fill in the first blank. My list includes planning for meetings, planning trips, planning events.)

- *I feel energized when I am ______. Here is a list of other activities that involve using this word:*
- Use your green pen to circle the activity you enjoy the most of the ones you just listed.
- Recall the last time you were involved in the activity you circled in green. Write five or six sentences describing what you were doing and when it was.

Repeat the steps above using the other word from the last blank of part A. These statements are the beginnings of understanding your Activity Strengths.

For Young Children:

In your child's Strengths Journal, take note of the activities your child naturally likes to do. For each activity, try to isolate the part of that activity he or she most enjoys. You will know this by the amount of time spent on task or by a visible sense of joy or deep concentration. Sometimes when young children are deeply involved in activities, their faces contort or they stick their tongues out. Take note of any such gestures.

REFLECT

Find a partner to share all the choices you have made so far about what activities you like and which you don't like and discuss why. If you are a parent doing the exercise for yourself, discuss it with your children or your spouse. If you are a parent doing this with a child, you might ask your child to complete the exercise and let him know that you want to listen to his thoughts about it. Be clear that this is not a talk about assigning family jobs or making judgments. Here is a way you can open the conversation:

"I have come up with a list of things we do at home that I might feel energized by or depleted by. I want to share them so I can think about them some more. I'd like it if you could listen and then ask me why so I can think about it further."

It is important at this stage that no one gives judgmental feedback on these reactions. The purpose of the reflection phase is simply to share what you feel when doing things and why. This is not about saying you will or will not continue to do the activities you are describing.

If you are a parent and talking to a child aged eight to twelve, your goal is to follow the guidelines and take note, not to steer. Your child will know how she feels; you cannot tell her.

For Added Incentive:

Use this exercise to set up an allowance program. The reflection part can be used to discuss what kids believe certain jobs are worth. You can use this to talk about jobs and their value. Bring a level of economics to this discussion with older children by asking them why some jobs should be paid more than others. Make this a family talk that uses your examples as a stepping-off place to discuss world economics.

Using Photos to Think About Activities

The following exercises ask you to think about photographs or drawings or to actually make a drawing or take a photograph. Pictures and images can be useful in helping people recognize abstract concepts such as a feeling of strength. The photos are intentionally vague. There is no right answer.

There are four activities in this section, followed by a reflection.

CHOOSE AND DESCRIBE

- Have a look at the three photographs above. Which one do you find the most appealing and why? Write a few sentences about why you like it.

- Look at the following three pictures. Which one do you like least and why? Write a few sentences about why you don't like it.

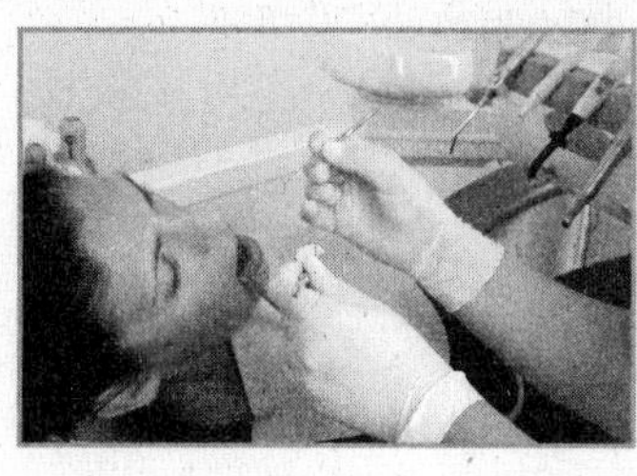

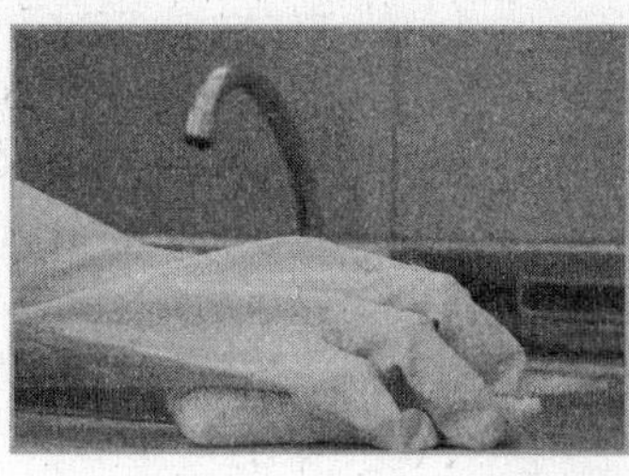

ATTRACTION AND FUNNELING

Directions: Look at the next set of six photos. Choose the two you are most *attracted to.*

> ***Note to parents:*** The photos are vague enough to suggest different kinds of activities rather than prescribe them. This is important because people are inclined to jump to a known category of activities and call one a strength. The goal is to discover the specific *part* of an activity that energizes your child. It is important to struggle some in the effort to name strengths. They are not obvious, or we would all know what ours are without hesitation.

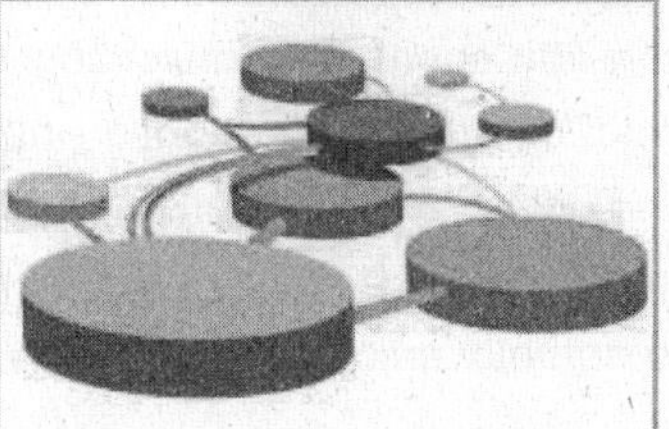

- Using the same six photos, rank them from 1 to 6 with 1 being the most appealing and 6 being the least appealing.
- Discuss why you found number 6 to be the least appealing. Write a few sentences or discuss this. Do the same for the one you find most appealing.
- Look at the top two photos that appealed to you. List all the activities that you can think of that come to mind as you look at these photos.

For Young Children:

Using several different children's books, find at least three but not more than four pictures of characters engaged in a variety of different activities. Ask your child to tell you what the character in the picture is doing. Then place the pictures alongside one another and ask your child to point to the picture of the thing she would like to be doing. Ask her several times if she would like to do the *activity* the characters are doing. Keep asking her until it is clear she has chosen one activity over another and is not simply responding to other enjoyable elements of the pictures. Keep track of this exercise in the Strengths Journal.

OBSERVE THE OBVIOUS

This activity involves taking photographs.

> ***Note to parents:*** At first glance, this activity may seem demanding, but children of all ages love to take photos. In my experience, now that so many kids have their own cell-phone cameras, the idea of having something purposeful to do with them or with a digital camera is a well-received assignment. This activity works in both schools and homes. If you have children between the ages of eight and thirteen, and you want to keep them busy while you are at the mall, have them complete this while you shop. If you do not have access to a camera, you can take notes in a field journal. The purpose of this activity is to have children begin to take notice of a variety of activities. They have already spent time observing their own, and now they are going to act as investigators observing others' activities. We think of jobs and activities in such broad strokes that we often miss the subtleties involved. It is those very subtleties that determine what it is we actually enjoy doing and why.

Directions:

- Go to a large establishment where there are many people working on different jobs: the grocery store, the train station, a shopping mall, a school, or a sporting event, for example. Using a camera, take between ten and twenty photos of all the various activities and jobs you see taking place.
- Look at the photos and write down all the tasks you can think of that are involved in each different job you photographed. For example, if you took a photo of an umpire at a baseball game, list all the things you think an umpire has to do as part of that job.

  Note to parents: Children often think they want to do a certain type of job in life but have no insight into the specific activities that are required as part of the job. The goal in this exercise is not to focus on professions but on jobs as complex systems in which a variety of activities take place. Younger children may not understand this distinction, but they can still do the activity.

- Print the photos and arrange them in groups of jobs that seem to have similar activities associated with them. Choose which jobs have the most activities that you believe would appeal to you and discuss or write several sentences why. Discuss or write several sentences about which activities would definitely not appeal to you and why.
- Is there a job among the photographs that you think you would like but that involves some parts you may not like?

For Young Children:

You can do this activity yourself and share it with a child who is too young to take photos but old enough to understand looking at them while you explain what you've discovered.

THE FIVE-WHY APPROACH

You need a partner for this activity. The example below has only three "whys," but you should do the exercise until you run out of answers to the "why" question. With your partner, take turns asking and answering the following questions:

1. What is your favorite sport?
2. What is your favorite hobby other than a sport?
3. If you could spend the whole day doing anything you wanted, what would you do?

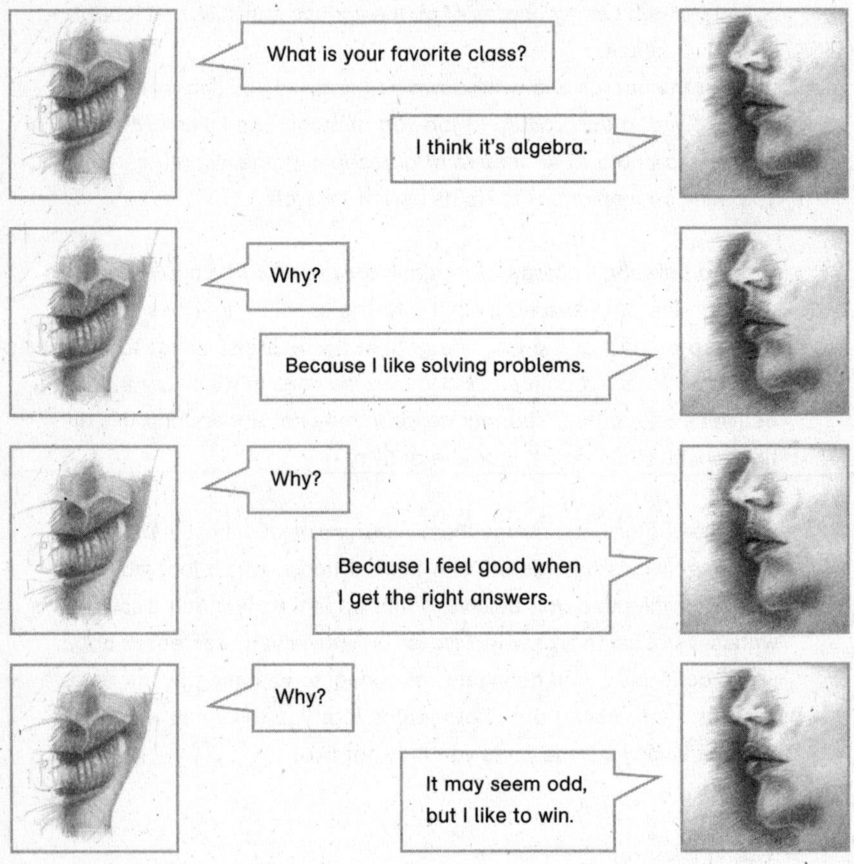

Note to parents: The Five-Why exercise forces people to examine and express the underlying reasons for a simple preference.

For Added Incentive:

Make this exercise a game you play when you are in the car. Each time someone has an epiphany—he learns something about himself that he was not conscious of before—give him a point. The first family member to arrive at ten points gets a prize. Hang a small white board in your kitchen to keep track of the points and the best epiphany of the week. If kids are reluctant to play, tease them and play by yourself, then reward yourself and put your points and your epiphanies up on the board. Let them see you give yourself cool prizes, and they may want to join in.

REFLECT

Look over the exercises you completed with the photographs. Choose one of the photos from any of the four exercises that has prompted you to realize an activity you feel strong doing. With that activity in mind, consider the questions that follow. You should think about these or take notes about them in your journal, or you can discuss them with a partner.

- Why do I like doing that?
- If I could substitute one thing I have to do for doing this instead, it would be . . .
- What are the other things I could do in my life that may be kind of like that?
- What are other activities that make me feel strong?
- How can I repeat those activities in my school, job, and personal life?
- How can I bring these activities to a team to help us win?
- How can I explain these strengths to others?
- What kind of people do I want to work with in my future?
- How will my boss be able to recognize my strengths?
- What qualities will my future boss need to activate my strengths?
- How can I best contribute to a team project?

Activity Epiphanies

By now you've thought through so many different activities and feelings that you are ready to come to a strength epiphany. A strength epiphany is an insight into what makes you feel strong and energized. It is a thought. It is an aha moment. This realization doesn't have to be earth shattering. Every day we experience many aha moments and don't even know it. We just need to learn how to recognize them when they happen. An aha moment is a beginning, not an ending. The more you think about it, the more you will begin to observe what you feel strong doing.

A strength epiphany is a statement that begins something like this: "Now that I think about it, I actually like to ________." The next two activities have to do with your Activity Strengths epiphanies.

OLD IDEAS INTO NEW

This activity is designed to show you what a general epiphany is like so you will begin to understand what a "strength aha" feels like. Most great creative ideas come from connecting two different, unrelated things. For example, someone combined a zipper and a plastic bag to create Ziploc bags. Someone else combined stuffed animals with slippers to create those fuzzy slippers people wear. Look at the next six pairs of words and come up with as many ideas as you can for new things that are a combination of the two. You can use your imagination, and the ideas can be as wild as you want. The point is to take two very different things and combine them to create one new thing.

- lamp and rug
- pillow and shoes
- chair and boat
- tent and envelope
- umbrella and watch
- paper clip and rubber band

COMBINE TWO INTO ONE

- Write down your favorite hobby, your favorite class, and your favorite sport.
- Now pick the one element of each of these activities that you like the best. (For example, if your favorite sport is fishing, you may best enjoy the moment you catch the fish. If your favorite hobby is computer games, you may like winning the best. If your favorite class is math, you may best like measuring geometrical shapes.)
- Take the one thing you like best from each category and combine the three to create a new activity that has all three things you like best in

it. (For example, I am going to come up with an activity that combines catching fish with measuring geometric shapes and with winning.)

- Look one more time at the three activities and the one thing you decided you like to do most about each one. For each of the three things, think of as many other similar activities as you can that would involve that one favorite element. (For example, solving geometry proofs in class, solving spatial problems when putting furniture in a room, designing buildings, rooms, etc.) You may need to talk with someone about this or even do some research.
- Write down an Activity Epiphany by filling in the blank: "Now that I think of it, I actually like to ________." Don't force yourself to come up with this. If you are not yet able to fill in the blank, go back and do any of the exercises you enjoyed again. If you are able to have an epiphany, go to the back of the book and find the *Strengths Profile.* You can write your first epiphany in the profile. This document is also available for download as a PDF for free from the www.strengthsmovement.com Web site.

DEVELOP

By the end of this section, you will be able to

- evaluate activities to determine whether they will engage your strengths and
- recognize whether or not an activity is going to be one where you will be able to volunteer strengths.

When you practice and commit to these simple exercises, you will begin to notice how you feel during your chores and activities. The next step is to decide what to do with that knowledge. The following exercises will further develop an understanding of Activity Strengths. The four exercises in this section are more involved than in the previous section. You can choose to try one or all of them. They do not follow any special order. They are meant as practice for developing ways your strengths can be used in group situations.

Imagine Yourself in This Scenario

This is a *hypothesis* activity.

Choose one of the following scenarios:

- You return from the store to find the house on fire; nobody is inside.
- You are locked out of the car in winter.
- The electricity in your house is not working.
- The president or a VIP is coming for dinner.
- A family pet is lost.

Answer the following questions in your journal:

- What is the single most important thing you see yourself doing to help in this situation? What do you think you will be able to do in this situation that no one can do as well as you?
- What are some of the first things you would do to help with this situation?

For Added Incentive:

Make this exercise the development of a family safety and security plan. Give each person a real role to handle in the case of any of these situations occurring.

Make a Family Plan

Note to parents: This exercise is for families, and so if you do not have a major event coming up, you can put it aside until you do. Read the entire exercise now to familiarize yourself with it so you will know when to use it.

Families encounter many events that are new and different and require everyone to pitch in. You may be getting a new pet, preparing for a big party, moving from one home to another, going on an extensive vacation, or even welcoming a new sibling into the family. You could be helping a family member through an illness or recovery from an accident, dealing with the fallout of a huge snowstorm, or needing to cut back significantly on spending. These big events require many actions on everyone's part. When they happen, you can use them as opportunities to enable everyone in the family to have a say in the decision making and volunteer their strengths to help the event be as successful and inclusive as possible. People will be more inspired to help if they know their strength will be necessary in order for the task they are assigned to be successful. (Remember Hawk in part 2?) This activity is easier if you use a chart. This chart is available for download from the Web site.

1. Once you have an event (for example, moving from one home to another), get everyone in the family together to brainstorm all the things that need to happen. (For example, "Moving Houses" Brainstorm: packing our things, deciding where things go in the new house, deciding what we need to do on the day of the move, unpacking, arranging things in the new house, settling in the pets, contacting the new neighbors, cleaning the old house.) This brainstorm may take several hours over a couple of days or even a week as you begin to determine all that needs to be done.
2. Discuss all the things that need to be accomplished and have family members volunteer to do the things they feel would energize them. This doesn't mean they are the only things someone will do; it just gives people a chance to do something they have a strength in. This activity doesn't require that you do anything very differently from the way you would normally, except that there will be a focus on strengths, which will make the activities more enjoyable and meaningful. If everyone has to contribute and help anyway, why not let people choose roles to play based on their strengths? One person may feel very strongly about greeting the new neighbors and another may want to help in decorating the new house and unpacking things. The roles and responsibilities in the example do not cover the entire scope of the move. There will be other roles and jobs that need to be accomplished. However, this piece of the planning gives children and parents authentic situations in which to volunteer and thus develop their strengths. **This exercise can be modified for the classroom and used when approaching any kind of group work.** By posting a chart of the division of labor, you reinforce the importance and the presence of strengths development in the home and in the classroom.
3. Make a chart of what everyone has volunteered to do. Have everyone discuss why he or she feels their chosen activity engages their strength.

EVENT: MOVE TO OHIO	DATE OF EVENT: JULY 12
TASKS WE NEED TO ACCOMPLISH	VOLUNTEERS
Pack kitchen	Mom, Chrissy
Be in charge of Buster (the dog)	Jason
Arrange family room	Jason, Chrissy

4. After the events you plan are complete, it is important for everyone to debrief on the event. Return to your chart with the goal of coming up with some strengths epiphanies. Ask all the family members if they enjoyed their role. What were the complications they discovered or the unanticipated problems or successes? Was there a new strength they noticed? This discussion is important, as it will inform and reinforce future behaviors.

Projecting Strengths onto Inanimate Objects

This activity asks you to think creatively about your strengths. It may seem odd. You may wonder, "What does this have to do with developing my strengths?" In order for you to understand and think naturally and consistently about your strengths, you need to reprogram your mind. The more engaging and positive ways in which you can consider Activity Strengths, the more conditioned your mind becomes. This won't happen by simply asking yourself what you like to do repeatedly. You need to exercise your thinking in a variety of ways.

Answer the following question, filling in the blank with each of the words on the list:

If you were a ________, what would energize you? What would deplete you?

- toaster
- river
- guitar
- watch
- basketball
- the sun
- spiderman

- map
- your best friend
- your identical twin

Seeing Strengths in Others

Watch your favorite television show, and as you are watching it, make a list of what you think the characters' Activity Strengths are. What energizes each character? What depletes them? What energizes you? What depletes you?

RELATIONSHIP STRENGTHS

AN INTRICATE WEB OF RELATIONSHIPS CONNECTS EACH OF US to others. Each relationship is different, yet we all have innate strengths to contribute to our relationships to make them more effective and rewarding. These are Relationship Strengths.

Relationship skills are imperative for children's success in the future, and their relationships will become increasingly complex as the world globalizes. As the world speeds up, so must our communication skills. First impressions are sometimes the only impressions we'll get, and so children will need to recognize the messages they send others, as well as make choices about the relationships they wish to sustain. Although children today boast of having thousands of friends on *myspace* and Facebook, the reality is that they will need to know how to choose and keep *real* friends. When time comes at a premium, sustaining relationships that are depleting or unrewarding becomes a waste. Children will need to understand the limits of their time and energy and make informed decisions about where and how to focus on other people.

Successful relationships depend on the ability to empathize, express gratitude, and forgive others. Children will grow into strong adults when they understand ways to learn and grow from the inevitable conflicts that happen in any relationship. The exercises in this section get children to think about these virtues.

Most of the exercises in this section will work with children aged eight and above. Where appropriate, I will offer suggestions for younger children. Most of my suggestions will ask you to make and record observations about your child's relationships with other people. Early observations are some of the most pure insights into the kind of person your child is, and you are encouraged to observe these behaviors without judgment. For example, you will begin to notice whether your child is introverted or extroverted—traits you cannot change. The insights you record will be invaluable in helping your child become self-aware and able to recognize her own strengths when she is ready.

DISCOVER

By the end of this section, you will be able to

- identify positive traits in yourself;
- apply those traits to a significant memory;
- distinguish between liking someone and friendship, friends, and best friends;
- comprehend rejection as a lack of energy;
- identify relationship strengths;
- create a relationship web; and
- apply relationship strengths to a relationship web.

Begin with Yourself

You are a unique individual with many talents to bring to the world. Relationship Strengths start with you. A positive self-image and an understanding of what you can contribute to your relationships will help you in your personal life as well as in your experiences in school. The four exercises in this section focus on identifying your positive personal traits.

For Young Children:

Use the words in the box below or substitute words that you believe describe your child. Be sure that all the words are positive words. Then continue with the exercise and record the profile in the Strengths Journal. Below the diagrams you create write this: "This is how I saw you at age (fill in blank). Look over the words in the book and choose how you see yourself today. How have you changed or grown since my perceptions?"

FOCUS ON YOU

- From the box below, choose the four words you think best DESCRIBE you:

able accepting adaptable bold brave calm caring cheerful clever complex confident dependable dignified energetic extroverted friendly giving happy helpful idealistic independent ingenious intelligent introverted kind knowledgeable logical loving mature modest observant organized patient powerful proud quiet reflective relaxed religious responsible responsive searching self-assertive self-conscious sensible shy silly spontaneous sympathetic trustworthy warm wise witty

- Look at the model on the next page and draw it in your Strengths Journal or download it from the www.strengthsmovement.com Web site. Place the four words you chose from the box above in the squares on the model.
- Look at the next set of words and pick two words that most APPEAL to you:

care encouragement love kindness trust play fun fairness acceptance respect safety listening inventiveness wonder equality cooperation order communication humor team

- Place the two words you chose in the circles on the diagram on the next page.
- Look at the next set of words and pick one that most ENERGIZES you:

fixing inventing planning helping writing teaching learning organizing directing setting-up listening computing playing choosing arranging

- Place that word on the rectangle on the diagram.
- Look at the diagram. Take about a minute to really study it.
- In your journal, write down anything that comes to mind about yourself when looking at the diagram. It can be anything at all.

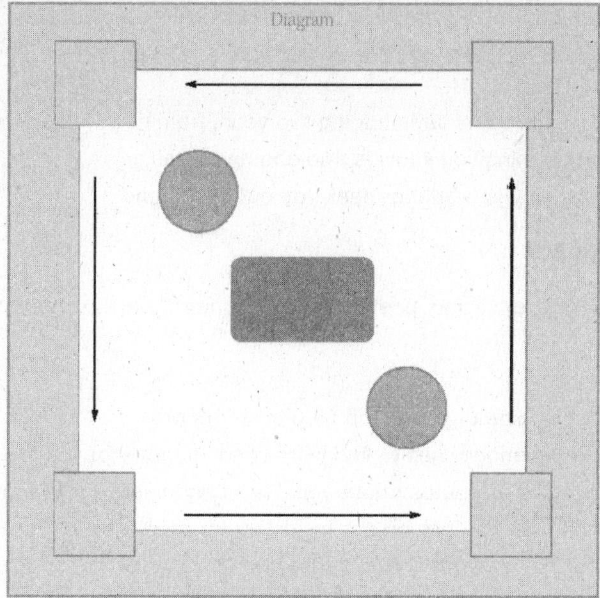

- With a partner, discuss your diagram and what you have written.
- Think of a specific positive memory about yourself. Use the diagram to help you think about yourself and write a description of yourself relevant to that memory. Be sure to end the description with a few sentences about how this makes you feel.

DOCUMENT IT

If your closet is like mine, you are starting to gather whole collections of home videos and DVDs. It has never been easier to document our lives in moving pictures. In this exercise you will document your strengths journey from the beginning. By videotaping yourself, you create your own personal record of growth. In five or ten years, when you reach up and pull this tape or disk from your shelf, you will be amazed to see how much you have grown in your thinking about strengths. This exercise is easy, and I guarantee that you will be happy you did it.

If you do not have access to a DVD or video recorder, you can document your journey by writing answers to the following questions in your Strengths Journal. The idea is to repeat this activity after four or five years have passed. Here are the questions for you to answer, either in writing or on tape:

- Look into a mirror. Describe the person you see.
- Do you think one person can change the world? Why? How? Why not?
- What do you see yourself doing five years from now? Ten? Twenty?
- Name one thing you know is true about yourself.
- Describe why your friends seek you out as a friend.

SELF-PORTRAIT

Make a self-portrait using poster board, markers, glue, scissors, and magazines.

- Draw an outline of your head on a poster board.
- Flip through magazines to find words and images that you feel reflect only positive attributes about you. Try to find images and words that describe who you are on the inside rather than who you are on the outside. You can use the diagram from the Focus on You exercise if you need some direction about what kinds of characteristics you are looking to represent.
- Cut words and images from the magazines and arrange them in any manner inside the outline of yourself on the poster board.

Now you have a self-portrait that represents your most positive qualities.

THIS IS ME

Write your name vertically down the left-hand side of a sheet of paper, writing each letter separately. For each letter, think of a word or phase that describes a positive statement or characteristic about you.

Example:

Makes people smile
Always willing to listen
Rarely has a conflict
You want to talk with me when you are down

Next, write a paragraph about yourself, making sure you talk about how these statements accurately represent who you are or who you want to be in the future.

Focus on Others

Many of us don't make the distinction between *liking* someone and *being friends* with someone. When we understand the qualities that attract people to one another, we recognize that relationships are about forces and energies *between* people rather than just about our personality traits. Sometimes when people reject us or don't like us, we think it is because something is wrong with our personality. That is not true. The following questions get you to think about the things you do with friends. There are four activities in this section.

> **For Young Children:**
>
> Use the questions below to make guesses about your child based on observations. Whenever you make a guess, provide a concrete example of an action that leads you to this belief.

FUNNELING RELATIONSHIPS WITH FRIENDS

- Make a list of five activities that you do with your friends.
- Put a positive sticker next to the one you like doing the most.
- Use your green pen to explain why you like doing that activity. How does it make you feel? Why do you think that is?
- Fill in this blank: *When I am with my friends, I am always one who ________, and this makes me **feel good.***
- Describe in detail a time you were involved in an activity with a friend and you felt good about something you contributed to the interaction.
- Use your green pen to underline the words in the description you just wrote that make you feel the strongest. You will just underline single words.
- Think of something a friend of yours enjoys doing that you don't. Use your red pen to describe why you think your friend enjoys the activity. What does he or she get out of it? Why do you think you don't like doing it?

MY SOCIAL PREFERENCES

Directions:
Make two columns on a page. Title one column "Activities I Enjoy" and the other "Activities I Don't Enjoy." Place each of the following descriptions in one of the columns, depending on how you feel about them:

ACTIVITIES I ENJOY	ACTIVITIES I DON'T ENJOY

- Giving advice
- Listening to problems on a regular basis
- Making time for one-on-one
- Being in large groups of friends
- Being there every time a friend needs me
- Coming in and helping in times of crisis
- Talking on the phone regularly
- Going to parties
- Responding to an instant message
- Adding my comment to a friend's social network
- Text messaging
- Sending gifts
- Planning get-togethers
- Never talking badly about anyone
- Making others laugh
- Understanding problems
- Going out with friends
- Feeling another's pain
- Having close intimate associations
- Working on a project
- Sharing a common sports interest

Look at the two columns and choose the top three things you like to do with others and the top three things you feel most uncomfortable doing.

From the following list, choose the four activities that would make you feel most connected to friends and write them down using your green pen:

- Going to a party
- Playing cards
- Attending a sporting event
- Playing a game
- Going out with two or three friends
- Hanging out with just the two of us
- Eating lunch
- Eating dinner
- Going to your house
- Having you come to my house
- Meeting with a book club

USING PHOTOS

Look at the following photos and choose the one that seems to portray how you are with family and friends. In your journal, write about why you chose this photo. Then choose the one you believe *least* portrays you and write about it in your journal.

REFLECT

Find a partner to talk about the things you wrote in the section you just completed.

- What is it that you feel you bring to these relationships?
- Why?
- Is there something you don't like to do that other people seem to like to do?
- Why?
- Are there things that others expect of you that you don't feel you are able to bring to the relationship?
- What can you do instead of those things?

Finding Friends

There is a difference between liking people, having acquaintances, and forming lasting friendships. In order to recognize Relationship Strengths, you need to know how they differ so you can choose which strengths are appropriate to bring to each kind of relationship. Four exercises and one reflection segment make up this section.

FAMOUS PEOPLE YOU ADMIRE

- Choose a famous person, either a real person or a character whom you "like." Brainstorm why you "like" this person. Write down all the reasons you can think of. This may involve some online research, a visit to the local library, or watching a television show to take some notes about the person who plays the particular television character you like.

> **For Young Children:**
>
> The famous person can be a famous character from a favorite book or movie.

ACQUAINTANCES

An acquaintance is someone you know. Some acquaintances are people you like but with whom you have not yet established a friendship. Some acquaintances are people you neither particularly like nor dislike. You feel neutral.

Other acquaintances are people you don't like. List one person you know for each category:

- An acquaintance I like: ________
- An acquaintance I don't have any real strong feelings for either way: ________
- An acquaintance I don't like: ________

Think of three people whom you have never liked. What is it about these people that you don't like? Write about it in your journal.

LET'S BECOME FRIENDS

- With your partner, have a short discussion about your experiences of meeting three new people you like. Write down the reasons that you like those people. Compare them. Are any of the reasons the same or different for each person? What do you believe makes you like one person and not another?
- Friendships evolve over time. Just because you are acquainted with someone and like someone doesn't mean you are friends. There is a stage between knowing someone and becoming true friends. Make a list of the things that you believe have to happen between you and someone else in order for that person to become your friend. This list should be about actions and activities rather than personality traits.

FRIENDSHIP STATEMENTS

What does it mean to be a friend? What kind of things do you expect from your friendships? What are the things you are willing and ready to do for others? Having a good sense of these things in advance will help you set expectations and navigate relationships. You can begin by making a Friendship Statement that will help you think about what Relationship Strengths you might have that you are willing to bring to your friendships. Fill out the Friendship Statement Work Sheet in the appendix. This can also be downloaded or copied into your journal.

> ***Note to parents:*** Girls may be more open to completing these friendship statements than boys, but boys and girls who are friends could benefit greatly from doing them together. Children between the ages of ten and fourteen may be willing to do this activity, especially in school or right after there has been conflict. Anytime a child has

a new friend, this work sheet can serve as a good conversation starter.

Many parents wonder how they can prevent their children from experiencing pain in their relationships. They cannot. Pain and disappointment are a natural part of growing up. However, this work sheet can serve as a tool to guide you and your children through understanding and talking about relationships.

REFLECT

Just because you like someone does not mean she or he will like you back. With your partner, think about and discuss a time that someone you liked did not like you back. What was it you liked about that person? How did you feel when he or she did not like you back? Why do you think that was the case?

Relationship Webs

Next, you are going to make a relationship web.

- Review the following list and use your green pen to copy five phrases you believe describe how you consistently act in a variety of relationships with others. Place a positive sticker beside the three that make you feel the best, or the most proud, when you do them for others.

I feel my best when I . . .

plan events
give advice
provide coaching
initiate activities
consult on ideas
coordinate events
create new ideas
detect concerns, flaws, and inconsistencies
discover new friends and new things to do
listen
mediate a conflict
assert myself
give honest feedback
am discreet and keep a secret
exert a calming influence
am social
follow through on commitments
act as a motivating force
feel continually positive
act as a stabilizing force
bring humor to a situation
take things seriously
provide intimate one-on-one interaction
am available to talk anytime

introduce new people, ideas, and places
make things
solve puzzles, problems
am patient
organize something
tolerate difficult things
instruct others
prove reliable
have been loyal

- On a piece of paper, draw a circle and put your name in it. Draw five or six more circles around the one with your name on it. (See the sample diagram in this section.) Inside each circle, write categories of people you have relationships with. Then draw an arrow from your name to each circle. This will become your relationship web. This template is also downloadable from the Web site.
- Next, draw a box in the lower-left-hand corner of the page. In that box write down three specific things you feel good and proud about doing in *all* your relationships. You can choose these character traits from the list you just put stickers next to or come up with some of your own. (Some examples are listening to others' problems, having regular ongoing conversations, helping people out of a jam, hosting parties, giving gifts, explaining things, and giving advice.) The things you choose should be things you think you do well for the relationships and that you feel you can continue to do for all the relationships. These character traits represent some of your chosen Relationship Strengths.

Look at the relationship web you've drawn, and on each arrow between you and the other people, write down the Relationship Strength you think you can bring to the relationship listed in the center circles. Choose from the strengths you have listed in the box on the diagram.

Relationship Web Diagram

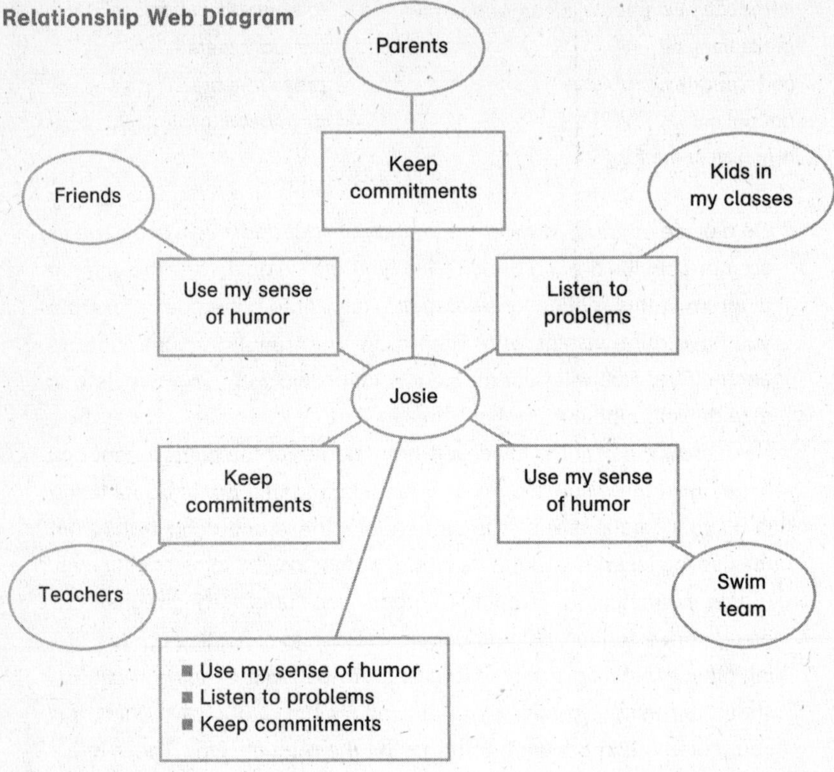

- Now, think back and try to recall specific positive things you have named in the sections "Focus on Others" and "Finding Friends." Make a list of things you do most often that make you feel good and proud. These are your Relationship Strengths. They are not your only Relationship Strengths, but they are ones you can work on developing now. You don't have to be everything to everyone all the time, but you can consistently do certain things for everyone in your life and use these to improve your relationships.
- Now list these Relationship Strengths on your Strengths Profile.

REFLECT

The activities you worked on should have given you a few relationship epiphanies. You can begin to think about them more deeply by talking about this with a partner. Share your diagram and have a conversation about your new insights.

It will help your relationships if you let the people involved know what your strengths are. It will also help if you tell them the things you are not able to do and explain why you are not always good at those things. This exercise will allow you to be clear about expectations others have for you. Your conversations may sound something like the following four examples:

"I can't make it to all the events and the get-togethers you plan. I'm so sorry. I'm just busy. This doesn't mean you're not important to me. What I can promise is that if you ever call me with anything you want to talk over, I will respond to you and listen. Listening is a relationship strength of mine."

"I'm really good at solving problems. If you ever have a problem you have to work through, I would love for you to come to me with it so I can work to help you solve it. I am not that good at talking about relationships, but if you have logistical issues or can't figure out what to do about a schedule or how to manage something, I would love to be the person you turn to for help."

"I'm not especially comfortable in big groups, so I'm not always eager to join in the activities you plan with lots of other people. I do really well one-on-one, and I would love to find time where we can meet and have some individual time together."

"Don't take it personally that I don't respond to e-mails. I may not be good at returning short e-mails, but I love having face-to-face conversations. I'd rather meet in person, and then I'd be more than happy to talk about whatever you want."

This kind of relationship-strengths volunteering will take practice. Not everyone will be receptive to this type of conversation, and that's okay. You need not have it with everyone. You can contribute your strengths to your relationships even without having this kind of talk. It will help you a lot if you continue to reflect on your encounters and think often about the specific things you consistently bring to them. Write your Relationship Epiphanies on your Strengths Profile.

DEVELOP

By the end of this section, you will be able to

- evaluate situations to determine where you can apply your relationship strengths and where this application is not useful.

Play with Relationship Strengths

This section has three exercises. All of them ask you to consider and get creative about how you see Relationship Strengths, your own as well as those of other people.

PERSONIFYING RELATIONSHIP STRENGTHS

Pretend that each of the items listed in the box that follows is alive. What kind of Relationship Strengths might each have? Make up and assign each item three Relationship Strengths.

Example: Tree—shares (shade, fruit); entertains (changes during each season); is dependable (always in same place, year after year).

> city car pencil bird moon building stoplight refrigerator river song ocean bridge book

FAVORITE CHARACTER'S RELATIONSHIP STRENGTHS

Choose a favorite movie or television show to watch. Select a character to observe, and compile a list of the character's Relationship Strengths as you see them. Explain the ways in which these strengths helped the character cope with adversity or enjoy some time spent with other characters.

APPLYING RELATIONSHIP STRENGTHS

Look at the following three pictures:

- Choose one of the pictures and imagine you are in the picture. Create a story about the picture that involves you using one of your relationship strengths in any way you think it can be helpful. Either write this story in your Strengths Journal or tell it to a partner.
- Find two photographs of you with another person. It should be the same person in both photos. Think of a time you had a conflict with

that person. Discuss or write down everything you can remember about it. Now, choose one of your Relationship Strengths and think about how you could have reached a different outcome by using that strength in the conflict. Write or tell your partner a short story about how things would have been different.

YOUR RELATIONSHIP STRENGTHS

You and Your Friends

- Consider the following scenario and determine how you would bring your Relationship Strengths to the situation. If you prefer, discuss with a partner how you would handle the situation.

You are at a baseball game and your friend has a poor seat. There is a very tall person in front of him. You have waited a long time to see the game. Your other friend is not as interested in the game, because she just found out her dog has cancer. She wants to take some time and talk about this with you. You really value your friendship with both of these friends, and you are excited about watching the game, too.

You and Your Parents

- What are some things that kids say that are guaranteed to close down a conversation with parents? Make a list.
- What are some things that parents say that shut things down? Make a list.

Create some rules that would help make relations between parents and kids better. Decide how you can use your Relationship Strengths to formulate and support some of these rules. Parents and children should discuss the rules with one another.

Develop Empathy

The activities in this section are appropriate for children in grades six through twelve.

For Younger Children:

Teach your young child to develop empathy by having her take care of a plant or a pet. You can also ask her to describe how she feels when she is not having a good day. This will get her thinking about her feelings, which is the first step toward being empathetic.

Empathy is what allows people to live together harmoniously and to work together effectively. Empathy is one's ability to recognize, perceive, and feel directly the emotions of another. Empathy can be characterized as the ability to "walk in another's shoes." It is what enables people to bond with one another, to support and trust one another, and to help one another. The ability to empathize is a necessary skill both for recognizing strengths in others and for knowing how to use one's own strengths to help others. When people learn how to be empathetic, it leads to greater personal openness, mindfulness of others' needs in conflicted situations, improved teamwork, and greater job satisfaction. In the next few exercises you will develop your Relationship Strengths by first finding other people who share your Relationship Strengths and then seeing how you can use your own Relationship Strengths to help others. There are two exercises in this section.

MODEL YOURSELF AFTER A HERO

Several Web sites feature modern-day heroes. One site is www.giraffe.org and another is www.myhero.com. Both sites have dozens of examples of modern-day heroes.

From www.giraffe.org: "Who are Giraffe heroes? They're men, women and kids, and they're from many races, religions and backgrounds—all sticking their necks out for the common good. They're truck drivers, students, retirees, artists, waitresses, doctors, homemakers, business people and teachers.

"Since 1982, the Giraffe Project has found over 900 of them, then told their stories in national and local media, and in schools—inspiring others to take on the challenges they see.

"Giraffes are working on many different issues, from poverty to gang violence to environmental pollution. One element that is common to all of them is that they lead meaningful lives. Win, lose or draw they're living fully, giving their all. They know why they get up in the morning, why they do things that may be scary and difficult but must be done if their cause is to be served."

MY HERO is a not-for-profit educational Web project that celebrates the best of humanity. Its mission is to enlighten and inspire people of all ages with an ever-growing Internet archive of hero stories from around the world. MY HERO uses current Web technologies to provide a unique educational experience that promotes literacy and cross-cultural communication. When you visit this site, you'll see dozens of examples of heroes as well as short films about them.

- Visit both sites and search for a hero who you believe shares some of the Relationship Strengths you have.
- Print out the description of this hero, and in your journal write about the ways in which you'd like to emulate this person.
- Create your own personal hero profile and submit it to the MY HERO Project online.

COMPASSIONATE RESPONSE

- Take a look at the following three photographs:

- What do you feel when you see the people in these photos? Disgust? Indifference? Compassion?
- Now imagine the people in these photos are you. How would you want people to think about you?
- Imagine for a moment that the people in each one of these photos have come to you for something. Given what you have already decided about your Relationship Strengths, make up a scenario in which you use your Relationship Strengths to help them in some way.
- Think of the person you like the least. Now select two or three things about that person that you find the most admirable. Then think of three ways you see those virtues in yourself.
- Describe the most annoying habit of the person closest to you. Think up six ways that you could help him stop the habit. Then think of two creative ways to communicate this to him without hurting his feelings.

A Different Perspective

Meaningful and strong relationships are those that can be sustained and even grow through times of misunderstanding and conflict. Relationship Strengths are needed for people to see past their own hurt and embrace another's perspective. Once you have learned the skill of empathy, you will be on the road to cultivating the ability to put yourself in another person's shoes, and that is how you build trust. These next three exercises are ones in which you can practice seeing situations from a different perspective.

SHIFT THE PARADIGM

With your partner, look at the following three photographs and come up with as many positive captions as you can.

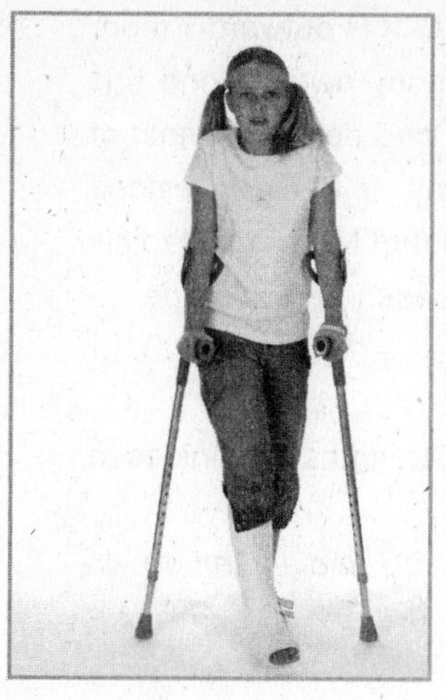

A.

B.

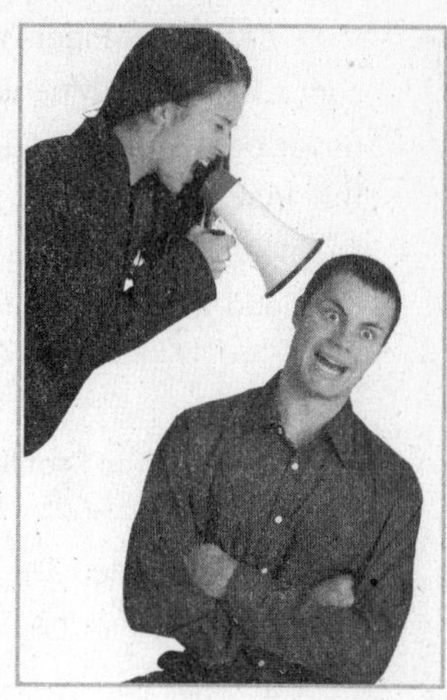

C.

Examples:

For A: They said I would never walk again, and look at me!

For B: Thank goodness, they found that car; there's a million dollars in the backseat!

For C: These new high-tech earplugs need one more test.

RETELL THE STORY

Recall the story of "Little Red Riding Hood." Retell this story as seen from the viewpoint of the wolf, and make him a sympathetic character. You can do this with any fairy tale you wish.

WALK IN HER SHOES

Look at the following photograph and read the facts listed about it below. Your job is to write or tell a story from the woman's point of view, making it sympathetic. Then write or tell it from the man's point of view, and make it sympathetic as well.

The facts: Maggie and Cliff are brother and sister. Cliff is outwardly more successful than Maggie. He gets good grades, wins many awards, and has never been in any kind of trouble. Maggie is asthmatic and demands most of the family's attention. Their parents have missed many of Cliff's milestone events due to Maggie's illness. Now Cliff has discovered that Maggie lied to his girlfriend. Invent more facts and then tell the story from each person's side.

WRAP UP

In your Strengths Profile, list three of your Relationship Strengths and link each one to a goal.

For example: *My Relationship Strength is _______, and I plan to do _______ with it in the next few weeks.*

LEARNING STRENGTHS

EVERYONE LEARNS IN DIFFERENT WAYS. IN ORDER TO LIVE PROductive lives, children must understand how they learn and be able to communicate that to others. How many children fail in school simply because the teacher cannot figure out their respective learning style, and the student lacks the language to explain it? How many adults fail in jobs because they are not able to articulate how they learn, and their bosses do not know how to make simple adjustments so learning can happen? Failure in our society is too often the terrible consequence of an inability to effectively communicate about Learning Strengths or to challenge the dominant learning and teaching styles of the environment.

There are many valid and useful ways to classify and think about learning. Some of the models we've looked at are learning styles, multiple intelligences, and neurological constructs. Educational researchers have come up with many enlightened paradigms for viewing how we learn, and many of them are complementary. The following section is not intended to be diagnostic; rather, it provides exercises that will give insight into the learning styles of children and adults. The more everyone is aware of Learning Strengths, the better advocates we can be for ourselves in the classroom and the workplace.

This workbook does not provide all the answers for the places where you experience challenge. What it does is stops *blaming you* for feeling challenged. Learning Strengths are both the ways in which we *prefer* to learn and the mode in which we learn *best.*

Test grades are just one indicator of what and how well someone is learning. Learning Strengths inform you about how you learn best. As we saw in part 1, the kinds of tests we get in school do not always measure what we really know.

You can do well on a math test in school because you memorized the formulas, but you may know little to nothing about math. Learning Strengths show you the ways in which you learn. You will keep learning for the rest of your life. The person in charge of understanding how you learn outside of school will be you. This information will help you engage your Learning Strengths now and in the future, both at school and beyond.

DISCOVER

By the end of this section, you will be able to

- comprehend your Learning Strengths,
- describe your multiple intelligence style,
- comprehend the way the environment many affect your leaning, and
- communicate what your learning strengths arre to others.

In the Classroom

Although most of the things we learn in life do not take place in a classroom, we spend much of our early lives in schools of one kind or another. The three exercises in this section focus on classroom and school experiences.

MAKING CHOICES, FUNNEL TO NAME

- Look at the photographs and choose the one that best represents the way you like to learn. In your journal, write a few sentences describing it.
- Use your green pen to underline the words in your description that you like the most.
- Fill in the blank: *I am having the most fun in a class or a learning situation when we are* ________.
- *It is fun because* ________.
- If you could do one learning activity in school all day, what would it be?
- *I enjoy this specific thing about that activity:* ________.
- Make a list of your classes or think back to when you were in school. Put a star next to the classes you like/liked and an X next to the ones you don't/didn't like.
- Complete this sentence: *If only more teachers would* ________, *more students would succeed.*

MY PREFERENCES

- Choose one word or phrase from each column that best describes the way you prefer to learn, and write them in your journal.

In groups	Independently
Hands-on	Listening to the teacher
Tests	Projects
Listening	Speaking
Following along	Leading

- Now choose three of your classes, and in your journal write down two activities that you regularly do in these classes.

Name of class: ________
Activities: 1.
2.

Place a positive sticker next to the activities you like the best and circle in red the ones you like the least.

DIGGING DEEPER

Next, you will find a list of random activities. Make two columns in your journal, "Energizes Me" and "Depletes Me." Place each activity on the list in one or the other column, depending on how the activity makes you feel.

- Speak in front of your class
- Research your family history
- Rearrange your bedroom
- Help a classmate come up with a plan to take a year abroad
- Plan a trip to Africa
- Listen to a friend's concerns
- Come up with a new invention
- Attend a religious service
- Share your potato chips
- Rescue a hurt animal
- Join a competition between the students and the teachers
- Make a list of all the things you want to accomplish
- Write for the school newspaper
- Untie a knot
- Decorate the house for a party
- Shop for new shoes
- Conduct a lab experiment
- Win first place in a competition
- Participate in a scavenger hunt
- Map out the quickest way to get to somewhere
- Search for facts on the Internet

In the "Energizes Me" column, choose two of the activities that energize you most and place a star next to each.

In the "Depletes Me" column, choose the two activities that deplete you the most and underline them in red.

- Now, writing in your journal, fill in the following blanks using the starred phrases you chose from the "Energizes Me" column. *I think I would like to ________ because I really like to ________.*

  Do the same for the ones that deplete you most, changing the sentence to *"I think I would not like to . . ."*

- Recall a time you failed at something. What were you doing? Why do you think you failed? What was the specific activity you were not able to do? Why do you think you were not able to do this?

Fill in this sentence: *If only I could have ________, I think I might have experienced more success.*

Things That Affect My Learning

The environment, your attitudes about success and failure, and your natural preferences all affect the way you learn and should be considered when you are developing your Strengths Profile. The next three sections give you a snapshot of the ways these factors influence your learning.

THE ENVIRONMENT

Everyone's ability to learn is affected by the environment she learns in, and everyone has a different optimal learning environment. Some people learn best when the room is completely silent, and they cannot understand how people can learn with music playing in the background. Do you like the room warm or cool? I cannot work well unless I am seated at a desk. In college, my roommate did all her work lying on her bed. When you optimize your learning environment, you increase your chance of engaging your Learning Strengths. Take this short environment assessment to figure out what kind of learning environment works best for you.

Environment Assessment

Choose the statement that best describes which you prefer:

Interaction

- ☐ Being with people who are quiet
- ☐ Being with a pet
- ☐ Being by myself with the door closed
- ☐ Talking or doing things

Sound

- ☐ Absolute quiet
- ☐ Some noise is okay (like cars or street noise)

- [ ] Music helps me concentrate
- [ ] People talking is okay

Body Position

- [ ] Sitting at a desk or table
- [ ] Sitting on the floor
- [ ] Lying on the bed, floor, or couch
- [ ] Standing at a counter

Food

- [ ] I get hungry before lunchtime
- [ ] I cannot miss breakfast or I crash
- [ ] I never eat breakfast
- [ ] I get hungry between lunch and dinnertime
- [ ] I am usually hungry when I get home from school
- [ ] I get hungry between dinner and bedtime
- [ ] I get thirsty a lot
- [ ] I usually don't feel hungry or thirsty
- [ ] Snacking helps me study

Lighting

- [ ] Bright light
- [ ] Low light
- [ ] Sunlight (outdoors)
- [ ] Light from a window
- [ ] The kind of light does not matter

Temperature

- [ ] I get cold easily; I like it warm
- [ ] I don't like the room too warm
- [ ] I like the windows open
- [ ] I like to keep the windows closed
- [ ] I often need my sweater or sweatshirt
- [ ] I would rather wear shorts most of the time
- [ ] Any temperature is usually fine for me

Time

My best time of day, when I have a lot of energy, is ________

My worst time of day, when I have no energy, is ________

Color

My favorite or best color is ______

My least favorite or worst color is ______

Take the answers you checked from each category and write them in your Strengths Journal. Your best learning environment will have all these elements in it. Now think of where you usually study. Are these elements present? What can you do to make studying more comfortable? Enter some of this information in your Strengths Profile. You will work more with the environmental factors that affect your Learning Strengths in the "Develop" section.

MY ATTITUDES TOWARD LEARNING

Some of us have experienced feelings of weakness in learning for so long that our attitudes can get in the way of our ability to use our Learning Strengths to the fullest. We simply do not believe we have what it takes to be successful. The following questions ask you to consider your attitudes about learning and success. You must believe that you have Learning Strengths before you can discover and develop them.

Consider the following questions and mark whether you (1) agree, (2) somewhat agree, (3) are undecided, (4) somewhat disagree, or (5) disagree.

- ☐ I believe I can be the best at something.
- ☐ The people who are the most successful have the fewest number of friends.
- ☐ I enjoy telling people when I have done something well.
- ☐ I would love to win an award at the school assembly.
- ☐ I don't like to win because people will think I am a snob.
- ☐ It embarrasses me to get compliments.
- ☐ It is extremely important for me to do well in everything I try.
- ☐ I am happy doing better than others are.
- ☐ I am constantly struggling to get ahead.
- ☐ I don't care if I don't do well; my friends like me anyway.
- ☐ At school they think I am easygoing.
- ☐ Other people think I work hard.
- ☐ My classmates are/were people who studied very hard.
- ☐ Good relationships with teachers are very important to me
- ☐ I am usually bored.

Discuss your answers with someone. Are you someone who feels afraid to be successful? Is this the result of past failures? What does it take for you to feel good about winning something or being the best at something?

MY LEARNING STYLE

As we saw in part 2, learning can be categorized in many ways. In this section you will find a description and a simple checklist for three basic learning styles.

Three Kinds of Learners:

Kinesthetic learners learn best through *movement* and *manipulation.* They like to find out how things work and are often successful in the labor trades and in the industrial arts, such as carpentry or design. It is estimated that nearly half of all children aged twelve to eighteen are this kind of learner and have difficulty learning in a traditional setting

Visual learners learn by watching. They call up *images* from the past when trying to remember. They *picture* the way things look in their heads. Approximately 40 percent of children aged twelve to eighteen fall into this category.

Auditory learners learn by *listening,* and they remember facts when they are presented in the form of a poem, song, or melody. *Rhythm* and *sound patterns* help them learn.

Learning-Style Checklist

Check the statements that apply to you. The category with the most check marks may be your dominant learning style.

Kinesthetic

- ☐ Enjoy running around
- ☐ Can't seem to sit still
- ☐ Chew on ends of pencils and pens
- ☐ Like to touch things, disturbed by Do Not Touch signs
- ☐ Begin to dance and tap feet when hearing music
- ☐ Enjoy sports and games
- ☐ Get right out of bed in the morning
- ☐ Use gestures to get attention

Visual

- ☐ Turn to the pictures in magazines before reading
- ☐ Drawn to colors and flashy objects
- ☐ Like to watch movies and can sit through them for longer periods of time than other kids
- ☐ Notice things out the window while driving
- ☐ Enjoy reading
- ☐ Like to write
- ☐ Understand maps
- ☐ Read the back of the cereal box

Auditory

- ☐ Like to listen to books on tape
- ☐ Enjoy music all the time
- ☐ Talk through steps of activities involving sequences
- ☐ Ask many questions when doing an activity
- ☐ Interested in listening to others' conversations
- ☐ Volunteer to read aloud
- ☐ Explain by talking
- ☐ Follow oral directions well

For Young Children:

You can observe your child by watching her in play and when socializing with others. Pay attention to how she uses her imagination, looking for any of the themes below.

GROUP 1: KINESTHETIC

- Enjoys building with blocks
- Curious about how things work
- Enjoys puzzles
- Can't seem to stay near you in the store

GROUP 2: VISUAL

- Becomes excited by colors and flashy things
- Reacts to facial expressions like frowning or winking
- Points to pictures in books
- Prefers watching movies or television

GROUP 3: AUDITORY

- Hears music and starts dancing
- Enjoys listening to music
- Enjoys listening to someone reading books
- Picks up vocabulary easily

If you've made the most check marks in the kinesthetic category, here are two things to do with your child:

1. Give your *kinesthetic* child a lot of physical reinforcement in the form of pats of encouragement or hugs.
2. Have many areas around the house specifically for physical activities, such as a mini-basketball hoop or a craft area.

If you've made the most check marks in the visual category, here are two things to do with your child:

1. Keep a big, colorful map on the wall in a prominent room in your house. Make up games involving finding things on the map. Keep track of where you have been using pushpins.
2. Have many books in the house. Give books as gifts to the visual learner.

If you've made the most check marks in the auditory category, here are two things to do with your child:

1. Allow her to listen to music as she does tasks.
2. Buy books on tape and let her listen as she reads along.

Look over all the information in this section.

- What do you think your Learning Strengths are? Add them to your Strengths Profile.
- In what situations do you believe you are able to best use these strengths?
- In what situations do you believe you are not able to use them?
- Come up with two suggestions for a partner about how you think he can use his Learning Strengths in the situations where he doesn't think he can.

DEVELOP

By the end of this section, you will be able to

- use your Learning Strengths to choose activities that will develop your abilities.

Plan for Learning

Your life doesn't just randomly unfold. You usually know the big things that are coming up or what your weekly schedule is. You can plan for the times you will be learning something new and bring your strengths to them if you think ahead a bit. The next three activities will help you plan to bring your Learning Strengths to work or school.

PLANNING TO USE STRENGTHS

- There is not one way to do things. You will enhance your learning when you put your Learning Strengths to use in the subjects you need to learn. Think about the classes or learning situations you'll encounter in the upcoming week. Pick the one thing you are least looking forward to and the one thing to which you are most looking forward. Write these down in your journal. Now choose one of your Learning Strengths. You may be looking most forward to Spanish and looking least forward to math. You may be looking most forward to a research project and least forward to an oral presentation. Now think of a way you can apply your Learning Strengths to both situations.

For example:
"I have a learning strength in writing. I can learn best about something by writing about it. I am looking forward to the research project; I can do all kinds of writing for that. I can also use my writing strength to better learn math. When there is a problem I am not grasping, I can write about it. I can write about all the ways I think the problem should be solved and all the ways I am having difficulty. I can share this with the teacher. I can share it with a friend or a partner. I can use the same technique in science, in foreign language, and in anything I struggle with."

Now it is your turn. Try to think of all the ways you can use your Learning Strengths in your classes. If you cannot come up with ideas, get a partner to brainstorm these strategies with you. Together, you will be able to arrive at a few great ideas for how to put your Learning Strengths to work in all your learning activities. This will not be easy. It will not ensure success every time, but it will begin to help you see how you can volunteer your strengths to help in various learning situations. You will be more successful in your learning situations if you share your strengths with your teachers. If you have a job, you should tell your employer about your Learning Strengths, too.

- Name or describe a positive learning experience that has occurred for you in the classroom.
- Describe a positive learning experience that happened at school but outside the classroom.

PREPARING YOUR ENVIRONMENT

Go back to your environment assessment and take a photograph of the place you study the most. See if the picture is in alignment with the way you like to learn. Draw a picture of your ideal learning environment.

MONITORING YOUR PROGRESS

As students, most of you have weekly organizers you use to plan out your days, but this is a little different. Copy the chart below into your journal or download this from the Web site and use it at the end of each day. This will help enrich your thinking about learning. When you are faced with challenges, you can talk to people about them, but more important, you can begin to focus on talking about the things that make you feel strong in your learning. When you focus on developing your Learning Strengths, you will be more successful in all your classes.

	How my week engaged my Learning Strengths				
	MONDAY	TUESDAY	WEDNESDAY	THURSDAY	FRIDAY
These classes made me feel energized and in the flow:					
This is what we did in them:					
I told my teacher when I was feeling strong (yes/no):					
These activities depleted me:					
I was able to tell my teacher when I felt depleted (yes/no):					
On a scale of 1 to 5 with 5 being fantastic, here is how I rate my day:					
Here are two things I would change if I had the day to do over:					

Parent-Teacher-Student Partnership

The conversation about changing our minds, our schools, and our nation to a paradigm that focuses on strengths begins with parents and teachers. Parents, teachers, and students can begin to form a strength alliance between the home and the school. If you are a parent and use this book at home, share it with your school. Likewise, if you are a teacher and practice these exercises and philosophies with your students, waste no time in sharing them with your students' parents. Here are some exercises to help advance the strength alliance.

- Draft a one-page letter to your child's teacher if you are a parent, to a child's parent if you are a teacher, or to both your teacher and your parent if you are a student. In the letter, describe the Learning Strengths of the child in question in as much detail as you can. Include how he—or you, if you're the student—likes to learn, what things he enjoys doing most, what type of environment works best for him, and what he finds difficult. Share this letter with the person for whom you wrote it. If you are a parent, bring the letter to parent-teacher conferences.
- Read the following case study and answer the accompanying questions.

Yolanda's Day in School: Yolanda is a focused student. She takes everything she does in class very seriously and listens very well to the teacher. She does not like to participate in group activities, and she does not raise her hand much or contribute to class discussions unless the teacher calls on her. Although she completes all her assignments, sometimes her work is not correct. At recess, Yolanda likes to sit in the shade and read. She has a few friends that sit with her, but she does not like to join in the large group activities on the playground.

Given what you know about Learning Strengths, create a learning profile of Yolanda. Ask a teacher or another parent to do the same, and then compare your decisions and insights.

- Arrange for a conference with your child and his teacher during which you discuss only the positive aspects of his or her learning. Bring the *Strengths Profile* to the conference.

Whether or not your child struggles in school, he or she will need his or her strengths to find success, happiness, and fulfillment in the future. Whether through conferences or phone conversations, you should be in touch with *all* your child's teachers, not just the ones whose classes present a challenge. Consider spending more time talking to the teachers in whose classes your child does well. They will provide you with greater insight into your child's strengths and therefore deserve your attention. Many parents of students who do well in school skip the conferences altogether. This will certainly not guarantee that you, your child, or the teachers will comprehend and develop your child's strengths.

Good grades are not a conduit to your child's finding work he loves and relationships that are meaningful. Your attention is. When you go to parent-teacher conferences or call to talk with teachers, ask what your child's strengths are. You may have to phrase the question several ways. You may ask, "What things does my child do that he really enjoys doing?" or "What activities does my daughter feel most successful doing?" Remember, history is not a strength; it is a subject of study. Do not ask the teacher what your child is good at doing; you can figure that out easily. Instead, inquire about what your child likes to do in the classroom. The next question can be, "How is your class engaging my child's strengths?" If the teacher does not know, you can offer to help. Teachers dislike confrontation as much as anyone, so keep in mind that these questions are not meant to be accusatory or confrontational. They are designed to shift the focus of the conversation from weaknesses to strengths.

- Ask to see your child's assessment—which is another word for tests, quizzes, and projects—as these are all the ways a teacher determines what your child knows. Have the teacher show you the way she or he breaks down the components of your child's grade. Is the bulk of the grade based on only one way of demonstrating knowledge? A school that focuses on student strengths will assess your child's knowledge in a variety of ways, not just pen and paper recall. You can ask your child's teachers to assess understanding in a variety of ways and have those different ways count as much as the traditional way. A teacher should be able to explain the way she or he came to grade your child and show you how your child's strengths were reflected in that grade.

LOOKING TO THE FUTURE

I'VE HAD MY SHARE OF CHALLENGES AND SETBACKS, YET I FEEL MY life is strong and meaningful in every way. You could consider me lucky, and to some degree I have been lucky. However, my sense of purpose and fulfillment is more than the result of dumb luck. It is the result of my ability to rebound from setbacks, to take responsibility for my actions, and to plan for future success. I wrote this book because I want to reach as many young people as I can and show them how they can have lives that are exciting and rewarding. There is nothing better than having a passion for your work and a passion for your family. If you have both, you are in the minority. More people deserve to have both. This section offers a few activities to get you thinking about the future and how to keep centered on your strengths so that they will lead the way to the future you deserve. Some of these activities are better done at school, and I have included them here for teachers to consider. I hope that this book will serve as a beginning and that you will add ideas and activities to mine. Strengths are not something you can turn your attention to one day and forget the next. What follows are suggestions for some ways to stay focused on them.

Envisioning the Future

This activity is appropriate for high-school-aged students and some middle school students.

Look over the following list of questions and choose the two you think are the most important. Copy them into your journal using a green pen.

- Who do I want to be in the future?
- How do I decide what I will do for my life's profession?
- What do I do if things are not working out as planned?
- How can I make my best contribution for the longest time?
- How can I make strengths last into my future?
- What do I need to be successful?
- What will make me happy in the future?
- What do I have to give the world?

Now, pretend you are the expert. You are able to offer advice! Pick what you think is the best answer to the two questions and pretend you are responding to all teens in the world asking these two questions. You can either give the advice in a letter or, if you have access to a movie camera, you can make a film of yourself talking as though you are a talk show host. If you do the film, you can upload it to the Strengths Movement Web page, and it will become part of a collection called "Teens Give the Best Advice." You can do this with your whole class or at home as an individual project.

Self-profile

This exercise will help you identify with your best self, something you need to do to engage your strengths.

- To begin, find a favorite photograph of yourself and some of your favorite things. The photo and the items you choose should have sentimental meaning for you. These things will help stimulate ideas about your life.
- Next, use your journal to create a chart like the one below and fill it in as best you can.

	Self-profile	
	POSITIVE QUALITIES	NEGATVE MEMORIES
Elementary School		
Middle School		
High School		

- When done, look at the chart to make some decisions about what parts of your past you want to have in your future. Now go on to try the next exercise.

Mapping the Past and the Future

This activity is appropriate for seventh grade and up.

In this activity, you are going to envision your past and the future in the form of two maps. We'll start by making the map of the past. First, list all the major successes of your life. Then list any significant regrets or mistakes. Take these lists and create a map of the Land of the Past. Make the map as though the events were countries or states. You can use any kind of materials to add color and visual distinction. The biggest successes occupy the largest territory on the map. You can place the mistakes that have most influenced you closer to your successes on the map, rather than off in the distance. It's up to you. Next, you can create a map of the Land of the Future. Incorporate into the map some events you look forward to, as well as what you hope will be the major and significant contributions you will make to realize your future.

Birthday Letter

Write a letter to yourself to read on your ninetieth birthday. This letter should describe who you hope you have become and what you hope to have accomplished. It will describe the life you hope you will have lived. Set it aside to read sometime in the future to see if your priorities are still on target.

Future Portrait

Create a self-portrait, of you as you would like to be seen in the future. This can be made with photographs in Photoshop, drawings, a painting, a collage, or a model that represents you. This portrait will represent all your various strengths. Keep it in a special place in your house. Even if you are not good at art, you can create an image of yourself that speaks to you on some level and then guides you to become the person you envision yourself being.

Strengths Artifacts

Take some time to review your journal. Next, list some of your strengths. Then find one item that you believe best represents each of the strengths you have listed. For example, a pair of glasses might represent a strength at seeing patterns in things, or a rock might represent a strength in being consistent. Keep these objects in a special place. They will become your strength symbols.

Bounce Back

Everyone experiences setbacks. Here are some tools you can use to plan your recovery.

- Name a time when you failed. How did this feel? What did you do to get over the bad feeling? Write about it.
- Have you ever broken up with a boyfriend or a girlfriend? How long did it take you to get over that? In your journal, make a list of three things you remember doing to get over this kind of setback.
- Pick your favorite outfit, the one that makes you feel the most comfortable and alive. This is your strengths outfit. Wear it on days when you feel down.
- Make a list of five songs that get you pumped and make you feel alive. These are your strengths songs. Make several copies of these and tell your friends to do it, too. Swap strengths songs.
- Search the Internet for three funny sites that you can bookmark. When you are having a bad day, spend some time on these sites.
- Create a psych-up plan. This is a written plan for how you are going to get yourself out of the funks you get into when you have a setback. You may use the attached example. If you create this template on your computer, you can import actual photographs of your friends, and add colors, songs, and links. You can keep this template on your desktop and open it whenever you want. I have included a copy in the appendix of what mine looks like. I keep it on my desktop.

My Psych-up Plan

These are my strengths:

These are my strengths songs:

These friends give me the most strength:

This is my strengths color:

Three funny Web sites:

Whenever I feel down, if I ________, I can perk up.

My top three strengths quotes:

IS THIS THE ANSWER TO OUR FUTURE?

YOUNG PEOPLE WHO ARE WORKING ON DISCOVERING AND DEVELoping their strengths now will be more self-aware and self-directed in the future. Parents and teachers who work alongside children in developing their strengths have something significant to talk about with them. Parents can tell their children how they are developing their strengths at work, and children can tell parents about what is happening at school. In this way, strength conversations are a new kind of glue to bond families. These individual conversations might lead to a more collaborative discussion about how to plan the family's week, what a student might do over the summer, or any other decision involving how to activate strengths in the family.

Given some common language, everyone can participate in this process. The activities in this book can also bond teachers with parents. Parents know their children better than anyone else does. They should be in partnership with the schools. We have so many good things to learn from one another. One of the great disappointments of my career is that parents and schools increasingly see one another as adversaries.

The reality is that there is simply no time for blame. Everything is changing, from the way we do business to the way we relate to one another. Schools must change to keep pace with the world. That is a certainty. How they change is up to us. Parents have a vital role to play in the changes our schools will implement in order to remain viable and relevant in the twenty-first century. We all have a shared responsibility to speak up about how our children will be educated; we will do justice to all children by demanding a focus on strengths. As the world speeds up and information expands, bringing out the best in our children becomes an ever-greater imperative. And we all must figure it out together. Strengths are for the future. They never go out of style. They are generative—they keep pace. They will help our children make sense of the hyperreality we find ourselves in today. They will provide meaning for us as we move full speed ahead into a future that we have not yet imagined.

Our schools need strengths not only in concept but also in practice, tightly woven into the fabric of the curriculum and the culture. Now that you know what to do, how can you possibly turn away without doing something? Join this revolution by taking this step. Focus on strengths. It is up to you to do so, and in this practice you will have the power to change the course of history.

ACKNOWLEDGMENTS

The following people played a significant role in making this book possible. I am grateful to each of them beyond measure.

Rick Lavoie, who in the summer of 2006 encouraged me to write this book.

The Purnell School. Dawn Frost: your creativity, intelligence and sense of humor made this book happen.

The Blank Page: Brian and Tania. Gary Douglas. Best Buy, for supporting the Strengths Movement, especially Stacey Boggs, Jeff Peterson and Steve Prather.

From Viking Penguin: my editor, Alessandra Lusardi, whose amazing patience with my scattershot process and her expert advice made this book possible. Molly Stern, whose encouragement and support kept me going, and the whole crew at Viking—the best team for which a writer could hope.

The Marcus Buckingham Company opened so many doors for me. Marcus, for everything—most especially for believing in me. Mike Morrison, for taking it to the next stage. Robert Levi.

My agent, Jennifer Rudolf Walsh, one of the great *real* people and a super star literary agent.

The Siewerts: Pat, Dick, Jake, Christine, Jim, Alysa, and Aniseh.

Laura Dickerman, the best friend a person could have; where others may have envied, you cheered.

Lizapalooza, one of the last great extended families. In the final days of my writing this book, you all visited, ensuring the completion of my work.

My family: Bill, Mark, George, Tim, Fay, Natalie, Matt, Martha, Jeff, Jaxon, Stephen, Marie, Michael, Karen, Dad, Mom—your support and love make me strong. Nick, you are the constant one.

APPENDIXES

Appendix A

MY STRENGTHS INVENTORY: HAT, VEST, SHOES

MY STRENGTHS INVENTORY IS AN *UN*TEST. YOU KNOW ALL THE answers before you begin. This inventory will allow you to take everything you know about yourself and place it in an organized place, kind of like a closet. Your strengths come in so many categories and are always changing and combining with other strengths, and this useful tool will give you a way to group the broader themes. The themes that are chosen here for you are not describing your personality; rather, they describe your preferences: the way you prefer to learn, the way you prefer to relate with others, and the activities you prefer to do.

You are a unique combination of many strengths. Once you begin to try on your strengths and wear them around, you will see that you have the ability to choose which strengths to bring to which activities. To help get you there, the three kinds of strengths in this inventory are likened to items you can pick out of your closet and wear. Learning Strengths are called Strengths *Hats,* because they are the strengths that are associated with your brain, or how you think. Since all people exhibit some degree of each learning style, this *un*test allows you to change your "hat," or choose your strength, according to the task. You may be both a visual and a kinesthetic learner, for example, and when learning a new sport, you may be inclined to put on your kinesthetic hat, whereas while learning about the latest genome, you may desire to put on your visual hat.

Your Relationship Strengths are your Strengths *Vests*. You wear them next to your heart. As with the Strengths hats, your closet will be full of "vests," and there will probably be a favorite that you wear most of the time. However, it will not be appropriate dress for every relationship occasion, and you may choose to put on a different vest at a different time, depending on the situation.

Finally, your Activity Strengths are the things that get you moving down your strength path, so they are referred to as your Strengths *Shoes*. This collection of shoes will be important. You will choose to wear different shoes all the time.

The strengths wardrobe is mix and match. The hats, vests, and shoes combine to create different styles of the strong person you are meant to be. Once you complete the inventory, you can go to Strengths Island in Second Life and meet other people from around the world who share your strengths. You can even dress your avatar up in strengths outfits to get the day going right. Now let's take the inventory and see which strengths suit you.

I. Your Strengths Hats: Learning Strengths

Directions: In each section, rate each statement 1, 2, or 3.

1 = Not like me

2 = Somewhat like me

3 = A lot like me

Logical-Mathematical

- ☐ My room is rarely messy
- ☐ I like directions that are given one step at a time
- ☐ I am good at problem solving
- ☐ Disorganized people drive me crazy
- ☐ When I cook, I measure things exactly
- ☐ I like puzzles
- ☐ I can unscramble letters to make a word
- ☐ I can't begin an assignment until my materials are on hand
- ☐ I need to know there is a right answer
- ☐ I need structure
- ☐ I enjoy fixing things
- ☐ I am frustrated when things don't make sense

Total for Logical-Mathematical ______

Social-Interpersonal

- ☐ I am considered a leader
- ☐ I am concerned about issues that are about people
- ☐ I believe in fighting for a cause
- ☐ I have close friends
- ☐ People often come to me with their problems
- ☐ Parties are one of my favorite things
- ☐ I could see being a counselor
- ☐ I am a "team player"
- ☐ Friends are more important to me than to most people
- ☐ I like to belong to clubs or organizations
- ☐ I like to listen to people's problems
- ☐ I want to work in a career that helps people

Total for Social-Interpersonal ______

Bodily-Kinesthetic

- ☐ I learn best by active involvement
- ☐ I like to do things with my hands, like knit, carve, sew, and build things
- ☐ I can show you better than I can tell you
- ☐ My hobbies are physical
- ☐ I find it hard to sit for a long time
- ☐ I love to dance
- ☐ I enjoy exercise
- ☐ If I am not exercising, I start to feel bad
- ☐ I like to be very busy
- ☐ Hands-on activities are fun
- ☐ I live an active lifestyle
- ☐ I talk with my hands a lot

Total for Bodily-Kinesthetic ______

Auditory

- ☐ I focus in on noise and sounds
- ☐ Moving to a beat is easy for me
- ☐ I love seeing musicals

- ☐ I can tell if someone is singing off-key
- ☐ I play a musical instrument
- ☐ I enjoy making music
- ☐ I respond to sounds
- ☐ I like to listen to books on tape
- ☐ I remember sounds and words after hearing them once
- ☐ I need to have music on to study
- ☐ Musical patterns are easy for me to hear
- ☐ I like to sing and harmonize
- ☐ Remembering song lyrics is easy for me

Total for Auditory ________

Linguistic

- ☐ Foreign languages interest me
- ☐ I enjoy reading books, magazines, and Web sites
- ☐ I like to write letters
- ☐ I volunteer in class to read out loud
- ☐ I enjoy class discussion
- ☐ I keep a journal
- ☐ I read for pleasure
- ☐ Taking notes helps me remember and understand
- ☐ I faithfully contact friends through letters and/or e-mail
- ☐ It is easy for me to explain my ideas to others
- ☐ I write for pleasure
- ☐ I enjoy public speaking and participating in debates

Total for Linguistic ________

Spatial

- ☐ Rearranging a room and redecorating are fun for me
- ☐ Packing the car is something I am good at
- ☐ I can see how things fit together
- ☐ Charts, graphs, and tables help me remember facts
- ☐ I pay close attention to the colors I wear
- ☐ It is easy for me to find my way around unfamiliar cities

- ☐ A music video can make me more interested in a song
- ☐ I can recall things as mental pictures
- ☐ I am good at reading maps
- ☐ Three-dimensional puzzles like the Rubik's Cube are fun
- ☐ I can visualize ideas
- ☐ I have a well-organized closet or workspace

Total for Spatial ______

Now add up your numbers and place your Learning Strengths in descending order with the one that has the highest number at the top of the list. Put these on your *Strengths Profile.*

1.
2.
3.
4.
5.
6.

Remember, to one degree or another, everyone has a combination of all the learning styles. This is simply a way to determine your dominant style.

The table below illustrates ways in which you can use your Learning Strengths to demonstrate knowledge.

VISUAL	Chart, map, cluster, or graph Create a slide show, videotape, or photo album Create a piece of art that demonstrates a concept Draw models; write things down Illustrate, draw, paint, sketch, or sculpt
LOGICAL-MATHEMATICAL	Translate into a mathematical formula Design and conduct an experiment Enjoy logical arguments, reasoning Make up analogies to explain Detect the patterns or symmetry

BODILY-KINESTHETIC	Create a movement or sequence of movements to explain Make task or puzzle cards Build or construct things Plan and go on a field trip Use hands-on materials Enjoy sports, physical games
AUDITORY	Give a presentation with musical accompaniment Sing a rap or song to explain something Identify the rhythmical patterns of a song Explain how the music of a song is similar to something else Make an instrument Memorize by listening to music
SOCIAL-INTERPERSONAL	Talk about yourself and personal qualities Set and pursue a goal to better understand yourself Understand personal values Develop a sense of personal mission Enjoy keeping journals Assess your own work Enjoy self-improvement
LINGUISTIC	Use narrative to explain Debate, discuss, have a dialogue Write a poem, script, story, play, or news article Conduct interviews

II. Your Strengths Vests: Relationship Strengths

Directions: In each section rate each statement 1, 2, or 3.

1 = Not like me

2 = Somewhat like me

3 = A lot like me

Add the numbers and record the total at the end of each column.

Director

- ☐ In a group, I enjoy taking the lead
- ☐ I like that my friends depend on me to plan our fun
- ☐ A lot of our social time happens at my house
- ☐ I enjoy calling everyone and setting a time for events
- ☐ If we don't know what to do, I usually come up with the ideas
- ☐ I can get us through any problem
- ☐ I enjoy leading a group in activities
- ☐ I am ready to help my friends come up with a plan
- ☐ I enjoy helping others complete tasks
- ☐ I can help anyone finish things on time
- ☐ I like telling people what to do, and they want me to
- ☐ My biggest contribution is helping people get things done

Total for Director ________

Nurturer

- ☐ I am a good listener
- ☐ People come to me with their problems
- ☐ I will take care of people who are sick
- ☐ I call up friends if I know they are feeling bad
- ☐ I don't enjoy conflict
- ☐ If my friends are doing things well, I let them know I notice
- ☐ I care about people who are not my close friends
- ☐ I enjoy helping others with their homework
- ☐ I am friends with many different types of people
- ☐ I like babies and small children
- ☐ I have a lot of sympathy for less fortunate people
- ☐ I understand how people are feeling

Total for Nurturer ________

Truth Teller

- ☐ I think honesty is the best policy
- ☐ I have no problem saying what is on my mind

- ☐ I believe good friends should be honest with one another even if it is painful
- ☐ People know that I will tell them the truth
- ☐ I have strong opinions and share them
- ☐ I am not ashamed to tell people about my faults
- ☐ My life is an open book
- ☐ I never tell people what they want to hear just to make them feel good
- ☐ My family asks my opinion on things that are important to them
- ☐ Most things I do are things I feel good about
- ☐ I am able to tell what others are thinking even when they don't say anything
- ☐ Courage is saying what is really on your mind

Total for Truth Teller ______

Appreciator

- ☐ I remember people's birthdays
- ☐ I always thank people
- ☐ I am grateful for my friends and family and show them this
- ☐ I know when my parents' anniversary is
- ☐ E-mail can never take the place of making phone calls and seeing someone face-to-face
- ☐ I am happy to help clean up after the dinner or the party
- ☐ I usually bring my teachers end-of-the-year gifts
- ☐ When someone else drives, I offer to help pay for gas
- ☐ If someone does something nice for me, I always repay the favor
- ☐ I have some teachers who have made a huge difference in my life
- ☐ Mother's Day and Father's Day are important to me
- ☐ I thank my parents when they cook me meals

Total for Appreciator ______

Negotiator

- ☐ I like the challenge of finding the win-win solution for the problem or the deal
- ☐ I like the give-and-take of information, perception of the problem, and desired outcomes
- ☐ I like the thrill of finding that perfect balance between what everyone wants
- ☐ I like problem solving with others
- ☐ I like to get the best deal for everyone
- ☐ I like back-and-forth interaction
- ☐ I like giving people advice
- ☐ I like to make deals
- ☐ I like to think I am logical
- ☐ People come to me when they need help with difficult people
- ☐ I like interacting
- ☐ Most relationship conflicts can end with everyone being satisfied

Total for Negotiator ________

Coach

- ☐ I can always see the good in everyone
- ☐ I help people believe in themselves
- ☐ I believe everyone can learn anything
- ☐ I like to teach people new things
- ☐ I love to see others succeed
- ☐ I cheer on my teammates
- ☐ I will attend my friends' sporting events
- ☐ I don't mind being on the sidelines
- ☐ I believe my friends and family are capable of winning
- ☐ I don't have to take credit for others' victories
- ☐ I know how to motivate others
- ☐ People say I inspire them

Total for Coach ________

Now add up your numbers and place your Relationship Strengths in descending order, with the one that has the highest number at the top of the list. Put these on your *Strengths Profile* in the Appendix.

1.
2.
3.
4.
5.
6.

Remember, everyone has combinations of all the categories. This is simply a way to determine your dominant style.

DIRECTOR	You enjoy taking the lead, and you feel good when people want your direction. In groups, you naturally take the lead, and leadership thrills you. You feel self-worth when you are directing others.
NURTURER	You feel good when you are taking care of others in some way; you enjoy listening to their problems, and you feel important when you can help someone out.
TRUTH TELLER	You feel you play an important role that few people do—you tell the truth and people respect you for this. Although it means you limit your relationships because some people are afraid of the truth, you feel fewer "real" relationships are better than more false ones.
APPRECIATOR	You get joy by showing appreciation for the people in your life; you remember birthdays, holidays, and special occasions. People are grateful for the ways you show appreciation, and your relationships are made strong by your attention and thankfulness.
NEGOTIATOR	You are a peacemaker and a deal maker. You believe everyone has something to gain, and you don't get caught up in petty conflicts. Because of that you build unique trust with the people in your life.

COACH	You are a natural teacher, and people come to you to show them how to do things. You give people confidence and believe in their ability to succeed. You get pleasure from passing on your skills.

III. Your Strengths Shoes: Activity Strengths

Directions: In each section, rate each statement 1, 2, or 3.
1 = Not like me
2 = Somewhat like me
3 = A lot like me

Investigator

- ☐ I like to problem solve
- ☐ I like books with complicated plots
- ☐ I like to see if I can predict how a book will end before I have finished the book
- ☐ I like to fix things
- ☐ I enjoy learning the causes behind the effects
- ☐ I observe things and see patterns
- ☐ I think facts are clues to an overall picture
- ☐ I don't mind losing things; I usually find them
- ☐ There is a reason for everything
- ☐ I like to ask many questions
- ☐ I am naturally curious
- ☐ I love the challenge of making something work right

Total for Investigator ________

Organizer

- ☐ I like to arrange things
- ☐ I enjoy editing
- ☐ My things are very neat
- ☐ I have no problem keeping my school things in one place

- ☐ I have a clear plan for everything
- ☐ I keep an appointment book
- ☐ I don't mind a challenge
- ☐ I can advance many projects at once
- ☐ I see sequences and patterns
- ☐ I am good at most board games
- ☐ I always know what is coming next
- ☐ I can see my way through a complex task

Total for Organizer ________

Verbalizer

- ☐ I prefer to talk on the phone
- ☐ I need to talk through my problems
- ☐ I prefer a discussion more than a lecture
- ☐ I need a job where we are allowed to talk a lot
- ☐ Sometimes I talk to myself as I am doing complex tasks
- ☐ After I see a movie, I need to talk about it to really understand it
- ☐ I am not afraid to talk to strangers
- ☐ I plan by discussing what is happening next
- ☐ I don't mind reading out loud
- ☐ I enjoy singing
- ☐ It is difficult for me to ride in a car in silence with someone
- ☐ I like to share with someone what I am reading in the newspaper

Total for Verbalizer ________

Creator

- ☐ I enjoy art
- ☐ I am able to invent things
- ☐ I have lots of ideas
- ☐ I write songs or stories
- ☐ Brainstorming is fun for me
- ☐ I keep things I made

- ☐ I give homemade gifts sometimes
- ☐ I would like to design my own house
- ☐ I wear outfits that others would not think of wearing
- ☐ Interior decorating appeals to me
- ☐ I rarely follow a recipe
- ☐ If I had a baby, I would give it an unusual name

Total for Creator ________

Collaborator

- ☐ I seek the advice of others
- ☐ I like to work in teams
- ☐ I rarely choose things on my own
- ☐ Two is company, three is even better
- ☐ Whenever I succeed at something, I always share the credit
- ☐ I don't mind sharing
- ☐ I enjoy group work
- ☐ I prefer team sports over individual ones
- ☐ I like family trips
- ☐ I like it when a group of people prepares a meal
- ☐ I enjoy meetings
- ☐ I don't like doing things by myself

Total for Collaborator ________

Explorer

- ☐ I like to surf the Internet
- ☐ I enjoy research
- ☐ I like to try new foods
- ☐ I enjoy fashion
- ☐ I like elective classes
- ☐ The idea of space travel intrigues me
- ☐ I can't wait to get out of my town
- ☐ I see myself in a big university
- ☐ I enjoy science

- ☐ I like to make predictions
- ☐ I think there is a cure for every disease
- ☐ I like to try new activities

Total for Explorer ______

Now add up your numbers and place your Activity Strengths in descending order, with the one that has the highest number at the top of the list. Put these on your Strengths Profile in the Appendix.

1.
2.
3.
4.
5.
6.

Remember, everyone has a combination of all the categories. This is simply a way to determine your dominant style.

INVESTIGATOR	You enjoy activities that allow you to analyze problems and investigate facts. You like to see all the parts and determine how they fit together; you like to research.
ORGANIZER	You like to arrange things, organize things, put like parts together, and make sense of things through their patterns and the order they are in. You like activities in which you can collect things and categorize things.
VERBALIZER	You like activities in which you can talk through things; you get a charge from talking through ideas and talking with others about ideas and events.
CREATOR	You like activities that ask you to make something new and different. You like to be creative; you enjoy design and coming up with innovative solutions. You like to invent things, and you crave originality.

COLLABORATOR	You like to work on teams. You enjoy doing tasks that involve others and like to problem solve in groups. You work best with others, and the tasks that call for multiple perspectives attract you.
EXPLORER	You like to discover new things and explore new possibilities. You look outward and are able to synthesize many different kinds of information. You enjoy making connections.

My Strengths Profile Top Three

LEARNING STRENGTHS (HAT)

I find it difficult to learn this way:	Learning Strengths: 1. 2. 3.	Favorite ways to learn: A. B. C.

RELATIONSHIP STRENGTHS (VEST)

Relationship Strengths
1.
2.
3.

These are my favorite things to do with people:
1.
2.

These are my relationship goals:
1.
2.

ACTIVITY STRENGTHS (SHOES)

Activity Strengths	Activity Epiphanies	Activity Interests

Appendix B

THE AFFINITIES PROGRAM

A GUIDE TO CREATING A SCHOOL ENVIRONMENT DEVOTED TO STUDENT STRENGTHS

INTRODUCTION

THE FOLLOWING PAGES OUTLINE AN ORGANIZATIONAL FRAMEWORK for creating a positive school culture that reinforces everyone's strengths. It includes a four-year high school curriculum that develops strengths at each grade level and teaches students how their strengths will enhance their futures.

As a parent reading this book, you may be inclined to skip the Affinities Program, thinking you do not understand how curriculum is written or thinking that since your children are young, a high school curriculum doesn't apply to your situation. Before you make that decision, consider the following: reading the Affinities Program outline will show you what is possible in schools.

As explained in part 2, families and schools can begin developing strengths in children between birth and eleven years by providing them with rich memories and a variety of activities to explore and by celebrating their innate personality traits. Active engagement in strength identification can begin when children are able to self-reflect, at around age twelve. Although this program is for grades nine through twelve, it could be adapted to work in middle school. In any case, it is important for parents to understand that whichever program a school is using, it will be successful only if it's sustained over time and involves progressive activities that build on one another to form lifelong habits. This requires using a variety of teaching methods to reach all kinds of children. The Affinities Program will show you what that looks like in a school setting.

HISTORY OF THE PROGRAM

The Affinities Program was first conceived and implemented in 2003 by Jenifer Fox at the Purnell School, a girls' boarding school in Pottersville, New Jersey, making the school America's first explicitly strengths-based high school. The mission of the school is to educate young women who have not realized their potential in traditional school settings. Before coming to Purnell, many of the students have been labeled as having learning disabilities. Educators at Purnell work to remove the labels and help the students grow in all areas by both managing their challenges and building on their strengths. Purnell draws its students from more than twenty-eight states and internationally. They come from public, independent, and nontraditional schools such as LD and Waldorf.

Since 1963, the school has graduated girls who go on to achieve wide-ranging academic success. While Purnell students have always had low aggregate standardized scores, the girls have nevertheless been admitted to competitive universities and colleges and done well, many going on to earn advanced degrees. Among Purnell's graduates (many who were told as early as grade school that they would not be able to find success in college) there are news correspondents, teachers, professors, artists, business owners, and real estate agents. Because of the strengths-based environment, one girl, who was told by teachers in her middle school that she could never learn a foreign language, today not only teaches French but is married to a Frenchman and speaks French almost exclusively in her home. Girls who were bullied and put down in other environments come to Purnell to become class presidents, captains of sports teams, and stars in school musicals. Most of the school's twelve hundred graduates attribute their success and satisfaction in life to their positive experiences at Purnell.

Until 2003, the program for that success evolved intuitively. In 2003, Jenifer Fox implemented her Affinities Program as a means of advancing, measuring, and tracking that success and, in doing so, developing a model that both public and independent schools can replicate. In 2005, the program won a Leading Edge award from the National Association of Independent

Schools in the category of Equity and Justice. This distinction put an indelible stamp on the Strengths Movement, signaling that developing strengths is every student's right.

The Affinities Program began as an organizational approach that inculcates the students to a school culture that gives them a sense of belonging and control—the two things most children need to feel successful. In 2007, Purnell began adding the grade-level courses taught by the Affinities coordinator. Strengths-based approaches are not only for students who struggle. All children can benefit from this approach because it gives students a sense of purpose and direction—necessary elements for remaining engaged in learning. Engaged learners are the ones who find success academically and in life.

Purnell is an intentional community. That means that very little is left to chance and in every realm—from the residence halls to the cafeteria—throughout the entire school year, the school has created systems, rituals, practices, and traditions to reinforce the positive and provide community members opportunities for volunteering strengths. This approach heightens the sense of belonging. The journey toward a successful future begins with the belief that every girl has strengths and that she is someone with unique abilities to offer the world. In order for that potential to be fulfilled, the community starts by stating and restating, over and again, its belief in the girls. In this way, students come to experience more than a school; they find a community that supports and cares for them, one that won't give up until they find success.

THE AFFINITIES PROGRAM AS PREPARATION FOR THE WORKPLACE

In the twenty-first century, success in the workplace depends on performance criteria that are increasingly mental and less physical. This shift applies across the board in businesses. For example, in the past, an auto mechanic could learn the job by observing the behavior of other people at work. Today, cars run on computers, and learning through observation is not as useful as technical training. Consider these estimates:

- There are 1,000 words added each day to the English language.
- One week's worth of the *New York Times* provides more information than most people in the 1800s consumed in an entire lifetime.

- Every month there are 2.9 billion Google searches.
- Of today's top 10 most sought after jobs, none of them existed in 2004.
- Technology information doubles every year. This means that the information available to students entering a four-year college will be outdated by their third year.

In an age when information increases exponentially every month and is globally hyper-accessible, where most jobs require intuitive decision-making and mental activities replace physical ones, traditional instruction and assessment (i.e., the teacher demonstrates how to do something and the student who repeats the performance best receives a high grade) is ineffective. The twenty-first century puts a new premium on creative problem solving, teamwork, and collaboration. The Affinities Program was developed with these realities in mind. With so much information and so many options, the people who know their strengths and how to put them to use will be the ones who find success.

The program helps students discover their strengths through reasoning and inventing. Not only do students prepare their minds for effective ways of thinking about problems, tasks, and activities, they also discover the best personal qualities they can bring to those problem-solving challenges.

While preparing the students for participation in the global economy is a real concern for educators, an equal concern is preparing them for a life that offers not only success but also significance. Without an inherent sense of meaning, one's daily activities are simply empty tasks. The value of our relationships and the quality of our work are the two cornerstones on which rest most other measurements of a meaningful life. Ultimately, they are what determine happiness.

WHAT IS INVOLVED

The program sets out a clear progression of lessons and activities designed to unite schools in the Strengths Movement, not just by talking about it, but also by taking action. A survey prepared by the Gallup Organization revealed that fewer than two out of ten people report consistently playing to their strengths at work. *Two out of ten* will not sustain the workforce of the future. This program makes a significant effort toward ensuring that your students are among the two out of ten and that that number grows.

Many of the ideas in this program are new, and some come from other programs to naturally integrate into this strengths-based framework. Most of the activities are simple, and with a bit of innovative thinking they are easy to accomplish. There is an intentional focus on creativity, especially around the activities that require the students to determine how to bring their strengths to teamwork. All the assessments are authentic and are performance or product based. The curriculum contains practices that individual teachers can adopt in their classrooms, but the focus of the Affinities Program is the whole school culture. The culminating assessment, the Presentation of Learning, is a public performance involving community members, business leaders, and outside educators.

When you read the curriculum, you will see that it guides children toward strengths discovery through hands-on, interactive assignments. The curriculum touches on a wide variety of topics organized as a teen's personal journey toward the future. This is accomplished using interactive games, group activities, films, books, field trips, technology, and presentations. The strengths approach presented here prepares children to

- understand a wide variety of ways they can be successful;
- feel passionate about work, given a wide spectrum of career choices:
- think about careers without focusing too narrowly on one kind of job or one topic;
- feel confident knowing what they love to do; and
- know what to look for in life, relationships, and work.

Strength development is an ongoing process that needs to be rich and layered to make any real and lasting change. We can't introduce strengths concepts in one unit of a class as an add-on. For a child to own his strengths to the extent that he can build a future on them, he must rigorously and consistently engage in activities that inspire their growth. The whole school must form a culture that delivers transformative messages.

HOW IT WORKS

The Affinities Program is a four-year curriculum with four interdependent courses, one at each grade level (9–12). At the same time the courses are being taught, the whole school is also involved in events, traditions, and rituals that communicate and build a strengths culture. It is helpful to create several all-school activities that can rotate in and out of the school routine when they begin to feel manufactured. There are some ideas to get you started listed in the sections following the course descriptions. In order for the culture to be transformative for both the students and teachers, there must be evidence of practice in every arena in the school. While the practices change and evolve, there should always be strengths concepts at work in tangible and visible ways to communicate the intended culture in the school environment. Faculty, staff members, and parents can all play significant roles in building a culture of strengths and should be considered in any planning.

Course Components

Each grade-level course divides into units. There are sixteen units total: six in the ninth grade, four in the tenth grade, four in the eleventh grade, and two in the twelfth grade. The units divide into lesson plans designed for sixty- to ninety-minute classes. Each grade level course has twenty-five lesson plans.

You will find the program outline and the grade-level course outlines in this appendix on the following pages. There is a Web site where you can get the rest of the components. The outline is not a lesson plan; it is an overview of what happens in each unit.

www.strengthsmovement.com

The Strengths Movement Web page is an international gathering place for strengths zealots, teachers, parents, schools, and bloggers. On the Web site there is an Affinities Program page on which you will find the following:

- A Resource Guide containing
  - 100 lesson plans to accompany the Affinities Program units,
  - a list of all the games, videos, and activities used in the program and where to find them, and
  - all handouts and work sheets used in the program;
- a student workbook: *Create Your Future, Play to Your Strengths;*
- the Strengths Journal—to accompany the workbook in part 2 of *Your Child's Strengths;* and
- Developing Strengths portfolio folders on the Web.

On the Web site you will also find

- The Strengths Movement in Schools—an international consortium of schools and organizations dedicated to promoting strengths-based approaches. This portal has an idea exchange for teachers and a place for you and your school to sign up and become supporters;
- an OnLine Strengths Community;
- a Portal to Strengths Movement Island in Second Life and Teen Second Life with a calendar of strengths events taking place on the island; and
- a strengths blog "roundup," which is a "reader" for the best of the strengths blogs on the Web.

Affinities Coordinator

The Affinities coordinator is the teacher who serves as point person, motivator, organizer, and coach for implementing the program. That person may also teach classes, coach teachers, and organize events. She is the person who ensures that the program reaches students with a wide range of talents and abilities. This position is described later in this guide.

Scheduling

There are many ways to schedule the program. Purnell School teaches it in a block schedule, opposite a study hall. It occurs one day a week for seventy minutes all year long. The school in Aiken, South Carolina, is teaching it as part of a "Student Success" class. The class meets every day for fifty minutes. One day a week is set aside to teach the Affinities Program as a subpart of the Success curriculum.

A Word About Assessment

Traditional, standardized assessments are ineffective in measuring individual feelings of accomplishment and well-being. Simply put, you cannot measure something completely new with outmoded and ineffective indicators of success. Research is currently under way to discover a method to document the Affinities Program's relationship with improved performance. The goals of the program are affective, and the competencies that result include the students' abilities to find meaningful work and develop positive relationships. Standardized tests cannot measure this success, but this doesn't mean that some measurement cannot be devised. These concepts have proved to be effective in other arenas, such as business. Companies that have adopted a strengths-based approach report increased profit and worker satisfaction. We cannot measure school success the same way, but Purnell School sees improvements every day, and schools that take the initial leap of faith to develop their own Affinities Programs will as well. As schools use this program, people will discover increasingly creative ways to implement and improve it. In this way, it is generative and evolutionary. This is the first step. Welcome to the Strengths Movement in Schools.

Course Outline

Ninth Grade: CONNECTING

PREACTIVITY: DOCUMENT IT

RELATIONSHIPS BY DESIGN

UNIT 1: FOCUS ON FRIENDSHIP

UNIT 2: DISCOVER RELATIONSHIP STRENGTHS

UNIT 3: DEVELOP EMPATHY

UNIT 4: CREATE A MENTAL MODEL

LEARNING STRENGTHS

UNIT 5: LEARN ABOUT LEARNING STRENGTHS

UNIT 6: ILLUMINATION OF LEARNING

Tenth Grade: ACTIVATING

UNIT 7: DISCOVER ACTIVITY STRENGTHS

UNIT 8: VOLUNTEER STRENGTHS TO TEAMS

UNIT 9: WORK WITH AUTHORITY

UNIT 10: DESIGN PROJECT

Eleventh Grade: ENVISIONING

UNIT 11: FIND THE FUTURE

UNIT 12: CHOOSE A PATH

UNIT 13: BOUNCE BACK

UNIT 14: MAKE IT LAST

Twelfth Grade: PROCLAIMING

UNIT 15: GIVE A STATEMENT

UNIT 16: PAY IT FORWARD

POSTACTIVITY: LEAVE A LEGACY

Ninth-Grade Course

CONNECTING

To grow mature is to separate more distinctly, to connect more closely.

—HUGO VON HOFMANNSTHAL

Preactivity: Document It
Unit 1: Focus on Friendship
Unit 2: Discover Relationship Strengths
Unit 3: Develop Empathy
Unit 4: Create a Mental Model
Unit 5: Learn About Learning Strengths
Unit 6: Illumination of Learning

OVERVIEW

Meaningful relationships create meaningful lives, yet it is rare that schools actually teach students skills to promote long-term success in their relationships. As discussed in the book, specific relationship skills will become imperative for success in the future. Today's students need to be prepared to make good choices about how they will spend their time outside of work and with whom they will spend it. They need to understand how to learn and grow from the inevitable conflicts that happen in any relationship. The successful people of the world will find ways to feel empathy for and connectedness to all people they encounter. **Connecting** begins with self-awareness and moves to an understanding of others. **Connecting** teaches the students how they can avoid the aimless wandering around in relationships that leads to so much confusion, conflict, and betrayal. **Connecting** teaches the students how to act when confronted with others who weaken them or cause them to feel depleted.

Connecting Essential Questions

- What events in the past can I use to help make choices about who I am today?
- Who are my friends?
- How did I choose my friends?
- What does it mean when someone rejects me?
- What is a relationship?
- What do I bring to my relationships?
- What can I expect from my relationships?
- How can empathy help me become a better, stronger person?
- How can I understand how others are feeling so I can work best with them?
- How do I learn?
- How can I let others know how I learn so they can help me learn better?

PREACTIVITY: DOCUMENT IT

Behavior is the mirror in which everyone shows his or her image.

—JOHANN WOLFGANG VON GOETHE

Each student answers the following questions. These responses may be voice recorded, filmed, or written in a journal. The most powerful method of documentation will be filming. The responses are to be archived until the final year of the Affinities Program.

Questions:

1. Pretend you are looking into a mirror. Describe the person you see.
2. Name or describe a positive learning experience that has occurred in the classroom for you.
3. Describe a positive learning experience that happened at school, but outside the classroom.
4. Describe your learning style.
5. Do you think one person can change the world?
6. What do you see yourself doing five years from now? Ten? Twenty?
7. Name one thing you are certain is true about yourself.
8. Describe why your friends seek you out as a friend.

At the beginning of the twelfth-grade year, seniors are taped again, responding to the same questions. The students compare and contrast the tapes. The two tapes (before and after) serve as preparation materials for the culminating activity in the Affinities Program: Presentation of Learning that is explained in the twelfth-grade course. They also serve as evidence of progress in self-understanding.

The teacher will have each student keep a Developing Strengths Portfolio. In this portfolio, students store all the activity sheets that come from the course units. The portfolio assists the students in charting their journey to discovering their personal strengths and will be an essential tool in creating their Presentation of Learning. Teachers can use folders, files, or any method of portfolio keeping they feel comfortable using. There is a custom portfolio folder available on the Web site.

RELATIONSHIPS BY DESIGN

Unit 1

FOCUS ON FRIENDSHIP

Fate chooses your relations, you choose your friends.

—JACQUES DELILLE

By the end of this unit, the students will be able to

- IDENTIFY positive traits in themselves,
- APPLY those traits to a significant memory,
- DISTINGUISH between liking someone and friendship, and between friends and best friends,
- COMPREHEND rejection as a lack of energy,
- UNDERSTAND ways in which e-mail, instant messages, and online social networks can help and harm friendships, and
- SYNTHESIZE knowledge from situations outside of class.

The ninth grade is fraught with uncertainty. The students arrive at school apprehensive and anxious about who they are, how they will fit in, and who they are going to become. Most students need immediate help identifying their positive personal qualities. Students' personal lives are enriched when they have positive self-concepts and they are able to understand the ways they can use those to contribute to their relationships. The students who begin acting out in high school usually do so because they have uncertainty about who they are and where they fit in. Ninth graders have the most uncertainty, since they are newest to the environment.

In this unit, the students begin by selecting words that best describe their positive attributes. After choosing three words from a work sheet (found in the Resource Guide), they move to placing the words onto a diagram on the work sheet and using the diagram to describe themselves in positive terms.

Many of the exercises in this course direct the students and teachers to apply interpersonal feelings and abstract thoughts to concrete physical models. By synthesizing the information from the diagram with personal memories, students gain a positive understanding of themselves that they can talk about with others. They practice this outside of class.

This unit moves from developing a positive self-concept to creating a definition of friendship. First, the students distinguish between *liking* and *being friends* with someone. They learn about the qualities that attract people to one another. This information is useful in developing an understanding of how they influence their relationships. Most young people view the successes or failures of their interpersonal relationships as consequences of their personalities rather than the result of actions people take or the energy that exists between people. This unit reframes this understanding, giving the students greater control over their interactions.

In the Resource Guide, there is a *relationship matrix,* which is a hierarchal table that classifies relationships in increasing levels of intimacy, moving from affiliation to unconditional love. The students fill in the attributes of each level of intimacy on the matrix and then discuss the concept of rejection. In this discussion, they learn that when others reject them, it doesn't mean there is something wrong with them.

Next, the students create Friendship Statements that teach them to think about the expectations they have for others and themselves. In this activity, they outline what they are willing to contribute to their friendships and what they expect from friends. Many relationships are conflicted because there are unclear expectations. The students can learn how to examine their expectations and how to articulate them to others. Before making new friends, the students consider what they believe a good friendship entails. They are encouraged to use these as guidelines when selecting new friends. Clear expectations always help alleviate disappointment and aid in negotiating inevitable conflict.

Finally, there is a lesson plan on exploring online friendships and virtual communications to identify ways that e-mails, instant messages, and online social networks can both help and harm relationships. The students discuss their experiences and bring examples of e-mails to read. The Resource Guide outlines an activity in which the students look at real life examples of ambiguous e-mail and instant messages, then discuss what they think the tone and intention of each e-mail is. Using a projector and a screen, the class analyzes different Facebook and *myspace* pages and share impressions about what each is communicating. This discussion concludes by learning what is and isn't appropriate to communicate online. They learn that withholding judgment is important when receiving e-mails and to recognize how hasty decisions and impulsivity can lead to misunderstandings. The lesson plan in the Resource Guide has these discussion guides for teachers.

At the end of this unit, the Affinities coordinator has five essential words from the first activity and the Friendship Statements to keep in student portfolios.

Unit 2

DISCOVER RELATIONSHIP STRENGTHS

> *Every person, all the events of your life are there because you have drawn them there. What you choose to do with them is up to you.*
>
> —RICHARD BACH

By the end of this unit, the students will be able to

- IDENTIFY relationship strengths,
- CREATE a relationship web,
- APPLY Relationship Strengths to a relationship web, and
- EVALUATE situations to determine where they can apply their Relationship Strengths and where this application is not useful.

An intricate web of relationships connects each person to others. Every relationship serves a different purpose, and everyone has innate strengths to contribute to relationships to make them more effective. These are Relationship Strengths. Relationship Strengths have their roots in character virtues. Although the ideal is to develop as many character virtues as you can, the strengths approach recognizes that children come to school with some character virtues that are more developed than others. While people can learn many character virtues—such as compassion, generosity, and forgiveness—some qualities are innate and feel more natural. In developing character virtues, the students begin identifying the ones that naturally strengthen them. They use these virtues as a basis for guiding their relationships. Once their natural tendencies are engaged, many more character virtues or Relationship Strengths will develop.

To initiate the discovery of Relationship Strengths, the students use software such as Inspiration or Inspire Data to create *relationship webs.* Both pieces of software are tools students can use to create concept maps or graphic organizers. Many concept-mapping programs can found by doing an online search. Inspiration can be found at www.inspiration.com. As outlined in the Resource Guide's lesson plan for this unit, the concept maps are used to create a web of all the relationships in which students are involved. This web includes siblings, classmates, grandparents—all the major categories of relationships they have. This web is used to determine specific things the students can do to strengthen each relationship. In the next activity, the students become more specific and identify the things they *consistently* do for their relationships that give them strong feelings of personal pride. Then the students find patterns for the activities that engender these feelings and use them to name their Relationship Strengths. This process is investigative and accomplished through a series of activities found in the lesson plan.

Once the students discover Relationship Strengths, they return to the web and, working in pairs, make decisions about how to effectively apply the strengths to their relationships. Using a weekly schedule that they create in class, they make choices about how much time to spend on any given relationship. Then they complete activities from the Resource Guide to identify situations in which their Relationship Strengths will add value. These activities may include interviewing their friends and family members or creating a calendar to plot out occasions to use their Relationship Strengths. The students also brainstorm plans for how they will respond when their Relationship Strengths are not creating the kind of energy needed to sustain a positive relationship, and they discuss when to let relationships go dormant.

At the end of this unit, the Affinities coordinator adds the Relationship Strengths to the portfolios.

Unit 3

DEVELOP EMPATHY

If your emotional abilities aren't in hand, if you don't have self-awareness, if you are not able to manage your distressing emotions, if you can't have empathy and have effective relationships, then no matter how smart you are, you are not going to get very far.

—DANIEL GOLEMAN

By the end of this unit, the students will be able to

- DEFINE empathy,
- EVALUATE ways in which other people use empathy to enrich their lives,
- EXAMINE role models to see how their Relationship Strengths are used to show empathy,
- DETERMINE ways empathy can be used to turn negative perceptions about other people into positive understanding,
- APPLY empathy to situations in order to seek and offer forgiveness,
- EVALUATE situations with empathy in order to experience gratitude, and
- CREATE an action plan for developing empathy.

Empathy is what allows people to live together harmoniously and to work together effectively. It is what enables people to bond with one another, to support and trust one another, and to help others out. The ability to empathize is a necessary skill both for recognizing strengths in others and for knowing how to use one's own strengths in the service of others.

After defining *empathy,* the students read about "heroes"—other people who have made significant contributions to society by being empathetic. Students can find heroes for this unit at the Giraffe Project (www.giraffe.org) and the MY HERO Project (www.myheroes.org). Both hero projects provide excellent examples of people who have developed exceptional empathy skills. The students also view films from the Little Pearls project (www.littlepearls.org). Little Pearls are free films that inspire empathy and are useful for writing about and discussing how empathy helps build relationships. Students can watch these films and decide what they think the characters' Relationship Strengths are. Then students outline the conditions and attributes they would need to become heroes themselves. The Resource Guide describes these activities in detail.

Next, students learn how Relationship Strengths can turn around negative situations. They view clips from inspirational films that challenge their perspective, and through guided discussions they learn how forgiveness can solve relationship problems. The Resource Guide suggests a clip from the movie *Pay It Forward,* which brings up many issues that hit home for kids today and provokes many positive discussions about how we can respond to what life throws at us. For example, this film addresses forgiveness head-on. The alcoholic mother, Arlene, struggles with the alcoholism and abuse in her own past, holding her mother responsible for all that happened. Her grudge against her mother kept their relationship at a distance until, in a powerful moment in the film, Arlene forgives her mother. The Resource Guide has discussion questions to accompany this clip. Of course, there are any number of films you may find to illustrate this concept.

The virtues explored in this unit are necessary in all avenues of life. Anytime someone encounters conflict, the way to move past it is by being able to acknowledge and to understand another person's point of view and to be able to forgive others for both intended and unintended hurt. Near the end of the unit, students participate in several exercises that challenge them to see situations in a variety of different ways. The teacher uses film clips from unfamiliar movies with scenes in which the characters are involved in obvious conflicts. These scenes are used to practice seeing situations from multiple perspectives. Suggestions for the film clips and discussion questions are noted in the Resource Guide.

The students review their own encounters, recalling one that ended in hurt, confusion, or embarrassment. Personal photographs help students remember times from their past. Although the photographs are not documentations of negative experiences, they can remind students of a variety of experiences not found in the pictures. When students recall a time that ended negatively, they talk with a partner, explaining how the photograph reminded them of an experience and what happened. A work sheet from the Resource Guide helps them imagine what the past conflict would have been like had they used their Relationship Strengths. Students consider the points of view of the other people who were involved in the conflict. This exercise ends with the return to a discussion on forgiveness.

At the end of this unit, the Affinities coordinator will enter the name of the student's hero into the portfolio.

Unit 4

CREATE A MENTAL MODEL

The only way to predict the future is to invent it.

—ALAN KAY

By the end of this unit, the students will be able to

- UNDERSTAND their relationships as systems of interaction,
- CREATE a new mental model representing their relationships as a way to remember how to apply Relationship Strengths,
- APPLY knowledge of different perspectives and creativity to their concepts of relationships,
- UNDERSTAND the design concept of forgiveness and the strategies that make it work, and
- APPLY the design concept of forgiveness to their mental models of relationships to gain new perspectives.

Most students enter ninth grade thinking that each of their relationships is individual and separate from the others. They believe they need to come up with a new set of governing rules to operate each one. However, this is not so. Often, the trouble people have with their relationships is that they have not fully developed a positive mental picture of how the "system" of relationships works, and when one breaks down, they don't know how it can be fixed.

A mental model is someone's perception of how something works. It can be abstract or concrete. People understand and interact with systems and environments based on mental representations developed from experience. For example, when a certain person enters a shoe store, her mental model includes a process in which she looks at several pairs of shoes, and after finding one she likes, she sits in a chair to signal to the salesperson that she is ready to try on shoes. When this same person goes into a store like Payless Shoes or T. J. Maxx, that mental model becomes ineffective because there are no salespeople to assist with the shoes. A road map is a concrete example of a mental model. It represents a system of travel between one place and another. The map serves as an organizational tool. Once the model is clear in our heads, we may no longer need the map.

We have thousands of mental models to represent all the systems with which we interact. We often choose to represent abstract mental models concretely as images, drawings, graphs, or any number of ways to make the ideas more familiar and to make the systems we think about more obvious. The relationship webs that students create are mental models of their interactions with others. This unit expands on that concept.

We would be hard-pressed to interact without mental models in today's world. We construct mental models from our wide range of experiences, and generally they serve us well. They allow us to make complex decisions in the blink of an eye; they allow us to focus our analysis on the difficult or novel portions of a larger issue. Throughout history, a generally accepted set of mental models has governed society's behavior. As we look back, it is easy to recount any number of invalid models that have held back human progress. Consider the mental model of the world as flat. This model most certainly slowed new exploration because people feared they would fall off the edge of the earth if they went too far. When ineffectiveness results from old mental models, we need to create new ones so that people can change their perceptions.

When we share systems with others but have different mental models for that system, there is room for uncertainty and ineffective behavior. For example, in the United States we have a mental model for how to go to the movies. We expect people to be quiet during the movie and remain seated until it is finished. This model doesn't work in Turkey, where people do not whisper when speaking and the movie stops halfway through, sometimes in the middle of a scene, for an intermission.

This unit introduces the idea that relationships are systems for interacting with others and that we have many mental models for how they work. Students will see how conflict happens between people when they are operating from ineffective, different, or outmoded mental models for these systems. They will devise working models of relationships that will have a strong likelihood of resulting in healthy outcomes.

In this unit, students begin by revisiting their relationship webs and then, in small groups, developing metaphors for their relationships as a way to begin identifying their mental models for relationships. For example, some people may use a bank account as a metaphor for relationships, with interactions described as deposits or withdrawals. Relationships can also be represented as clocks, where the hours represent those people with whom the most time is spent and the minutes representing people with whom less time is spent. Other metaphors, such as gardens, the seasons, houses, and so forth, can be used to conceptualize relationships. A work sheet in the Resource Guide helps the small groups come up with these metaphors. Once students agree on a metaphor, the group members each individually interview between eight and ten people outside of class to get information on "Important Aspects of a Relationship" using the following questions:

1. What are the three ways you discover new friends?
2. What are the two most important things to do to keep relationships positive?
3. What determines how much time you spend with other people?
4. What are things that can break a relationship?
5. How do you repair the relationship when it is broken?
6. When do you know a relationship is beyond repair?

After students gather this data, they compile it and discuss people's responses to the questions in an effort to find similar themes or shared concepts for how people interact in relationships. They organize and group this information into graphs or a chart until they have a shared concrete mental model for how relationships work. This mental model will incorporate the data they gathered from the interviews as well as their own beliefs about how effective relationships should work.

In the next part of the unit, students become designers. All good designs are governed by certain principles. One such principle is the concept that a design has a built-in quality of *forgiveness*. Unlike the kind of forgiveness studied in the last unit, this principle applies to *things,* not people. The forgiveness principle assumes that with any material things that people use, there will be an inevitable margin of human error. When a product's design accounts for forgiveness, it has a built-in mechanism that allows users to recover from their errors. For example, word-procressing programs have "undo" functions so people can add back text they accidentally deleted. Software programs that incorporate this feature thus have a built-in principle of forgiveness.

Students will then compare the design of their system of relationships (as represented in the mental models they created) to products that incorporate the design principle of forgiveness. They will do this to deepen their understanding of their relationships as systems, with the goal of learning to become more effective in them. Before they make the comparison, they look at the following common strategies for incorporating forgiveness into designs as outlined in *Universal Principles of Design* by William Lidwell, Katrina Holden, and Jill Butler (Rockport, 2003):

- Good Affordances—physical characteristics of the design that influence its correct use
- Reversibility of Actions—one or more actions can be reversed if an error occurs or the intent of the person changes (e.g., undo function in software)—that is, how actions can be changed or backed out of if things are not going the right way
- Safety Net—device or process that minimizes the negative consequences of a catastrophic error or failure (e.g., pilot ejection seat)
- Confirmation—verification required before a critical action is allowed (e.g., a lock that must be opened before equipment can be activated)

- Warnings—signs, prompts, or alarms that notify of imminent danger (e.g., a road sign warning of a sharp turn ahead)
- Help—information that assists in basic operations

Once students understand these strategies and are able to identify how they are incorporated into products and systems, they think about how their relationships can become more effective if they utilize some of the same strategies. In relationships, the strategies can translate as follows:

- Good Affordances—what relationships are used for
- Reversibility—ways relationships can be changed or backed out of if things are not going the right way
- Safety Net—ways to minimize the consequence of negative encounters
- Confirmation—feedback before taking any critical actions, such as breaking up or cutting off the friendship for good
- Warnings—signs that the relationship is unhealthy or destructive
- Help—places to get advice about the relationship

After discussing how these strategies can work to understand and improve relationships, the students return to the mental models and the metaphors they created for their relationships. The final activity is to build a physical model representing their relationship. The physical model will have at least two of the strategies of forgiveness in its design. The students will explain their models, and the models will be displayed in the school in an exposition format like a science fair. Readings, directions for each activity, and discussion questions are in the Resource Guide in the lesson plans for this unit.

At the end of this unit, the model becomes an artifact in the student's portfolio.

LEARNING STRENGTHS

Unit 5

LEARN ABOUT LEARNING STRENGTHS

To learn anything fast and effectively, you have to see it, hear it and feel it.

—TONY STOCKWELL

By the end of this unit, the students will be able to

- COMPREHEND their Learning Strengths,
- DESCRIBE their Learning Strengths,
- USE their Learning Strengths to choose activities that will develop their abilities,
- APPLY knowledge of Learning Strengths to understanding why they are successful in and enjoy certain class activities more than others,
- CREATE an ability profile based on an understanding of their Learning Strengths, and
- SYNTHESIZE their knowledge of Learning Strengths into a presentation to teach others about them.

Everyone learns in different ways. Students can understand how they learn and how to communicate that to others. How many students fail in school simply because the teacher doesn't understand how he learns, and the student lacks the language to explain it? How many adults fail in jobs because they are not able to articulate the ways in which they learn, and their bosses do not know how to make simple adjustments to facilitate their learning style? Failure in our society is too often the terrible consequence of an inability to effectively communicate about learning styles or to negotiate within the dominant style of the environment.

All students have Learning Strengths. Learning Strengths is a term that refers to how students naturally and most enjoyably receive content and produce a product. There are many valid and useful ways to classify and think about learning. These ways are called learning styles, multiple intelligences, and neurological constructs. Adjusting teaching to engage these various classifications is known as *differentiated instruction* or *multiple teaching and learning modalities*. Differentiated instruction includes individualizing the content, the process, and the product in the classroom.

This unit involves using exploratory stations on two separate occasions, viewing a variety of films, and filling out questionnaires to determine Learning Strengths. The first part of the unit begins with two classes in which the students explore various learning styles based on Howard Gardner's Multiple Intelligences:

- Linguistic intelligence ("word smart")
- Logical-mathematical intelligence ("number/reasoning smart")
- Spatial intelligence ("object and picture smart")
- Bodily-kinesthetic intelligence ("body smart")
- Musical intelligence ("music smart")
- Interpersonal intelligence ("people smart")
- Intrapersonal intelligence ("self-smart")
- Naturalist intelligence ("nature smart")

During the class, students visit a variety of learning stations set up by the teacher. Each station has small activities for students to explore. The Resource Guide describes the stations and the activities in detail. They include a logical-mathematical table where students work to solve puzzles; a visual table where they use paints, markers, or pictures from magazines to illustrate something; and a spatial table where they fit smaller shapes into larger ones.

In the first activity, the students are free to choose at which station they want to work. They must visit at least three stations. As they participate, the teacher makes observations on a form that is provided in the Resource Guide, and the students reflect on their choices, deciding where they felt the most engaged. This class is followed by a meta-cognitive lesson in which the students learn about the various intelligences from watching the educational video *Multiple Intelligences: Discovering the Giftedness in All,* available at www.nprinc.com/mult_int/midg.htm.

The next three classes focus on the eight neuro-developmental constructs as identified by Dr. Mel Levine:

1. Attention
2. Temporal-sequential ordering
3. Spatial ordering
4. Memory
5. Language
6. Higher-order cognition
7. Social cognition
8. Neuromotor function

Using Dr. Levine's constructs as the content, the students participate in another activity using experiential stations. As in the multiple-intelligences exercise, the teacher sets up the stations as described in the Resource Guide, and the students choose which stations they want to explore. At each station, they participate in activities that engage the various constructs. Afterward, they view educational films from the series *Developing Minds,* available on DVD at www.shop.wgbh.org/DevelopingMinds. After the films, the class discusses both the Gardner and the Levine frameworks so students will understand their own Learning Strengths as well as others'. Once the students have a firm sense of their Learning Strengths, they create a Learning Strengths Profile. This profile is included in the Resource Guide.

The profile becomes part of the student's portfolio and is shared with classmates and teachers in a mini-Presentation of Learning. This is where each student in the class creates a five- to ten-minute presentation about their dominant learning styles to share with faculty members, whom they invite to watch their presentation. The rubrics for the presentations are in the Resource Guide.

At the end of this unit, the Learning Strengths are entered into the portfolio.

Unit 6

ILLUMINATION OF LEARNING

Mystery is but another name for ignorance; if we were omniscient, all would be perfectly plain!

—TRYON EDWARDS

By the end of this unit, the students will be able to

- EVALUATE their learning challenges and strengths,
- CHOOSE strategies for using Learning Strengths in classes, and
- CHOOSE strategies for accommodating their learning challenges.

Illuminations of Learning (IOLs) are meetings that happen between a student and a teacher or adviser who has assembled information regarding the student's Learning Strengths and challenges. The information comes from questionnaires that are in the Resource Guide. The student, his teachers, and his parents complete these questionnaires about how the student learns. The responses to the questionnaires are integrated into a learning plan that suggests strategies for managing around his areas of challenge and building on his strengths. Teachers share the plan with the student at the Illumination meeting, and the student chooses which strategies he feels will be the most helpful to him.

One class period familiarizes the students with the concept of Illumination. This is followed with a discussion after viewing DVD examples of other students during their Illuminations. The DVDs, filmed at Purnell School, are part of the Resource Guide. Illuminations of Learning last between thirty and forty-five minutes. Because every girl who attends Purnell School has an IOL as part of the Affinities Program, there is a lot of information about scheduling and school communication available by contacting the school at www.purnell.org. The handouts, Illumination forms, and the DVD example in the Resource Guide will get you started.

At the end of this unit, the students' parents learn about the Illumination, and the Affinities coordinator enters strategies for developing Learning Strengths and supporting learning challenges into the portfolios.

Tenth-Grade Course

ACTIVATING

> *You need to claim the events of your life and make them yours. When you truly possess all you have been and done, which may take some time, you are fierce with reality.*
>
> —FLORIDA SCOTT MAXWELL

Unit 7: Discover Activity Strengths
Unit 8: Volunteer Strengths to Teams
Unit 9: Work with Authority
Unit 10: Design Project

OVERVIEW

In tenth grade, the students are full of energy: emotional energy, physical energy, and mental energy. They become frustrated and bored very quickly when they are not active, so the tenth-grade course is an active one. It is an ideal time for the students to begin to explore their unique Activity Strengths.

The activities in **Activating** give tenth graders a sense of control, freedom, and independence. Knowing strengths is empowering and self-fulfilling if they are put to use.

Parents and teachers are often good at seeing the potential talents in the students. They point them out and then hope that the students will decide to develop them. However, in order for their true strengths to emerge and grow, the students will need to discover their strengths for themselves, because they are the ones who know best which activities make them feel strong. Teachers can assist in this process in a variety of ways using the activities in this section.

Activating has four units. The first unit, Discover Activity Strengths, is the shortest, but it is ongoing through use of a student workbook described in part 3 of *Your Child's Strengths*. The other three units put the strengths to work on teams and in work-related relationships. **Activating** uses these experiences to *activate the feelings of strengths*. **Activating** does not explore team theory or address the development phases of teams. Instead, it puts the students to work and then asks them to reflect on their positive team experiences.

Activating Essential Questions

- What are the activities that make me feel strong?
- How can I repeat those activities in my work and personal life?
- What can I bring to the team to help us win?
- How can I explain my strengths to others?
- What kind of people do I want to work with in my future?
- How will my boss be able to recognize my strengths?
- What qualities will my future boss need to activate my strengths?
- How can I best contribute to a team project?

Unit 7

DISCOVER ACTIVITY STRENGTHS

What makes the engine go? Desire, desire, desire.

—STANLEY KUNITZ

By the end of this unit, the students will be able to

- IDENTIFY their Activity Strengths,
- DESCRIBE their Activity Strengths to others,
- EVALUATE activities to determine whether they will engage their strengths, and
- RECOGNIZE whether an activity is going to be one in which they will be able to volunteer strengths.

For the purpose of the Affinities Program, in order for something to be identified as an Activity Strength it must

- be a verb,
- make you feel good and strong when you are doing it,
- be something that can be transferred to a variety of activities,
- be innate—neither given to you by someone nor removable,
- be used to engage talents, and
- be able to combine with other strengths.

An Activity Strength is something people *do* and feel good doing. Some activities naturally engage an individual's strengths. Other activities are not natural "fits" with strengths. However, a person can learn to see the activity through a "strengths lens" and figure out how to apply strengths to activities that do not seem at first to match up. Contrary to popular belief, the opposite of strength is not weakness—it is depletion. If an activity is not engaging an individual's strengths, and thereby energizing, the activity is depleting.

To discover strengths, students will

- DESCRIBE a specific activity that makes them feel strong,
- IDENTIFY (name with precision) which part of that activity is causing the feeling of strength,
- REVIEW the events and activities that they are engaged in during a typical school week to recognize other activities that cause that feeling of strength,
- REFLECT with a partner, and
- CREATE new opportunities for practicing their strengths.

The unit begins with an introduction to a student workbook called *Create Your Future, Play to Your Strengths,* available at www.strengthsmovement.com. This workbook becomes a reference throughout high school for ongoing practice. The first unit begins with in-class completion of the section on "family activities," followed by a discussion. Next, students learn how to funnel the descriptions of their activities and separate them into discrete parts to reach a core understanding of precisely what makes a person feel energized.

The students examine their activities across a week using the funneling activities found in the section on Activity Strengths in part 3 of *Your Child's Strengths* or the Affinities Program workbook that is found on the Web site. Next, teachers choose film clips from contemporary films and characters from literature to illustrate ways in which the main characters use strength both positively and negatively. The students analyze characters in the films and books to begin to reflect on their own actions. The lesson plan for this unit is in the Resource Guide.

Unit 8

VOLUNTEER STRENGTHS TO TEAMS

Talent wins games, but teamwork and intelligence wins championships.

—MICHAEL JORDAN

By the end of this unit, the students will be able to

- UNDERSTAND the purpose of teamwork,
- ANALYZE tasks and roles of team members,
- PREDICT which of their strengths will help the team,
- APPLY prediction of strength to a variety of situations,
- REFLECT on what it feels like to activate a strength,
- CREATE strategies for dealing with team conflict,
- EVALUATE their own roles in bringing their strengths to the team, and
- APPLY gratitude at the end of a project.

Most teachers ask the students to complete their work independently. But consider this: how many times while in the workplace will someone who is solving a problem be asked to return to their office because the company demands that he solve his problem on his own? This is misguided. Teams of people working together accomplish most of the important work in both businesses and families. Schools must begin to focus on teaching the students how to participate on teams. Most team development models lay out negative and positive roles that people play on the teams and then show the participants how to avoid undesirable behaviors. While this may be a useful exercise, it is a reflective exercise best left for *after,* not *before,* a team works together. A better method is to set the people up for success before they enter the team. A focus on "what not to do" never clarifies what a person is capable of doing for the team.

This unit focuses attention on all the ways the students can bring their strengths to teams. It is not the be-all and end-all for learning about teamwork; rather, its focus is on learning how to do it *right* by getting in and trying. The more the students are engaged in solving real-life, team-oriented problems in all their other classes, the more effective these units will be.

Prior to this unit, the students will have identified their respective Relationship, Learning, and Activity Strengths. Now it is time to take those strengths and apply them to teams. Teamwork often requires many roles. The students are most successful when they have a hand in selecting the role they play based on an understanding of how that role is a good match for their strengths. The classes begin with the students examining a list of team roles and then choosing one to take on based on their strengths. Each "role" has an accompanying set of team expectations about how the team member will act. These expectations are included in the Resource Guide. After choosing a role, in a short written assignment the students defend why they believe their strength will work well in their chosen role. The Affinities Program uses the following team roles:

- Leader and Organizer
- Coach and Empathizer
- Innovator and Designer
- Implementer and Communicator
- Detail and Follow-up Agent

It is important for the team to discuss each of the roles in order to reach a common understanding about their importance. It is equally as important that teammates recognize that roles are not *in*dependent of but rather *inter*dependent on group dynamics. Next, there are class discussions about how to choose roles and ways to allow individual strengths to be expressions of the interdependent team.

PUT THE TEAM TO THE TEST

For the next two to three classes the students play an interactive class game, Putting Your Strengths to the Test. This game tests their assumptions about roles and strengths. It introduces several simulated problems that require team solutions. Players choose roles and then follow steps as described in the simulation description. This game can be found in the Resource Guide.

For example, one of the problems describes a family reunion with people flying in from all over the country. A severe storm blows through the area, causing flight delays and cancellations and messing up the yard where two days of picnicking and barbecues are to take place. There are interpersonal struggles that factor into the event—family hopes and anxieties surrounding the event are high even before the storm. The team's task is to make the reunion as positive an experience for the family as they can.

The students choose roles and determine which Relationship, Activity, and Learning Strengths they can bring to it, then follow the directions about what tasks they are to complete. Every team member participates in forming group goals and agrees to adhere to them. The main activity of the game involves a group meeting, where the team creates a plan to address the problems.

PLANNING FOR CONFLICT, ESTABLISHING AGREEMENTS

Effective teams are committed to working from mutually agreed-upon ground rules. Every member of a team has to accept the purpose of the team and its goals and objectives. Without mutual understanding or shared purpose on the part of team members, any team will find success difficult, if not impossible. Diverging from topics, not having an agenda, or lack of planning are examples of things that keep a team from being effective. By establishing mutually agreed-upon ground rules, team members are able to keep focused on strengths.

The next part of this unit involves watching a film of a team at work. Good examples of teamwork can be found in the movie *Apollo 13,* when the spacecraft is having trouble and the team on Earth has to come up with a way to get them home. Other examples can be found in sports films in which the team has to overcome great odds to win.

These examples allow the students to reflect on their own process. Next, the students write Conflict Strategy Statements by first brainstorming, then making a web of all the possible kinds of conflicts that may come up on teams. After creating the web, the students write team agreements for how they will respond when faced with conflicts. These agreements can include anything from seeking third-party mediation to preestablishing a "parking lot" protocol (a strategy that involves hanging up a large sheet of paper outside the room, and when conflicts or questions arise, students write them on the paper and "park" their concerns for later, when there is time to address them systematically. In this way, the teacher can see what is brewing as well as help out without the students having to stop everything and confront the issues. This strategy works with minor conflicts that can wait or that need time to simmer). The Conflict Agreements must come from the students.

This exercise

- builds team trust by agreeing beforehand that conflict is expected and does not have to break the team apart, and
- allows team members to be proactive about conflict, the first step in becoming active agents in solving the problem.

APPLYING GRATITUDE

The final class in this unit is about the ways in which gratitude can benefit teamwork and relationships in general. Often overlooked as a tool for building effective performance, gratitude can help teams feel confident about coming together again. In the class on gratitude, the students begin by discussing how their team was effective. They discuss ways to offer support, praise, and thanks to one another. Finally, the students discuss the general concept of gratitude and look at the places in their lives where they can enrich their relationships by showing that they are grateful for other people's efforts.

Unit 9

WORK WITH AUTHORITY

By working faithfully eight hours a day, you may eventually get to be boss and work twelve hours a day.

—ROBERT FROST

By the end of this unit, the students will be able to

- COMPREHEND how a boss can be a partner and an ally,
- PREDICT situations in which their own strengths will assist the boss,
- UNDERSTAND better the give and take in an employment relationship,
- EVALUATE an organizational scenario and comprehend the big picture in order to empathize with the boss, and
- CREATE an "ideal boss" profile.

Job satisfaction, performance evaluations, and career progress all depend on the ability to manage relationships effectively with the leaders and bosses in organizations. People begin forming their thinking about their relationships with authority figures early in life, when parents and teachers are the first role models of authority. High schools do little to teach the students how to think about these important relationships, and often the students simply react to authority—for better or worse—in the same ways they did with their parents and teachers. The Affinities Program includes this unit on authority as an opportunity for the students to learn how they can bring their strengths to these relationships as well as how to look for styles in future bosses that may match their strengths. Not all bosses and leadership styles work for all people. The students who know what to look for beforehand will choose a job in which the leader has a style that they feel allows them to work best, or they will recognize the need to adjust their own style to be accommodating to the boss's.

This unit begins with a discussion about students' attitudes toward authority figures. A case study from the Resource Guide illustrates the politics that can take place in the work setting. The students discuss how they can use their strengths to contribute to the boss's leadership challenges as described in the case example.

Next, the students put themselves in the position of the boss using You're the Boss, a fun game that puts the players in a number of positive and negative work situations in which they have to be the boss. (This game is available at www.franklinlearning.com.) The simulation helps the students empathize with bosses by actually becoming one for a while. The students then reflect on how a positive or strengths approach could improve various game situations.

Through the case studies and the game, the students learn what the big picture means in an organization. They consider where their strengths might contribute to meeting an organization's goals.

As a synthesizing activity, the students list five types of organizations that spark their curiosity. They ask "bosses" at different levels (managers, CEOs) to come and participate on a panel to answer the students' questions about ways in which the boss would engage employee strengths in their organizations. They also ask about their managerial and leadership styles. After the panel leaves, the students reflect on what they saw and heard. To end the unit, the students create an authority profile, describing the kind of boss they would like to work for in the future. This profile includes five questions they think are essential to ask in an interview to determine if the style of the boss will enable them to bring their strengths to the job.

Finally, the students create profiles for future bosses and interview volunteers from the community to see if their expectations of bosses match up with the strengths they can bring to the job. This step involves a field trip to local businesses. Many business leaders are looking for ways to contribute to their local schools. The students travel to meet business leaders onsite to experience what a real interview feels like.

Unit 10

DESIGN PROJECT

Originality is the essence of true scholarship. Creativity is the soul of the true scholar.

—NNAMDI AZIKIWE

By the end of this unit, the students will be able to

- APPLY their strengths to work on a team,
- CREATE a project that will engage their strengths,
- BRAINSTORM ideas with a team to arrive at a decision,
- EVALUATE their strengths as used on a team, and
- APPLY all team strengths to think innovatively about learning.

The unit focuses on creativity and innovation. By this time in the course, the students need opportunities to practice their strengths to further synthesize their knowledge. In this unit, students form teams and design projects that teachers in other classes can use. Once teams are assembled, the students work through the steps previously learned in team development (choose team roles, decide strengths, make working agreements and conflict statements).

Next, the students choose from three options for designing their project based on IDEO Method Cards, a deck of cards displaying fifty-one design methods used by IDEO, an international design firm. The cards are used to spark new ideas and push through mental barriers. These are available for purchase at www.ideo.com.

The fifty-one cards are divided into three categories: "Learn," "Look/Ask," and "Try." After dividing the cards into the three categories, the students read all the cards and then choose a category they want to work with. Each card describes a method that IDEO has used to invent an innovative new design. The students choose one of the methods to design their own projects. For example, student groups might develop a project for a science class, for an art class, or for a math class. Here is an example of a project students created using the card:

Jim has strength in fixing things. He loves the feeling he gets when he puts things together and they work just right. He has an interest in science, so he joins the team that is working on developing a science project for another class. Jim is a hands-on learner who feels a sense of pride when he helps people solve problems. Because of these strengths, he chooses to take on the role of Project Implementer & Communicator. He tells his teammates this is his choice and why.

The team decides to pick one of the "Try" cards to brainstorm a project. They read all the cards and choose the Scale Modeling Card. On the back of this card it says, "How: Use scaled, generic architectural model components to design spaces with the client, team and/or users. Why: This spatial prototyping tool provides a way to raise issues and respond to the underlying needs of different stakeholders."

The chosen IDEO card says that IDEO used the method to design home office products and used scale models to allow people to explore various use scenarios. The students will read this card and then brainstorm ways in which a science class might use this method—building a scale model—to learn something new in class. The Affinities class students write a thorough plan for the science teacher to consider, and pitch the project idea to the teacher to see if he will use it. If the teacher accepts, the Affinities class students will design the problem for the science students.

This unit is intentionally fuzzy at the onset, forcing the team to work through a certain amount of frustration and uncertainty in order to arrive at something original. The activity in this unit stretches students' thinking and is easily implemented by following the accompanying lesson plan.

Research demonstrates that all real talent develops when people stretch and practice just beyond the comfort zone. To get the students there, teachers must go there first. This unit stretches everyone. Its activity falls outside of the traditional curriculum, yet also connects back to it. In the end, the students gain enormous pride when they see their projects realized by other students in the school.

Eleventh-Grade Course

ENVISIONING

We don't receive wisdom; we must discover it for ourselves after a journey that no one can take for us or spare us.

—MARCEL PROUST

Unit 11: Find the Future
Unit 12: Choose a Path
Unit 13: Bounce Back
Unit 14: Make It Last

OVERVIEW

The eleventh grade is a time for thinking ahead. Life begins to get a little more serious for the students at this stage. Either the students can become anxious about their futures or they can embrace the possibilities in positive and decisive ways. **Envisioning** is affirmative, exploratory, and hopeful. It is about *inventing* the future. The students invent their futures based on what is good, meaningful, and effective in their past and present experience.

Envisioning uses all three kinds of strengths as the determining factors for future choices. For the students, the future must be framed with respect to the here and now, because ultimately it is *themselves* they take with them into the future. Too often schools frame the future as "the real world," making it seem as though when students get there they will somehow miraculously transform into different people. That is simply not true.

Many of the activities in **Envisioning** focus the students on various narratives. They write about their memories and then about who they want to be in the future, imagining the kinds of jobs, homes, and relationships that allow them to use their strengths. The students learn the importance of bouncing back from defeat. They practice gratitude as a virtue that will enable them to keep attracting positive experiences. **Envisioning** is a serious course with a serious goal: a well-lit path and a map. In effect, this course asks the students to believe, to envision, and then to act.

Envisioning Essential Questions

- Who do I want to be in the future?
- How do I decide what I will I do for my life's profession?
- What do I do if things are not working out as planned?
- How can I make my best contribution for the longest time?
- How can I make strengths last into my future?
- What do I need to be successful?
- What will make me happy in the future?
- What do I have to give the world?

Unit 11

FIND THE FUTURE

If stories come to you, care for them. And learn to give them away where they are needed. Sometimes a person needs a story more than food to stay alive.

—BARRY LOPEZ

By the end of this unit, the students will be able to

- CONNECT their past to their future,
- CREATE a personal narrative describing their past,
- SYNTHESIZE a personal narrative from the past and a narrative of their future, and
- CREATE a representation of their narrative, highlighting their strengths.

Storytelling is in our genes. Stories are powerful teaching and learning tools. They are the vehicles that carry emotions from one person to another. Stories teach us about our past and help us create our future.

This unit is about the power inherent in telling stories. Students use their own and others' stories to envision their futures. They learn that how they experience themselves today will determine who they become. The future is more than just a place with a college major or a job waiting for them; the future is where they will continue to evolve with purpose and find greater meaning.

In this unit, students become autobiographers, writing about both their past and their future. Lasting eight to ten class periods, the unit culminates in an exhibition of student stories called "Composing a Life."

During the initial class, the students free write about their past using personal photographs and artifacts to stimulate their memories and generate ideas about their lives.

Next, they share their writing with a peer editor and choose the most important points. Then they use the writing to create a profile of themselves that encompasses all three years of high school. They refer to their Strengths Portfolios when making the profile. With a partner, the students select the things about themselves they want to ensure will also be true about them in the future. Then they write a story set in the future in which they are the main character.

In the next class, the students write letters to themselves on their ninetieth birthdays. This letter describes who they desire to become and what they hope to have accomplished. It describes the life they want to live. Following that, students make "future self-portraits" that are made from photographs, drawn, or painted.

Following the portraits, students find an item to represent a few of the strengths they have identified up to this time. It may be something like a pair of glasses to represent their strength at seeing patterns in things, or a rock to represent their strength in being consistent. They will use these objects to create metaphors for their strengths, and then they will use the metaphors in a creative writing project about them.

Finally, students put all these pieces together into a visual presentation in which they are the featured character. These presentations make up a school exhibit called "Composing a Life."

Unit 12

CHOOSE A PATH

Your work is to discover your work and then with all your heart to give yourself to it.

—BUDDHA

By the end of this unit, the students will be able to

- ASSESS jobs for the kinds of skills, abilities, and strengths that are called for in performing the role,
- CONNECT interests and strengths to a variety of jobs and possibilities,
- DEVELOP a list of careers to look into more closely,
- LEARN earning potential and job outlooks for various careers,
- CREATE an activities and abilities chart,
- DEFINE their ideal job,
- PROFILE the kinds of people they would like to work with,
- INTERVIEW people in jobs that seem appealing,
- CREATE a superior résumé, and
- MAKE a plan to move from school to work.

Most people end up spending over half their waking lives at work, yet statistics show that fewer than two out of every ten people report actually playing to their strengths at work. Work is not only our focus while we are on the job, but often what we think and talk about outside of the workplace. The more a job uses a person's talents, abilities, and strengths, the more opportunity the individual has both to enjoy that work and to make a meaningful contribution. Using Relationship, Learning, and Activity Strengths at work will create the difference between fleeting success and lasting significance.

This unit uses a variety of resources. In particular, classes use the *Occupational Outlook Handbook* (OOH), developed by the U.S. Department of

Labor, an Ability Explorer and Quick Job Search, all published by Jist Works at www.jist.com. These resources are statistical and provide mountains of useful information for the students, giving this unit a research focus.

The students view *Exploring Your Career Options* (www.jist.com). It is an excellent DVD for students in grades six through twelve. Real students describe their interests, what they like to do, and what they are good at doing. Then these students use their insights to identify occupations and careers for exploration. Teachers should emphasize that in the work realm, adults' greatest happiness and biggest contributions come when they choose professions that utilize their strengths. Following the DVD, the students complete an Ability Explorer, which is an excellent interest and talent inventory that focuses on activities rather than roles or general job categories.

Next, the students form groups according to the results of the Activity Explorer and complete a chart found in the Resource Guide to help them decide what general field they are interested in. Once they choose a broad category, they use the OOH to choose between five and seven jobs to explore. They fill out a job-preference profile (found in the Resource Guide) that compares their choices in the following areas:

- education/degrees needed
- salary outlook
- nature of the work
- working conditions
- job outlook
- related occupations

Students use the job-preference profile to give an oral presentation of the top five jobs they chose and explain how they think these jobs will activate their strengths. The students consider what they expect from life compared with what they desire to do. For example, a student may decide she wants to be a professional dancer, so she looks up the job outlook for that profession. The OOH will tell her how many jobs are expected to be open in the next five to seven years, what sort of professional training is required, and what the salary projections are. After gathering these facts, the students describe the kind of lifestyle they expect to have. They consider the kind of car they wish to drive, the type of place they want to live, the sorts of leisure activities they desire, and the costs involved. From this introspection, they create life budgets that determine how much they'll have to earn to live in the manner they desire. They compare these requirements to the sorts of jobs they seek and the projected pay of their chosen jobs. If the job ignites their passion and plays to strengths but doesn't match up with their expectations, then they are encouraged to seek other jobs that play to their identified strengths *and* meet their requirements, or they will have to make decisions about what they are willing to sacrifice. This activity is enormously important for young people who are encouraged to both follow their bliss and make compromises to live in ways that satisfy their desire for material things. It also helps them recognize what they have to accomplish to reach their dreams and fulfill their desires.

Finally, it is important for the students to get out and visit the workplaces they have chosen to test their assumptions. The students contact local businesses and arrange tours and interviews with people in their jobs. All the students participate in several of these field trips. When this part of the unit is complete, the students set up an internship for summer between the junior and senior year.

Unit 13

BOUNCE BACK

> *I postpone death by living, by suffering, by error, by risking, by giving, by losing.*
>
> —ANAÏS NIN

By the end of this unit, the students will be able to

- UNDERSTAND planning as a tool to recover from setbacks,
- APPLY plans to setbacks,
- DISCOVER ways to recover from setbacks using signaling, and
- CREATE definitions of happiness and create a concept map for happiness.

Things do not always go as planned. Setbacks are inevitable, and young people will greatly benefit from knowing how to recover when others ignore their strengths or when they feel they have veered off course from feeling good about what they are doing with their time. This unit focuses on the art of bouncing back from setbacks. In addition to learning how to be persistent and to plan properly, the students investigate laughter, play, color, and song as "bounce-back medicine." Finally, the students will see the importance of having a partner be there for them when they face setbacks. An important class in this unit is the class on happiness. Setbacks and disappointments are prime opportunities for people to consider what they are really looking for.

During the first class, the students will learn three steps to recovering from setbacks:

1. Become aware of your attitudes toward setbacks, obstacles, challenges, and failures.
2. Create at least three options. Avoid the win-lose scenario by creating additional possibilities for personal fulfillment.
3. Make a plan for doing things differently.

The students will read case studies as a way to coach others through setbacks. They will apply the steps to the case studies.

Next, the students think about ways they can keep themselves from getting into slumps or funks. The class outlines several ways that the students can use song, color, laughter, and play to bounce back from frustration. For example, the students choose a few motivational songs. These songs get them psyched up. They should keep these songs close by, even create a special list on their iPod for these songs. Teens are accustomed to indulging in sad, melancholy music when they feel bad; and happy, upbeat music when they feel good. This exercise is about creating a new habit of going right to the upbeat music when experiencing a major or even a minor setback. This will help them reprogram their thoughts.

The students select signature colors, the ones that make them feel the strongest while wearing them. Then, when they buy new clothes, they can be sure to buy ones in their strength color. They also select a *strengths outfit*—the clothes that make them feel the most powerful and positive while wearing. When a setback occurs, students can listen to their psych-up list and wear their strengths outfit.

Next, they research several funny Web sites on the Internet, doing a search with the terms "funny Web site" and "jokes, cartoons." Bookmarking these sites allows for handy access when things go badly. Students choose a psych-up partner, someone who will be there when they feel down, not to listen and empathize, but to inspire and encourage them to get back on track. In class, students work at developing key phrases and words of encouragement they would use as psych-up partners. Next comes the making of "psych-up plans." These are fun plans that include humorous ways for students to redirect their feelings when feeling weakened or depleted. They are outlined in the Resource Guide.

The unit ends with a focus on happiness. The teacher makes the distinction between pleasure and happiness, and students participate in a discussion about short-term versus long-term happiness. In pairs, the students create Happiness Mission Statements that they can take wherever they go, reminding them that discovering strengths and happiness are lifelong pursuits. The class reads excerpts from the book *Happier: Learn the Secrets to Daily Joy and Lasting Fulfillment* by Harvard professor Tal Ben-Shahar.

Finally, the students develop a Happiness Map. They create a definition and make a road map to happiness. This activity uses the concept of happiness in a representational diagram, and the students come up with goals to attain their own happiness in life. All the happiness activities are described in detail in the lesson plan for the unit in the Resource Guide.

Unit 14

MAKE IT LAST

And the day came when the risk it took to remain tight in the bud was greater than the risk it took to blossom.

—ANAÏS NIN

By the end of this unit, the students will be able to

- DETERMINE what things take them off their strengths path,
- DECIDE what they can control and what they cannot control in their lives, and
- APPLY strategies to their lives to keep them on their strengths path.

By this time, the students are aware that a strong life is possible. This unit gets the students to think about how to stay on their strengths path and to make predictions about what might take them off it from time to time.

The unit begins by viewing two short videos from the MY HERO Project at www.myhero.com. The first is the short film *Perseverance,* a true story about Liz Murray, a homeless girl who overcomes her difficult childhood to win a scholarship to Harvard. The second film, *Rashid Peters: Peace Activist & Music Hero,* is the true story of a peace activist and music hero from Sierra Leone. Both videos are examples of people who have persisted in reaching their goals in life despite difficulty and setback. After watching the videos, the students discuss what it is that enabled the people in the films to keep on pushing through to success.

Next, the students share their own stories about their personal journeys, focusing on where, when, why, and how they veered off their strengths paths in the past. Each student has a peer coach who will listen to her story and help her identify the themes, situations, and feelings that precipitated veering from the strengths path.

Together, student and peer coach will develop a summary of time off the path. After reviewing his or her strengths portfolios, each partner helps the other create an individualized plan for staying on the path. This plan is completed and then turned into a hypermedia document for the students to keep on their computers. The complete hypermedia document contains each student's path, with links to

- strengths affirmations,
- lists of activities that strengthen,
- things to do to bounce back, and
- a profile of a "future self."

A good hypermedia program to use is eZediaQTIA (www.ezedia.com). This software is good for making student portfolios that have a variety of media components. It is inexpensive and easy to use. At the end of this unit, the students will have created their Strong-Life Profile and a hypermedia document for their computers to keep with them forever.

Twelfth-Grade Course

PROCLAIMING

Your time is limited; so don't waste it living someone else's life. Don't be trapped by dogma—which is living with the results of other people's thinking. Don't let the noise of others' opinions drown out your own inner voice. And most important, have the courage to follow your heart and intuition. They somehow already know what you truly want to become. Everything else is secondary.

–STEVE JOBS

Unit 15: Give a Statement
Unit 16: Pay It Forward
Postactivity: Leave a Legacy

OVERVIEW

The students in their final year of high school are the leaders. What they do, think, and say become the predominant values of the culture because all the other students watch them and follow their lead. A school focused on strengths will capitalize on this year as a way to inform the rest of the school about what matters. **Proclaiming** is a course in which the students make plans about how to leave their lasting impressions on the school. It also gives students the opportunity to reach beyond the school walls and with their presentations show the outside world who they have become. **Proclaiming** is a time to express gratitude and appreciation. The students bring it all together and then move on in the course.

Several major activities happen during **Proclaiming**. The students prepare final summative statements called Senior Speeches. They write their college essays and synthesize all their learning from the four years into a Presentation of Learning that they give to an audience of people from both inside and outside the school. They also make personal plans for ways they can advance the Strengths Movement and demonstrate gratitude.

Proclaiming Essential Questions

- What have I learned that is of enduring value?
- How can I make a difference to my school?
- How do I want to represent myself to colleges and universities?
- What can I say about my journey?
- How can I thank people for believing in me?
- What does it mean to be human?

Unit 15

GIVE A STATEMENT

Do the hardest thing on earth for you. Act for yourself. Face the truth.

—KATHERINE MANSFIELD

By the end of this unit, the students will be able to

- SYNTHESIZE their knowledge into a powerfully written college essay and
- SYNTHESIZE their knowledge into a dynamic, moving Senior Speech.

It is time to pull it all together—all the learning, understanding, and experiences from their classes, relationships, and activities of the previous four years. Up to this point, the courses and the school atmosphere for the senior class were about taking in the culture; this unit is about giving back to the school.

The unit begins by reviewing the Strengths Portfolios, Strength Viewer, and the workbooks. Then the students complete several prewriting activities to begin their college essays. This process can take anywhere from three to five classes, until the students have given it their best effort. The students who finish this process before others will work as peer editors.

The next few classes focus on preparing the students to give senior speeches. A full class is spent developing public-speaking techniques, and another on brainstorming speech ideas and ways to enhance the speech through use of props, media, or activities. Lesson plans for these classes are included in the Resource Guide.

Following the initial preparations, the students write their speeches. The purpose of the speech is to leave a lasting impression on everyone in the school and to explain what values they take away from their high school journey. It makes sense to allow the strongest, most innovative students to speak first as an example for the rest of the students. It is important that these speeches not be like Academy Awards acceptance speeches. The students are discouraged from publicly thanking individuals. When this is allowed, the speeches become too personal to serve any teaching purpose. The students should keep their speeches focused on the positive journey and relating it in a universal way.

A collection of all the speeches makes a nice artifact that can be used in a variety of ways. All the speeches can be printed and placed in a book for auction as a class fund-raiser, or they can be videotaped and used by students as graduation gifts to their parents. You can invite parents to Senior Speeches, making the event an important rite of passage.

Unit 16

PAY IT FORWARD

Gratitude is the fairest blossom which springs from the soul.

—HENRY WARD BEECHER

By the end of this unit, the students will be able to

- UNDERSTAND gratitude as a universal virtue,
- COMPREHEND how gratitude can work in their daily lives, and
- APPLY the understanding of gratitude to a commitment to following strengths.

Gratitude adds a final touch of energy to strengths education. This unit is about learning to cultivate gratitude in one's life in order to use strengths to make a significant impression on the world.

The unit begins with the students reading several quotes about gratitude that are provided in the lesson plan for this unit and choosing the one with which they most identify. They make signs out of the quotes and hang them up around the school.

The students next write letters of gratitude to the people they feel helped them make it though high school. These letters are to be very thoughtful, detailing exactly how their relationships contributed to the development of particular strengths in the student.

Next, via the Internet the students research the ways that people around the world express gratitude, demonstrating that gratitude is a universal principle. The class makes Gratitude Resolutions, and every evening they write about the specific things for which they feel grateful and come up with an action item for expressing that gratitude. Student Gratitude Resolutions become part of their Presentation of Learning.

POSTACTIVITY: LEAVE A LEGACY

No legacy is so rich as honesty.

—WILLIAM SHAKESPEARE

By the end of this unit, the students will be able to

- SYNTHESIZE all the information they have gathered in the four years of the Affinities Program,
- CREATE a multimedia, multimodal presentation of their learning and their strengths, and
- EVALUATE their own presentations and those of their classmates.

A personal journey . . . a significant contribution . . . a member of a family . . . a partner . . . a friend . . . a teammate . . . a coach . . . Each student has traveled through four years, and in that time each has become more of the person he or she was always meant to be. Now it is time for the students to leave a legacy—to determine what mark they will leave on the school—and to bring it all together in a final Presentation of Learning.

The Affinities Program culminates in the Presentation of Learning. The students spend most of the second half of their senior year preparing these presentations in their Affinities Course.

At the start of the unit, the entire twelfth-grade class determines an essential question around which they frame their presentations. Such questions may include the following:

- What does it mean to be human?
- How can we make happiness last?
- What is the purpose of life?

This is the time when the students once again view the original videos from ninth grade. First, the students rerecord themselves answering original questions. Next, they review the tapes from their ninth-grade year. This is a fun and exciting time for the students, reminding them how much they have grown. The tapes begin the brainstorming process for how they are going to construct their presentations. After choosing the essential question the whole class will focus on, the students create presentations that answer the question in the most personal and unique way they can. They bring their activities, their understandings of their strengths, some examples of their work, and stories about their experiences to answer the question. It is important that the presentations be more than just summaries of strengths and units learned in the Affinities courses. The students should end up with a new idea, a new direction, or an original contribution to the future. The presentations happen near the end of the academic year, before a panel of evaluators. The panels consist of educators from other schools, local businesspeople, teachers, and students from other schools. The school administration works with the Affinities coordinator to determine who to invite to participate on panels. These presentations can last for several days at a school and are one of the major rites of passage for the students. The logistics involved in setting up the visitors and arranging the schedules is indeed a challenge, but a happy, workable challenge for someone with a strength in such matters.

Each presentation lasts twenty minutes. Once the presentation is finished, panel members have ten minutes to ask the students questions. The students may also invite special friends and family members to the school to view their presentations. The school should involve as many other students as possible in active roles in the presentations: they may guide tours, introduce presenters, staff refreshments and information booths, film the presentations, and so on.

The four courses are now complete, and the students are ready to move on, knowing what their strengths are and how to use them to live a fulfilling life.

Get Started

CREATING A STRENGTHS ORGANIZATION

This guide for schools can serve as a window into how all organizations can create a culture that builds on and leverages people's strengths. Many of the suggestions can serve as stepping-off points for your own creative ideas.

THE AFFINITIES COORDINATOR

Wanted: Full-time Affinities Coordinator

JOB DESCRIPTION

1. The Affinities coordinator is the person responsible for keeping the Strengths Agenda moving forward in the school. While it is everyone's responsibility to be involved in the strengths-based culture, it is the role of the Affinities coordinator to work with school leadership to keep the strengths agenda hot.
2. The Affinities coordinator acts as a liaison between teachers and students. She helps teachers come up with units, activities, and assessments that involve using students' strengths and affinities. She reviews curricula to see if there are opportunities

for weaving in student talents. For example, if the students are learning word problems in their algebra classes, the Affinities coordinator may point out the students' mutual interests, which the math teacher can incorporate as topics of her word problems. Likewise, the English teacher may assign reading and writing lessons around student interests.

3. In conjunction with school leadership, the Affinities coordinator works to advance teacher and student strengths by paying attention to the overall culture and proposing whole school activities.

The Affinities coordinator

- acts as the major liaison between the parents and the school regarding student strength development;
- gives presentations at faculty meeting to keep everyone up-to-date on the latest discoveries regarding student strengths;
- coordinates all activities of the Affinities Program, including Presentation of Learning; and
- works with the school college counselor.

PROFESSIONAL REQUIREMENTS

In a public school, the Affinities coordinator can be a certified English teacher; communications teacher; guidance counselor or learning specialist; or a paraprofessional who fits the personal requirements.

PERSONAL QUALITIES

- Above all else, the Affinities coordinator must see life in a positive way.
- She must see the possibilities inherent in challenges.
- She will need strength in creative implementation.
- She must have strength for innovation and drive, wanting to have a program that permeates the life of the school.
- She must have strength in communication, because she will have to communicate equally well and clearly on all levels.

- The Affinities coordinator must have strengths as a self-starter and for self-advocacy.
- She must have an uncompromising belief in the strengths and talents of the students and be able to rally others to see those qualities in them.

ALIGNING THE TEACHERS

Teachers can focus on strengths in two ways. They actively engage with school leadership to identify and develop their own strengths, and they collaborate with the Affinities coordinator to help the students identify and grow their strengths.

Staff and Faculty Strengths Development

School leaders can engage adults in the community in discovering and developing their own strengths the same way they do for the students. A number of tools can help adults identify some strengths, including an online assessment from the Gallup Organization and a character strengths assessment called VIA (www.viastrengths.org). The themes these assessments identify are initially energizing. They bring people together in a "strengths conversation," but this is not enough. Ultimately, people must continue to practice the art of using their strengths to keep the process evolving.

Go Put Your Strengths to Work: 6 Powerful Steps to Achieve Outstanding Performance by Marcus Buckingham offers active and concrete ways for teachers and employees to refine their strengths identity and make the practice a habit in the workplace. All employees and teachers can be given a copy of the book, meet to determine strengths goals, and then follow up with yearly conversations about their goals. Teachers are encouraged to join the online strengths community and write to it after each conversation. For example, a teacher may write, "I find myself feeling very strong when I sit down and plan for things. Over the past few days there have been many interruptions in the schedule, and I have felt jolted a bit from my strengths path because of this." Other adults in the community are able to log on and add their own reflections as well as read and respond to those of others.

Strengths-Based Performance Evaluations: How to Manage the Weaknesses

When all components in the school are in strengths-based alignment, it reflects in the performance assessment system for both employees and students. There are several strengths-based models for encouraging employees, but many of them leave the administrators asking, "*What if the employee is screwing up? How do we manage their strengths if they are displaying weaknesses?*"

Most negative attitudes in schools, in both adults and students, are the result of inadequate evaluation and grading systems. Many times administrators use the evaluation system to document poor performance or to correct perceived weaknesses in their teachers. This is problematic insofar as the entire performance evaluation system is perceived as a weakness indicator rather than a strengths indicator. Conversely, many administrators feel wary about a system that focuses on strengths because they feel it will not address real concerns about substandard employee performance.

The assumption of the Affinities Program framework is that traditional methods of evaluation are ineffective in achieving the improvements they are designed to enact. In our experience, speaking very broadly, there are four kinds of workers, as outlined in the following table:

Strong Performer Positive Attitude	Strong Performer Negative Attitude
Weak Performer Positive Attitude	Weak Performer Negative Attitude

The administrator's greatest challenge is in evaluating the strong performer with a negative attitude. Poor employee performance usually falls into two categories: *unprofessional behavior* (such as arriving late for work, not showing up for meetings, inability to get along with others), which is an accountability issue, and *task performance* (classroom management skill, ability to create meaningful lesson plans, content-area knowledge), which is a matter of professional growth in that area. Put another way, *unprofessional behavior* has to do with basic job requirements across all fields, and *task performance* denotes the behaviors that are specific to the industry. In schools, the task-performance-related topics include interaction with the students, constructing lesson plans, conversing with parents, and so on. Every industry has corollaries.

Confusion happens when these categories converge. In this strengths-based model, the accountability issues are managed by the Accountability Team. The Accountability Team is selected by management or, in the case of schools, the administration. Each employee chooses who will act as his supervisor on the team. Team members are responsible for holding these employees accountable to minimum job expectations. This responsibility works two ways: the employee is responsible for upholding the expectations, and the team member is responsible for ensuring the employee knows what the expectations are. This is different from a *task* performance evaluation.

In some ways, the Accountability Team's role is a communications one. Each organization will have to outline what minimum job expectations are and make sure they're made clear to all employees. These can include, for example, adopting attitudes such as acting in respectful and positive ways, or showing up for work on time and meeting deadlines. Team members alert their employees of changes in schedules, duties, and the like. The key is that the expectations are clear to all employees. When employees fail to meet basic requirements, an Accountability Team member schedules a meeting with the employee to discuss the reasons behind the behavior. The conversation is based on *benign assumptions*. A benign assumption is the belief that there is a good reason the employee is not living up to basic minimum expectations, and it is the Accountability Team member's role to figure out the reason and assist the employee in finding a solution to the problem. The benign assumption model does not initially assume that the problem is the fault of the employee. The problem may reside with the team member's failure to communicate the expectation. Let's look at an example where the employee is having trouble.

Suppose an employee is chronically late for work or meetings. In the traditional system, the employee would face a reprimand. If the employee is lucky and has a compassionate supervisor, the employee will first have a conversation with the manager to figure out what is going wrong. However, this is not always the case. Usually, someone notices the behavior, and often a conversation between managers ensues. It goes something like this:

"Did you notice Mary is late every day?"

"Yes. What are we going to do about that?"

"Well, the handbook is clear that they need to be on time."

"How many times are they allowed to be late?"

"I don't know. Look it up."

The handbook usually has a policy about tardiness, and it is the manager's responsibility to enforce this policy with the employee. By the time the manager gets the courage to talk to the employee, a certain amount of anxiety and aggravation has built up. Thus the conversation begins with the assumption that the employee is irresponsible. The reprimanding conversations are usually brief and point to the policy.

In the strengths-based model, it is incumbent upon the supervisor to assume that the employee needs some assistance and that the employee actually wants to do a good job but something is getting in the way. The assumption is also that the problem might reside with either the employee or the Accountability Team member. The Accountability Team member's job is to discover the obstacle and help remove it before resorting to *negative assumption.* This is the philosophy of the program, and it becomes a transparent shared value of the organization. In the case of the chronically late teacher, she may have an unreliable car and is therefore at the mercy of public transportation. The conversation should expose the issue, and together the team member and the teacher can brainstorm effective ways to ameliorate the problem.

When both the Accountability Team member and the employee are open and accepting of responsibility, and both show genuine interest in finding solutions, this ongoing intervention method helps resolve minor problems before they build up to cause bad feelings. Organizations waste far too much energy on negative assumptions. The benign assumption saves time and builds relationships. If it turns out that the employee is not living up to expectations, no time is lost figuring this out; it reveals itself in the first or second meeting. If upon the initial meeting the employee becomes defensive or argumentative, the team member knows that a different kind of intervention—one that is more evaluative in nature—is required.

With regard to *task performance,* the assumption is that every employee wants to learn and grow, and it is simply a matter of teaching the employees the right things in the right increments to allow them to realize their greatest potential. If an employee is not able to perform tasks with the ability needed by the school or business, then it will be the manager's job, not the Accountability Team member's job, to provide training. If, given training opportunities, the employee is *not open* to growing and learning, the matter reverts to an accountability issue.

On the other hand, if the employee is *not able* to learn how to do the tasks required for his success, he has a strengths conversation about the match between employee strengths and the needs of the school or company.

A STRENGTHS-BASED CULTURE IS INDIVIDUALIZED

At its core, the Strengths Movement is about celebrating diversity and the strength that the individual brings to the team. In all strengths-based organizations, individuality will be a central value, and the policies and procedures will reflect the commitment to individuality. In schools, staff and faculty members are treated as individually as the students, with particular attention and accommodation given to their strengths and learning styles. This is not to say that people are not responsible for the well-being of the community. People's strengths do not matter if they can't be put to good use in the service of others. A focus on an individual's strengths should make him more responsible to the whole community, and this should be an explicitly stated value in any organization that focuses on strengths, such as "*Your* strengths are needed for *our* success."

Here are some other ways to recognize individuality:

- Celebrate individual milestones. Birthdays and anniversaries are cause for recognition and sometimes celebration. Staff and faculty members are given complimentary days off to go to their children's graduations or to attend special family events. When there are family deaths, the community rallies to help individuals through their time of grief.
- Hold "Gratitude Parties," to which each guest brings five thank-you notes to colleagues they may have neglected to thank. Gratitude is encouraged at all levels of the organization.

- Have employees take learning styles profiles so employers can be aware of their Learning Strengths. Review job descriptions with this information in mind, asking employees in what ways they believe their job challenges their learning style.
- Understand that many adults learn differently from the traditional method and accommodate where necessary.

INFUSING THE CULTURE

Teamwork Is the Best Way for the Students to Volunteer Strengths

Project- and problem-based learning work best to support developing strengths because students work on teams, and the tasks and problems they are involved in are similar to those found in the world beyond school. The students should be encouraged to take risks and try new roles on teams. This may result in some failure, and if it does, accurate self-assessment and reflection regarding the breakdown can mitigate a poor performance grade. Schools have to become places where students are able to experience and learn from failure without harsh penalty.

The Students Participate in Assessments of Academic Progress

To engage students in learning, they must be part of the process of assessing their own work. A strengths-based school may hold student-led parent-teacher conferences and allow student participation in the form of comment writing about their work. This will help the students begin to identify areas where they do and don't perform well. During the conferences, the students tell the teachers and their parents how they used their strengths in the class and where they both succeeded and failed at this. It is important that the students show actual work during this discussion to provide concrete evidence for their work analysis.

Recognize More Than Grades as Indicators of Achievement

It is critical to focus more on learning than on grades. This new focus can be demonstrated in places like an academic awards ceremony, at which students are recognized both for achievement and for growth and persistence. These latter awards should be as prestigious as the achievement awards. Schools might also develop awards—such as for generosity or for tackling challenges with humor—that reflect achievement in Relationship Strengths. These awards will affirm the school's high regard for all aspects of student development.

THE SCHOOL ENVIRONMENT IS INTENTIONAL

Communities are powerful in their ability to relate values and norms. Every community has a culture, whether it is intentional or not. Strengths-based programs can intentionally pump positive messages about people throughout the entire organization, holding everyone accountable for communicating the messages, as well as including everyone in the benefits of the messages. The ideas in this guide give the whole community an opportunity to participate and to feel the positive results.

One class, a few teachers here and there, a unit once in a while, a project, a sign on the wall, none of these things by themselves will have a transformative effect. For a school to fully embrace the power of knowing and working in your area of strengths, it needs to be all the things mentioned in this guide simultaneously. That does not mean you have to go out and do them all at once. The point is to try many things, and when they work, keep using them until they stop working. If something doesn't work, waste no time in ending it and trying something new.

Some Ways the Whole School Can Participate in Strengths

- Make a Strengths Statement as you would a mission statement. Frame this document and hang it in areas of importance around the school.
- Have the students create artwork that is representational of student strengths and display the work in a "Strengths Gallery."
- Have the students create an online strengths blog. Have one student be the strengths blog moderator. The students can log in daily to report on times when they were using their strengths to capacity.
- Highlight strengths on bulletin boards around the school.
- Start a "positive rumor mill," which sends out "rumors" about people that highlight their strengths.

- Highlight one student and one employee a week by making a poster, such as an "employee of the month" poster, on which you showcase their areas of strength.
- Have the students choose songs that make them feel the way they do when they are playing to their strengths. Choose one student's song a day to play in the hallways or in the dining room.
- Set up discussion tents on tables where the students congregate; use the tents as discussion starters or mental reminders of the strengths of the other students.
- Create an Affinities Wall, a special place in the school highlighting student strengths.
- Arrange an activity on Second Life Strengths Movement Island.

CREATE STRENGTH OCCASIONS

SOME IDEAS

- Have "Dress to Feel Your Strongest Day." On this day, the students wear the clothing that they feel their absolute best in. Share with others why the outfit was chosen.
- Have a strengths-song time-out. During a stressful time, tell the students to bring their strengths songs, then stop everything and have everyone take three to four minutes to listen to his or her song. Watch everyone become recharged.
- Hold a Strengths Story Assembly, where there is an open microphone and people are encouraged to get up and tell their stories of when they initially discovered their strengths.
- Have everyone come up with something to fill in the blank: My strength in ______ is like ______.

Example:

My strength in creating ideas is like a pinwheel. When they join, they all start spinning around, and it's entertaining.

- Have everyone bring in that thing that represents his or her strengths. Everyone can talk about this throughout the day.
- Invite groups from other schools to come, and have the students give them a "strengths tour" of your school, pointing out all the

ways that your school has become a positive environment, focused on developing strengths.

STUDENT PROJECTS TO SUPPORT STRENGTHS IN LEARNING

SOME IDEAS

Have the students

- create short films about their strengths,
- design board games that have to do with strengths,
- create outdoor competitions for people of many strengths to participate in, and
- develop a strengths logo for your school to identify it as a School of Strength.

For school publications,

- have a "Spotlight on Strengths" column in the school newspaper;
- feature in the school magazine a monthly story of a success someone had while using his or her strength;
- have a parent's strengths featured in each publication;
- report on stories of local businesses involved in strengths; and
- have the students present the school program to local community members and announce the event in a local paper.

A FINAL WORD ON SCHOOL CULTURE

For our purpose—that of strengths education—to infuse means to gradually, but firmly, fix something in someone's mind. Culture is the sum of all that is communicated through the language, symbols, rituals, traditions, and values of any group of people. It is entirely possible to infuse any school culture with ideas about strength and thereby create hope for a better future. The whole school must evolve in concert for the culture to be one that transforms the people who enter it.

PARENTS AS PARTNERS

Parents are the school's most powerful partners, and they should be encouraged to focus on their own strengths as well as their child's strengths. When parents are working alongside their children at developing strengths, they have something significant to talk about. Parents can tell their children how they are developing their strengths at work, and children can tell parents about what is happening at school. In this way, strength conversations are a new kind of glue to bond families.

Here are some things the school can do to include parents in the strengths agenda:

- Highlight parents' strengths in the school newspaper or newsletter.
- Start a book club to discuss *Your Child's Strengths;* invite both teachers and parents to be part of the group.
- Organize the school's volunteer opportunities by categories of different strengths.
- Hold a reverse-conference day, where parents are invited in to tell the teachers what they have discovered about their child's strengths.
- Have a wall or bulletin board that displays family posters that students make with their parents to represent the strengths of family members.

QUESTIONS AND ANSWERS

Where can a traditional school with little flexibility fit this program into its overall schedule?

The Affinities Program is not an add-on program. Nor is it a program with courses that are easily categorized. Some of the classes appear to be service-learning classes, others character education, and some seem like art classes. The course is designed to complement other disciplines, not replace or fit into one. The Affinities Program is a twenty-first-century program, so it will not fit neatly into the twentieth-century schoolhouse. If you want to start this program, first you have to decide that its benefits will be felt throughout the school, in the students' work and beyond—in their lives past school. The best place to begin is to figure out how every student in your school can take one class for between fifty and ninety minutes once a week. Then gather your teams and work it in as if the future of your students depended upon it.

Once you read this curriculum, share it with the parents at your school. Hold meetings and ask this question: What is most important for us to do in the twenty-first century so our children are not left behind? Take your questions and your proposal for implementation to the school board level.

How do we note a program like this on school transcripts?

Your school profile should outline the details of the program so college admission counselors see the class as a plus. There are many colleges with strengths-based programs. You should consider contacting them to ask for their advice as to how they would want a course like this noted on the transcript. Colleges and universities are beginning to see human development and emotional intelligence as factors commensurate with the importance of traditional academic success.

How much will it cost to implement a program like this?

The Affinities coordinator is a salary cost, but many schools have positions that can combine with this one. A Learning Specialist, for example, can sometimes play both roles in an independent school where there are fewer learning disabled students. Otherwise, the materials cost will be less than that of implementing a new textbook.

How will the program affect our scores on tests?

The Affinities Program is designed to have a positive impact on tests designed to measure critical and divergent thinking. If followed, it should boost test scores that test for intuitive ability, emotional intelligence, and creativity in problem solving and conflict resolution. The course is designed to enable the students to improve all those skills.

This all sounds like a good idea, but it seems too much to implement.

The beauty of the Affinities Program is that, unlike other curriculum reforms, teachers do not need all-school training, nor do they need to alter their individual methods. The courses and the Affinities coordinator take care of all that. Within five years of implementing the program, all members of the school community will see such positive results that they will not want to return to not having the program in place. However, if after five years people think it is not working, all they have to do is cancel a class. There is a very low risk factor in implementing the program and a very high risk factor in not implementing it.

I want this in my school, but my principal would never go for it. He would think it costs too much. He is not a big fan of change. What do I do?

We need to take a hard look at how we measure "cost" in schools. The cost of not doing the program far exceeds the cost of doing it. That cost is measured later, when people are miscast in jobs, when businesses spend as much time turning over employees and training them as they do moving ahead. The cost is precious time wasted in depression and other clinical maladies and in a general sense of loss of direction. If these facts do not compel your principal, then get parents involved. School leaders often listen to groups of parents.

Can We Do Some of the Program but Not All of It?

Something is always better than nothing, but the program is not designed for individual teachers to pick and chose interesting lessons and avoid the rest. However, if you want to build a case for your school's implementing the entire program, you are encouraged to do some of the units and use the positive results to your advantage in persuading your school to include more of the program. Keep adding more each year until you have the whole thing. Another thing you can do is divide the units in each grade level across disciplines, so you will not need to add a new class for the program.

This program aims to change lives by having a significant impact on the individuals who participate in it. Significant impact is not achieved in a smorgasbord approach; it is achieved through rigorous practice and relentless belief that the process is worthwhile because the result will be seen in students who know how to live meaningful lives and make important contributions to the world.

Conclusion

The Affinities Program can be life altering. The goals of the program are more than good grades and college acceptances; they are lives well lived. Every year at Purnell School, girls are discovering their strengths and, in doing so, reclaiming their futures.

At Grace's school they told her she "could catch up later" when she fell behind. Grace didn't have that kind of time to waste. Beth's school couldn't figure out if she was talented or disabled. In one year she went from the gifted program to taking Ritalin. When Claudie was a sophomore, her father died of cancer, and in her junior year, her mother also passed away. An only child, Claudie says, "I am going to need my strengths more than anything. They are the only things I have left." Ashley's father was going to kick her out of the house because she refused to focus on anything serious. She was told that she probably wouldn't be admitted to community college—the one place that accepts everyone.

Grace, Beth, Claudie, and Ashley all found their way within the Affinities Program. Grace stars in school musicals, holds leadership positions, and has a good sense of who she is. Other kids are now trying to catch up with her. Beth and Claudie both see their self-confidence as gifts they can give to others. They are both top students with a clear understanding of how to engage their strengths in the future. Ashley, who was elected Student Council president, is now enrolled in a four-year college.

The results of the Affinities Program at Purnell School are clear. Any school can commit to these ideas and philosophies. For too long, schools have focused attention on weaknesses and challenges. The time has come for every school to balance the equation with an equal focus on strengths. The time to start is now.

Appendix C

RESOURCES

The Strengths Movement on the Web
www.strengthsmovement.com
jeniferfox08@gmail.com
This Web site is a portal for *Your Child's Strengths* downloadable PDFs, the Strengths Movement in Schools project, Strengths in Second Life, the Affinities Program® Resources, the home Web site of Jenifer Fox, and an online strengths community.

Strengths Insight
www.strengthsinsight.com
848-702-6686
jeniferfox08@gmail.com
Strengths coaching, consulting, keynote speaking, organizational preparedness and tools and curriculum for parents, organizations, and schools dealing with raising youth. Homeschooling, church and ministry groups, afterschool programs, public and independent schools, community colleges, school-to-work, juvenile justice, and career planning.

All Kinds of Minds
www.allkindsofminds.org
1450 Raleigh Road, Suite 200, Chapel Hill, NC 27517
888-956-4637
All Kinds of Minds is a nonprofit institute that helps students who struggle with learning measurably improve their success in school and life by providing programs that integrate educational, scientific, and clinical exper-

tise. They developed the process of demystification. Dr. Mel Levine, author and pediatrician, is affiliated with the institute.

American Waldorf Schools of North America
Patrice Maynard • Leader of Development & Outreach
65-2 Fern Hill Road, Ghent, NY 12075
518-672-7878
pmaynard@awsna.org
The Waldorf Schools employ one of the only international methods of teaching that can be considered truly strengths-based. According to the Waldorf philosophy, play is viewed as the work of the young child and integral to how the teacher works with the child. Individuality and a belief in each child's unique talents are core components of the curriculum. There are Waldorf Schools throughout the world.

The Marcus Buckingham Company
www.marcusbuckingham.com
Carlsbad, CA
760-602-0024
charlotte@marcusbuckingham.com
Business consulting company founded by noted author of books on strengths.

Core Yoga
Deborah R. Cohen
www.coreyoga.com
PO Box 380064, Cambridge, MA 02238
617-945-2811
drc@coreyoga.com
Ms. Cohen consults on ways to still the mind and focus on preparing the mind and the body for positive living.

Flourishing Schools, Positive Psychology for Education
Sherri Fisher
www.flourishingschools.org
consultants@flourishingschools.org
Ms. Fisher consults with schools and families about strengths-based education.

Dr. Howard Gardner
www.howardgardner.com
Harvard Graduate School of Education, 14 Appian Way, Larsen 201, Cambridge, MA 02138
617-496-4929
pz@harvard.edu
In 1999, Gardner's book *Intelligence Reframed* was published. This book contains a twenty-year update on the theory of multiple intelligences. The appendixes of this book are helpful for those interested in further researching the topic.

The Giraffe Heroes Project
www.giraffe.org
PO Box 759, Langley WA 98260
360-221-7989
office@giraffe.org
The Giraffe Heroes are people who stick their necks out for the common good. The nonprofit Giraffe Heroes Project tells their stories.

Dr. Ned Hallowell
www.drhallowell.com
Hallowell Center, 142 North Road, Sudbury, MA 01776
978-287-0810
Dr. Hallowell is a clinical psychiatrist and author who specializes in the positive aspects of ADD and ADHD.

IDEO
www.ideo.com
650-289-3400
feedback@ideo.com
IEO is an international design company that created the IDEO Method Cards, a deck of fifty-one design methods used by the company. The cards can be used to spark new ideas and push through mental barriers. They are available for purchase online at www.ideo.com/case_studies/Method Deck/MethodDeck/index.html.

Little Pearls

www.littlepearls.org

PO Box 8641, Asheville, NC 28814

Little Pearls is a nonprofit media organization that creates and freely distributes inspiring, thought-provoking "tiny films" for television, the Internet, educational programs, and grassroots sharing. The films are used for learning about empathy.

Mike Morrison, Ph.D.

University of Toyota

Toyota Motor Sales, 19001 South Western Avenue, MS80, Torrance, CA 90501

mike_morrison@toyota.com

Dr. Morrison is the author of *Leading Through Meaning* and the creator of the accompanying personal leadership program for educators and employees. He developed a strengths-based leadership program for teachers to use with the Affinities Program.

My Hero Project

www.myhero.com

1278 Glenneyre, #286, Laguna Beach, CA 92651

949-376-5964

myhero@myheroproject.org

The My Hero Project is a nonprofit organization with a Web site that hosts thousands of stories of remarkable individuals. These stories, written by children and adults alike, serve to remind us that we all have the potential to overcome great obstacles and achieve our dreams by following in the footsteps of our heroes.

Dan Pink

www.danpink.com

danpink@danpink.com

Dan Pink is the author of *A Whole New Mind,* published by Penguin Books in 2005.

The Wishfarmers, LLC
www.wishfarmers.com
PO Box 64, Sunol, CA 94586
510-508-8709
The Wishfarmers are a unique team of artists, technologists, and inventors with expertise in real and virtual design and development. They designed and developed the *Strengths Movement in Second Life*.

The following Web sites are resources in the field of educational school reform:

www.bigpicture.org The Big Picture Company's mission is to catalyze vital changes in American education by generating and sustaining innovative, personalized schools that work in tandem with the real world of their greater community.

www.edutopia.org This is the Web site for the George Lucas Educational Foundation (GLEF), founded in 1991 as a nonprofit operating foundation to celebrate and encourage innovation in schools.

www.essentialschools.org Guided by a set of Common Principles, the Coalition of Essential Schools (CES) strives to create and sustain a network of personalized, equitable, and intellectually challenging schools.

The following Web sites are resources in the field of education:

www.ldonline.org LD Online is an interactive guide to learning disabilities for parents, teachers, and children. LD Online provides access to articles on a wide range of topics, a national calendar of events, a network of resources, and much more.

www.nagc.org The National Association for Gifted Children (NAGC) is an organization of parents, teachers, educators, other professionals, and community leaders who unite to address the unique needs of children and youth with demonstrated gifts and talents as well as those children who may be able to develop their talent potential with appropriate educational experiences. **www.nagc.org/index.aspx?id=691** is a listing of state education agency Web sites.

www.ricklavoie.com A site with articles on living with and learning about learning disabilities by special education expert Richard Lavoie.

www.schoolmatters.com A place for parents, educators, and leaders to research information about public schools.

www.SparkTop.org SparkTop.org is the first Web site created expressly for kids with learning difficulties, including learning disabilities (LD) and attention-deficit/hyperactivity disorder (AD/HD). The site educates kids about learning styles, helps them recognize their strengths, showcases their creativity, and offers safe ways for kids to connect with one another.

The following Web sites are resources in the field of positive psychology:

www.apa.org/releases/positivepsy.html Positive psychology resources from the American Psychological Association.

www.appreciativeinquiry.case.edu AI Commons is a worldwide portal devoted to the fullest sharing of academic resources and practical tools on Appreciative Inquiry and the rapidly growing discipline of positive change.

www.AppreciativeLiving.com Appreciative Living is actively applying the principles of Appreciative Inquiry in personal life.

www.authentichappiness.sas.upenn.edu Dr. Martin Seligman is the founder of positive psychology. His Web page has many interesting resources.

www.gallup.com The Gallup Association provides consultation on building strengths in business and beyond.

www.ivofhope.org Images and Voices of Hope is an international conversation about the impact of images and stories on people, families, communities, cultures, and the world.

www.positivepsychology.net The Positive Psychology site has an abundance of resources for the study of positive psychology.

www.viastrengths.org VIA is an independent nonprofit organization founded to advance the science of positive psychology. In the pages of this site you will learn about positive psychology, the classification system and measurement tools of character strengths that serve as the backbone of this developing scientific discipline, and the ongoing work of VIA.

Index